# Vico: A Bibliography of Works in English from 1884 to 1994

## Collected Volumes Associated with the Institute for Vico Studies

*Giambattista Vico. An International Symposium.* Edited by Giorgio Tagliacozzo and Hayden White. Baltimore, MD: Johns Hopkins University Press, 1969.

*Giambattista Vico's Science of Humanity.* Edited by Giorgio Tagliacozzo and Donald Phillip Verene. Baltimore, MD: Johns Hopkins University Press, 1976.

*Vico and Contemporary Thought.* 2 vols. in 1. Edited by Giorgio Tagliacozzo, Michael Mooney, and Donald Phillip Verene. Atlantic Highlands, NJ: Humanities Press, 1979.

*Vico: Past and Present.* Edited by Giorgio Tagliacozzo. Atlantic Highlands, NJ: Humanities Press, 1981.

*Vico and Marx: Affinities and Contrasts.* Edited by Giorgio Tagliacozzo. Atlantic Highlands, NJ: Humanities Press, 1983.

*Vico and Joyce.* Edited by Donald Phillip Verene. Albany: State University of New York Press, 1987.

## Conferences Associated with the Institute for Vico Studies

"Vico and Contemporary Thought." Columbia University and The New School for Social Research. New York City, January 1976.

"Vico/Venezia." Giorgio Cini Foundation, Isola di San Giorgio Maggiore. Venice, Italy, August 1978.

"Vico and Joyce." Giorgio Cini Foundation, Isola di San Giorgio Maggiore. Venice, Italy, June 1985.

"Vico and Humanistic Knowledge." National Endowment for the Humanities Institute held at Emory University, Atlanta, Georgia, June - July 1993.

# Vico: A Bibliography of Works in English from 1884 to 1994

### Molly Black Verene

Published by

**PHILOSOPHY DOCUMENTATION CENTER
BOWLING GREEN STATE UNIVERSITY
BOWLING GREEN, OHIO 43403-0189
U.S.A.**

Philosophy Documentation Center 1994.    All rights reserved

Library of Congress Card Number:

ISBN 0-912632-97-6

# The Institute for Vico Studies

The Institute for Vico Studies is directed by Giorgio Tagliacozzo and Donald Phillip Verene. It was founded in 1974 to promote study of the thought of Giambattista Vico. The Institute became associated with Emory University in 1983 and began the publication of *New Vico Studies*, an annual journal of essays, notes, translations, and reviews reflecting the state of work on Vico's thought.

## *NEW VICO STUDIES*

Coeditors: Giorgio Tagliacozzo
Donald Phillip Verene

Review Editor for Italian Works: Gustavo Costa
Editorial Assistant: Molly Black Verene

## BOARD OF CONSULTANTS

| | |
|---|---|
| Andrea Battistini | University of Bologna |
| Isaiah Berlin | All Souls' College, Oxford University |
| Gustavo Costa | University of California (Berkeley) |
| Marcel Danesi | University of Toronto |
| Max Harold Fisch | Indiana University - Purdue University |
| Donald R. Kelley | Rutgers University |
| Giuseppe Mazzotta | Yale University |
| Michael Mooney | Lewis and Clark College |
| Leon Pompa | University of Birmingham, England |
| Alain Pons | University of Paris (Nanterre) |
| Nancy S. Struever | The Johns Hopkins University |
| Hayden White | University of California (Santa Cruz) |

For inquiries regarding the Institute or *New Vico Studies*, write:
Institute for Vico Studies
202 Bowden Hall
Emory University
Atlanta GA 30322

To purchase back issues of *New Vico Studies* or to become a subscriber, contact:
Humanities Press International, Inc.
Atlantic Highlands, NJ 07716-1289
Tel. (908) 872-1441 Fax (908) 872-0717

This bibliography marks the 250th year since Vico's death and the publication in Naples of the third edition of the *New Science*

# Vico: A Bibliography of Works in English from 1884 to 1994

## Contents

**Preface**

**Part I:** **Works on Vico**
- A. Books .................................................... 1
- B. Essays ................................................... 15
- C. Dissertations and Theses ..................... 61
- D. Reviews in English of Works on Vico in Other Languages ........................... 65
- E. Entries in Reference Works .................. 73

**Part II:** **Vico's Works**
- A. English Editions of Vico's Works ................ 77
- B. Reviews in English of Editions of Vico's Works in Other Languages ..................... 81

**Part III: Works Citing Vico** ............... 85

**Appendix: Bibliographies of Works on Vico** ............ 163

**Index of Names** ................................. 167

# Preface

In 1986, the Philosophy Documentation Center published *A Bibliography of Vico in English 1884-1984*. The Institute for Vico Studies then began its ongoing project (similar to the project of the Centro di Studi Vichiani, in Naples) to update that bibliography, starting with Volume 3 of its annual publication, *New Vico Studies*. The current bibliography is a combination of the 1986 book and its continuous update to 1994, with a substantial number of additions and corrections. The year 1994 marks the 250th anniversary both of the publication of the third edition of the *New Science* and of Vico's death in 1744.

*Historical Note*

The earliest known published mention of Vico (1668-1744) in the English language occurred during his lifetime. This notation is discussed by Gustavo Costa in "Vico e Michel de La Roche" in *Bollettino del Centro di Studi Vichiani* 2 (1972): 63-65. Vico's *De nostri temporis studiorum ratione* appeared in print in 1709 in Naples and was the subject of a notice that appeared in *Memoirs of Literature*, published in London on 11 December 1710. This work was compiled by Michel de La Roche, a French Protestant refugee living in Great Britain. It offered the English public "a choice of the most Curious and Useful Subjects" and was created "to render the Extracts of Books acceptable to the Publick." A second edition of the *Memoirs* appeared in 1722. Under the heading of works from Naples there is a 280-word summary of Vico's *De nostri*, ending with the claim that "the Author proceeds to Discourse of Printing; and pretends it has been of no great use for the Improvement of Learning. Bad Books, says he, have been multiplied by it; whereas, before it was found out, none but good Books were transcribed and read" (cf. sec. 13 of *De nostri*).

Until Costa's discovery of de La Roche, the first attention to Vico in English was thought to have occurred in the early 19th century. In "The Coleridges, Dr. Prati, and Vico" (*Modern Philology* 41 [1943]: 111-22), Max Fisch noted that Samuel Taylor Coleridge discussed "an admirable remark of Joh. Bapt. a Vico." This was probably written by Coleridge in 1816 but appeared only posthumously in Coleridge's *Hints towards the formation of a more comprehensive theory of life* (1848). The "admirable remark" that Coleridge presents is a paraphrase in Latin of a passage concerning demonstration in geometry, physics, and metaphysics from the *De antiquissima Italorum sapientia ex lingue latinae originibus eruenda* (1710). Fisch points out that this is most likely taken by Coleridge from Jacobi's *Von den göttlichen Dingen*, in which the same Latin paraphrase of Vico appears. Coleridge's direct acquaintance with Vico likely dates from 1825, when Prati lent him a copy of the *New Science*.

In 1834, Henry Nelson Coleridge, son of Samuel Taylor Coleridge, translated and published the first of Vico's own writings into English, "On the Discovery of the True Homer" (Book 3 of the *New Science*). In 1884 Robert Flint published the first book on Vico in English, in Blackwood's Philosophical Classics, which is the beginning of academic scholarship on Vico in English. This bibliography takes its beginning date from that event.

*Vico in Literature and the Arts*

The use of Vico in the works of James Joyce, especially *Finnegans Wake*, has been well documented. For example, Vico's name in its Latin form appears in the first paragraph of the work: "by a commodius vicus of recirculation." Vico appears in person as "the producer (Mr John Baptister Vickar)" (p. 255) and in Joyce's time machine, "Our wholemole millwheeling vicociclometer" (p. 614), and Joyce transforms Vico's three ages into four: "eggburst, eggblend, eggburial, and hatch-as-hatch can" (p. 614).

This bibliography lists some more recent important fiction in which Vico appears—such as *Possession*, the 1991 Booker Prize novel by A. S. Byatt; *Christopher Unborn*, a novel by Carlos Fuentes; and "The Immortal," which appears in *Labyrinths*, by Jorge Luis Borges. Vico is cited in various ways by writers from W. B. Yeats to John Updike.

Vico also appears in late 20th-century popular culture. "Vico's Little Circus," a painting by the Atlanta artist Todd Murphy, was recently purchased by the British rock musician Elton John for the entrance to his Atlanta condominium. In addition, Paul Muldoon published an odd little poem "[*Vico*]" in *MADOC. A Mystery* (Farrar, Straus, & Giroux, 1991); and Vico is included in a "documentary comic book," *Philosophy for Beginners*, by Richard Osborne with illustrations by Ralph Edney (1991). Several works of science fiction are found to contain some of Vico's ideas: Greg Bear's short story, "A Martian *Ricorso*," and a novel by Robert Anton Wilson, *The Earth Will Shake: The Historical Illuminatus Chronicles*. Several episodes of the popular television serial *Star Trek* concern a spaceship named "Vico" and use terminology from the *New Science* concerning myth and poetry.

Vico, recently termed "fashionable" by Anthony Grafton, in a review ("Fear and Loathing in Naples," *The New Republic* 4105 & 4107, Sept. 1993), has also entered the public press. During summer 1993, two newspaper editorials on Vico were brought to my attention. "Heroic Minds," by Paul Greenberg, appeared in the (3 August) *South Carolina Post/Courier*. In "Clintons Shouldn't Cater to Zealots" (*Conservative Chronicle*, 23 June), R. Emmett Tyrrell Jr. cited Vico's conception of society and history and claimed that [President of the United States] Bill Clinton could be expected to know something of Vico's thought.

## Contents of the Bibliography

In this bibliography, the entries are separated into eight parts, plus an appendix. Books (Part I: A) are separated from essays on Vico (Part I: B). Reviews and abstracts of books and essays on Vico are listed with each work reviewed. Dissertations and theses on Vico have a section (Part I: C), as do English-language reviews of works published on Vico in other languages (Part I: D) and entries on Vico in reference works (Part I: E).

All translations of Vico's works into English are in a special section, with reviews (Part II: A), followed by reviews in English of editions of Vico's works translated into languages other than English (Part II: B).

"Works Citing Vico" (Part III) is a collection of mentions, citations, and short discussions of Vico in English. We consider it both important and of interest to document the wide distribution of references to Vico in scholarly literature. A page or so, or only a comment by a major thinker, or simply Vico's presence in a particular work may be of greater interest and importance to a scholar's project than a whole article about Vico. Part III is a way to learn of a great many of these references, but no claim is made that all citations to Vico have been found. A few figures who mention Vico, or read or were influenced by him, are Herder, Goethe, Jacobi, Michelet, Cousin, Thomas Arnold, Comte, Sorel, Dostoevsky, Marx, Croce, Gentile, Toynbee, Trotsky, Eric Auerbach, and Edmund Wilson. The citations and mentions of Vico listed in Part III also document the beginning and progress of Vico scholarship in the Anglo-American world. Entries, for example, of works by Isaiah Berlin, R. G. Collingwood, and Northrop Frye demonstrate the progression of their interest in Vico.

The Appendix lists all the bibliographies on Vico that have been consulted for the preparation of the various bibliographies published by the Institute for Vico Studies.

The Index lists authors, editors, and translators of works on Vico and the names of all persons, including fictional characters, named in the titles of those books and essays (hence the many appearances of Dante, Descartes, Homer, Joyce, and Marx). Authors of works citing Vico are indexed, but names in titles of those works are not listed.

The enormous amount of work on Vico published in English in the past 25 years is a testament to the efforts of Giorgio Tagliacozzo, who has interested so many scholars from so many fields in the contemporary importance of Vico's ideas. Dr. Tagliacozzo's library of Vichian works, which is bequeathed to the Institute, is the prime source for this and all earlier bibliographies prepared in connection with the Institute, especially for the entries of works citing Vico.

I wish to thank Giorgio Tagliacozzo and Donald Phillip Verene, the Directors of the Institute, for their guidance and advice. I also acknowledge those graduate fellows in Philosophy who worked for the Institute for Vico Studies at Emory University to update the Vico in English bibliography for publication in *New Vico Studies*: Anna Nelli, Timothy Bergstrom, Jeffrey Wilson, Alexander Bertland, Jennifer Rust Murray, and Charlotte Smith.

This bibliography is intended to be a working list, to pass on to scholars interested in Vico what we in the Institute have found to exist in English, and such a work cannot claim to be perfectly complete or wholly free of error, although every effort has been made in these respects.

Molly Black Verene
Institute for Vico Studies
Emory University
Atlanta, Georgia

# Part I. Works on Vico

## A. Books

Adams, Henry Packwood. *The Life and Writings of Giambattista Vico*. London: Allen and Unwin, 1935. Reprinted: New York: Russell and Russell, 1970.
*Reviews:*
Gianturco, Elio. *Italica* 13 (1936): 132.
Jessop, T. E. *Philosophy* 11 (1936): 216-18.

Albano, Maeve Edith. *Vico and Providence*. Vol. 1 of Emory Vico Studies, ed. D. P. Verene. New York: Peter Lang, 1986.
*Reviews:*
Daniel, Stephen H. *The 18th Century: A Current Bibliography*, n.s. 12 (1986): 148-49.
Munzel, G. F. *New Vico Studies* 5 (1987): 173-75.
Simon, L. *Canadian Philosophical Reviews* 8 (1988): 335-37.

Avis, Paul. *The Foundations of Modern Historical Thought: From Machiavelli to Vico*. Beckenham: Croom Helm, 1986: 132-57.
*Reviews:*
Goldie, M. *History* 72 (1987): 84-85.
Haddock, B. A. *New Vico Studies* 5 (1987): 185-86.

Bedani, G. L. C. *Vico Revisited: Orthodoxy, Naturalism and Science in the "Scienza nuova."* Oxford: Berg, 1989.
*Reviews:*
Costa, G. *New Vico Studies* 8 (1990): 90-92.
Pompa, L. *Times Higher Education Supplement* (London) (9 Feb. 1990).
Kelley, D. R. *Isis* 82, no. 311 (1991): 140-41.
Matteo, Sante. *Italica* 70 (1993): 99-103.

Berlin, Isaiah. *The Divorce between the Sciences and the Humanities*. Second Tykociner Memorial Lecture. Champaign: University of Illinois, 1974 [originally published as "The Divorce between the Sciences and the Humanities." *Salmagundi* 27 (1974): 9-39].
*Comment:*
Pruitt, Raymond D. *Perspectives in Biology and Medicine* 25 (1981).

Berlin, Isaiah. *Vico and Herder: Two Studies in the History of Ideas*. London: Hogarth Press; New York: Viking Press, 1976.
*Reviews:*
Barnouw, J. *The 18th Century: A Current Bibliography*, n.s. 2 (1976): 390-93.
*BBC Book Talk* (8 March 1976).
Beatty, J. *Commentary* 62 (1976): 86-91.
*Birmingham Post* (5 March 1976).
Cranston, M. "Forgotten Heroes in the War of Ideas." *Washington Post* (18 July 1976): 62.

"Creative Thought." *The Economist* 258 (1976): 105-6.
Dallmayr, F. R. "Vico and Herder." *The Review of Politics* 40 (1978): 140-45.
Dray, W. H. *Canadian Journal of Philosophy* 9 (1979): 179-83.
Fyvel, T. R. "Fate of Ideas." *Jewish Chronicle* (5 March 1976).
Gardiner, P. *History and Theory* 16 (1977): 45-51.
Gustaitis, J. *America* (25 Feb. 1978): 152-56.
Haddock, B. A. "Vico and Anachronism." *Political Studies* 24 (1976): 483-87.
———. *Philosophical Quarterly* 27 (1977): 173-75.
*Hampstead and Highgate Express* (5 March 1976).
Kateb, G. "A Foxy Hedgehog." *American Scholar* 46 (1977): 124-30.
Kelley, D. "Connoisseurs of Causes." *Times Literary Supplement* (London) (9 July 1976): 839.
Kessler, E. *Journal of Philosophy* 75 (1978): 264-78.
*Kirkus* 44 (1976): 283.
Krois, J. M. *Philosophy and Rhetoric* 10 (1977): 276-80.
*Library Journal* 101 (1976): 1022.
Lively, J. "The Reconstructive Imagination." *Times Higher Education Supplement* (London) (5 March 1976).
MacIntyre, A. "Who Judges Whom?" *The Listener* 95 (1976): 251.
Momigliano, A. "On the Pioneer Trail." *New York Review of Books* 23 (11 Nov. 1976): 33-38.
Morrison, J. C. "Three Interpretations of Vico." *Journal of the History of Ideas* 39 (1978): 511-18.
Parker, D. "Writing on the Wall." *Times* (London) (26 Feb. 1976): 10.
Pompa, L. "What Were We Thinking Of?" *New Review* 23 (1976): 66-68.
Poole, R. "A Philosophy for Today?" *Books and Bookmen* 11 (1976): 28-32.
Quinton, A. "The History Men." *Observer* (29 Feb. 1976): 26.
Rosselli, J. "The Reality of the Past." *The Manchester Guardian* (20 Feb. 1976): 7.
Ryan, A. "Inside Knowledge." *New Statesman* 91 (1976): 261-62.
Schaeffer, John. *Religious Studies Review* 13 (1987): 321-24.
*Scotsman* (28 Feb. 1976).
Scouten, A. H. *Comparative Literature Studies* 15 (1978): 336-40.
*Spectator* 236 (1976): 21.
Steiner, G. "Pathfinders of the Mind." *Times* (London) (29 Feb. 1976).
Struever, N. *Modern Language Notes* 91 (1976): 1625-27.
Swoboda, W. "I'll See You and Raise You Schlegel." *New Boston Review* (Fall 1976): 14-15.
Updike, J. "Texts and Men." *New Yorker* (4 Oct. 1976): 148-56.
Valone, J. J. *Journal of Modern History* 49 (1977): 675-78.
Walsh, W. H. *Mind* 87 (1978): 284-86.
Warnock, M. "History of Ideas." *New Society* (26 Feb. 1976): 446.
White, H. *Political Theory* 5 (1977): 124-27.
Zimmer, L. B. *History: Review of New books* 4 (1976): 224-25.
*The 18th Century: A Current Bibliography*, n.s. 5 (1979): 588-89 [critique of A. H. Scouten's (1978) review, *above*].

Berry, Thomas M. *The Historical Theory of Giambattista Vico.* Washington, DC: Catholic University of America Press, 1949.

Brown, Norman O. *Closing Time.* New York: Random House, 1973.
*Reviews:*
Said, E. *New York Times Book Review* (9 Sept. 1973): 31, 32, 34.
Schwartz, A. "In the Waiting Room." *New Republic* (22 Sept. 1973): 23-25.
Hampshire, S. "Joyce and Vico: The Middle Way." *New York Review of Books* (18 Oct. 1973): 8, 9, 12, 14, 16, 21.
Goldfein, A. "The End?" *Commentary* 57 (1974): 161-64.
Struever, N. *Modern Language Notes* 89 (1974): 1049-50.

Burke, Peter. *Vico.* Oxford and New York: Oxford University Press, 1985.
*Reviews:*
Palmer, L. *New Vico Studies* 4 (1986): 199-204.
Cono, J., and J. M. Todd. *History of European Ideas* 8 (1987): 248-49.
Logan, O. *History* 72 (1987): 85.
Whitfield, J. H. *Modern Language Review* (Oct. 1987): 993-95.

Caponigri, A. Robert. *Time and Idea: The Theory of History in Giambattista Vico.* Chicago: Regnery; London: Routledge and Kegan Paul, 1953. Reprinted, University of Notre Dame Press, 1968.
*Reviews:*
Hampshire, S. *New Statesmen and Nation* (London) (19 Sept. 1953): 315-16.
Madden, E. H. *Philosophy and Phenomenological Research* 15 (1954): 132-33.
Tsanoff, R. A. *New Scholasticism* 28 (1954): 494-96.
Walsh, J. V. *Theological Studies* 15 (1954): 503-4.
Armstrong, A. M. *Philosophy* 30 (1955): 266-67.
Bergin, T. *Italica* 32 (1955): 200-3.
Long, W. *Personalist* 36 (1955): 291-92.
Shanahan, W. O. *Review of Politics* 17 (1955): 136-42
Rockey, P. L. *The Modern Schoolman* 33 (1956): 51-52.
Fisch, M. H. *Journal of Philosophy* 54 (1957): 648-52.

Chambliss, Joseph James. *Imagination and Reason in Plato, Aristotle, Vico, Rousseau, and Keats: An Essay on the Philosophy of Experience.* The Hague: Nijhoff, 1974.

Child, Arthur. *Making and Knowing in Hobbes, Vico, and Dewey.* Berkeley: University of California Press, 1953.

Croce, Benedetto. *The Philosophy of Giambattista Vico*, trans. R. G. Collingwood. London: Latimer, 1913. Reprinted Russell & Russell, 1964.
*Reviews:*
"Beginnings of Sociology." *Nation* 99 (1914): 46-47.
Cohen, M. R. *Philosophical Review* 23 (1914): 677-82.

Danesi, Marcel. *Vico, Metaphor, and the Origin of Language.* Bloomington: Indiana University Press, 1993.

Dickinson, George. *The Dynamic Principle of Historical Growth and the Vico Theory.* Albuquerque, NM: American Classical College Press, 1978.

Fink, Karl J., and James W. Marchand, eds. *The Quest for the New Science: Language and Thought in Eighteenth-Century Science.* London: Feffer and Simons; Carbondale, Southern Illinois University Press, 1979 [Abstract in *History and Theory* 19 (1980): 242.] [Contents on Vico listed separately in Part I B.]

Flint, Robert. *Vico.* Edinburgh: Blackwood, 1884. Reprinted Arno Press, 1979.
**Review:**
"Flint's Vico." *Saturday Review* (London) 58 (1884): 699-700.

*Forum Italicum* 2, no. 4 (1968). *A Homage to G. B. Vico in the Tercentenary of His Birth.* [Contents listed separately in Part I B: Essays.]

Frascari, Marco. *Monsters of Architecture: Anthropomorphism in Architectural Theory.* Savage, MD: Rowman and Littlefield, 1991.
**Review:**
Bitz, Diana. *New Vico Studies* 11 (1993): 108-11.

Gianturco, Elio. *Joseph de Maistre and Giambattista Vico: Italian Roots of de Maistre's Political Culture.* Washington, DC: Murry & Heister, 1937.

Grassi, Ernesto. *Vico and Humanism: Essays on Vico, Heidegger, and Rhetoric.* Vol. 3 of Emory Vico Studies, ed. D. P. Verene. New York and Bern: Peter Lang Publishing, 1990.
**Review:**
Verene, D. P. *New Vico Studies* 8 (1990) 99-100 [Abstract].

Grimaldi, Alfonsina Albini. *The Universal Humanity of Giambattista Vico.* New York: Vanni, 1958.
**Review:**
Berry, T. M. *Thought* 34 (1959): 456.

Haddock, B. A. *Vico's Political Thought.* Swansea: Mortlake Press, 1986 [Abstract: *New Vico Studies* 4 (1986): 182-83].
**Reviews:**
Barnouw, J. *Journal of the History of the Behavioral Sciences* 23 (1987): 186-90.
Hutton, P. H. *New Vico Studies* 5 (1987): 176-79.
Morrison, J. *Canadian Philosophical Review* 8 (1988): 268-70.
Vaughan, F. *Review of Politics* 50 (1988): 326-28.
Mooney, M. *American Historical Review* 94 (1989): 1336-37.

Harrison, Robert Pogue. *Forests: The Shadow of Civilization.* Chicago: University of Chicago Press, 1992. See "Vico's Giants," 3-13; see also 19, 35, 36, 54, 57-58, 101, 109, 114, 131, 165-67, 245, 251-52; xv (Vico quote as epigraph); xvi (*Dipintura*).

*Reviews:*
Haines, John. "Where the Wild Things Were." *New York Times Book Review* (7 June 1992): 16.
Price, David. *New Vico Studies* 11 (1993): 105-8.
Bate, Jonathan. "Cry Treedom." *London Review of Books* 15, no. 21 (4 Nov. 1993): 21.

Kunze, Donald Edwin Jr. *Thought and Place. The Architecture of Eternal Places in the Philosophy of Giambattista Vico*. Vol. 2 of Emory Vico Studies, ed. D. P. Verene. New York and Bern: Peter Lang Publishing, 1987 [Abstract: *New Vico Studies* 5 (1987): 207-8].
*Reviews:*
Pickles, J. *Environment and Planning D-Society and Space* 7, no. 3 (1989): 347-51.
Tuan, Y. F. *Annals of the Association of American Geographers* 78 (1988): 372-73.

Lamparska, Rena A. *Stanislaw Brzozowski: A Polish Vichian*. Vol. 18 of Studia Historica et Philologica. Florence: Le Lettere, 1987 [Abstract: *New Vico Studies* 7 (1989): 137-38].

Lilla, Mark. *G. B. Vico: The Making of an Anti-Modern*. Cambridge: Harvard University Press, 1993.
*Reviews:*
Burke, Peter. *Times Literary Supplement* (London) (2 July 1993): 30.
Grafton, Anthony. "Fear and Loathing in Naples." *The New Republic* 4105 & 4107 (20 & 27 Sept. 1993): 51-57.
Robertson, John. "History Man." *London Review of Books* 15, no. 21 (4 Nov. 1993): 19-20.

Lion, Aline. *The Idealistic Conception of Religion: Vico, Hegel, Gentile*. Oxford: Clarendon Press, 1932.

Littleford, Michael S., and James R. Whitt. *Giambattista Vico, Post-Mechanical Thought, and Contemporary Psychology*. New York: Peter Lang, 1988.
*Reviews:*
Buford, T. *Canadian Philosophical Review* 9 (1989): 273-75.
Giorgi, A. *New Vico Studies* 7 (1989): 122-25
Kelley, D. R. *Journal of the History of the Behavioral Sciences* 26 (1990): 87-88.
Sipiora, M. P. *Research in Philosophy and Technology* 11 (1991): 391-95.

McAllister, David W. *The Reconstruction of Giambattista Vico's Theory of the Cycles of History, with Applications to Contemporary Historical Experience*. Albuquerque, NM: American Classical College Press, 1983.

Mali, Joseph. *The Rehabilitation of Myth: Vico's New Science*. Cambridge: Cambridge University Press, 1992 [Abstract in *History and Theory* 32 (1993): 367].
*Reviews:*
Burke, Peter. *Times Literary Supplement* (London) (2 July 1993): 30.
Robertson, John. "History Man." *London Review of Books* 15, no.21 (4 Nov. 1993): 19-20.

Manson, Richard. *The Theory of Knowledge of Giambattista Vico: On the Method of the New Science Concerning the Common Nature of the Nations.* Hamden, CT: Archon Books, 1969.
***Reviews:***
Beitscher, H. *Review of Metaphysics* 24 (1970): 342.
*Choice* 7 (1970): 851-52.
Hershbell, J. P. *Library Journal* 95 (1970): 2485.
Wolff, K. H. *Annals of the American Academy of Political and Social Science* 391 (1970): 239-40.
Caponigri, A. R. *Journal of the History of Philosophy* 9 (1971): 98-101.

Mazlish, Bruce. *The Riddle of History. The Great Speculators from Vico to Freud.* New York: Harper & Row, 1966.

Milbank, John. *The Religious Dimension in the Thought of Giambattista Vico. Part I: The Early Metaphysics.* Lewiston, NY: Mellen, 1991.
***Review:***
Goetsch, James R. Jr. *New Vico Studies* 10 (1992): 93-95.

Milbank, John. *The Religious Dimension in the Thought of Giambattista Vico. Part II: Language, Law, and History.* Lewiston, NY: Mellen, 1992.

Miller, Cecilia. *Giambattista Vico: Imagination and Historical Knowledge.* New York: St. Martin's Press, 1993.

Mooney, Michael. *Vico in the Tradition of Rhetoric.* Princeton: Princeton University Press, 1984 [Abstract: *New Vico Studies* 2 (1984): 113-14].
***Reviews:***
Abbott, D. P. *Rhetorica* 3 (1985): 297-99.
Baker, J. J. *The Eighteenth Century: A Current Bibliography*, n.s. 11 (1985): 665-67.
Struever, N. S. "Rhetoric and Philosophy in Vichian Inquiry." *New Vico Studies* 3 (1985): 131-45.
Bevilacqua, V. M. *Quarterly Journal of Speech* 72 (1986): 100-1.
Cleveland, C. *Columbia Magazine of Columbia University* (April 1986): 47ff.
Haddock, B. A. *American Historical Review* 91 (1986): 385-86.
Moss, J. D. *Review of Metaphysics* 39 (1986): 574-76.
Barnouw, J. *Journal of the History of the Behavioral Sciences* 23 (1987): 186-90.
Costa, G. *Italica* 64 (1987): 323-25.
Hughes, P. *Philosophy and Rhetoric* 20 (1987): 274-77.
*Italian Journal* 1 (1987): 78.
Schaeffer, John D. *Religious Studies Review* 13 (1987): 321-24.
Vasoli, C. *Journal of Modern History* 59 (1987): 603-6.
Whitfield, J. H. *Modern Language Review* (Oct. 1987): 993-95.
Zobermann, P. *Romantic Review* 78 (1987): 242-43.

White, H. *Eighteenth-Century Studies* 22 (1988-1989): 219-22.
Pompa, L. *International Studies in Philosophy* 21 (1989): 137.

*New Vico Studies* 1983— [Vol. 11 (1993) includes index to Vols. 1-10]. [Contents listed separately in Part I B.]

**Reviews of Vol. 1 (1983):**
*Journal of Philosophy* 80 (1983): 628.
*Choice* 21 (1984): 1104.
Luft, S. R. *Journal of the History of Philosophy* 23 (1985): 429-31.
Pietropaolo, D. *Forum Italicum* 19 (1985): 352-54.
**Review of Vol. 2 (1984):**
Holub, R. *Italica* 64 (1987).
**Reviews of Vol. 3 (1985):**
Danesi, M. *Rivista di Studi Italiani* 4, no. 2; and 5, no. 1 (Dec. 1986; June 1987): 133-39.
Holub, R. *Criticism: A Quarterly for Literature and the Arts* 30 (1988): 403-7.
Jacobitti, E. *Differentia* 2 (1988): 267-75.
**Review of Vols. 4-6 (1986-1988):**
Kelley, D. *Journal of the History of Behavioral Sciences* 26 (1990): 87-88.

Paparella, Emanuel L. *Hermeneutics in the Philosophy of Giambattista Vico*. Lewiston, NY: Mellen, 1993.

Pietropaolo, Domenico. *Dante Studies in the Age of Vico*. Ottawa: Dovehouse Editions, 1989.
**Reviews:**
Mead, C. L. Quaderni D'Italianistica 10 (1989): 349.
Scaglione, Aldo. *New Vico Studies* 7 (1989): 139-40.

Piovani, Pietro. *Giambattista Vico: Our Perennial Standard*. New York: Istituto Italiano di Cultura, 1969.

Pompa, Leon. *Vico's Theory of the Causes of Historical Change* [Monograph]. Tunbridge Wells, Kent: Institute for Cultural Research Monograph Series, 1971.
_____. *Vico: A Study of the 'New Science'*. Cambridge: Cambridge University Press, 1975 (2d rev. ed. 1990).
**Reviews:**
Abel, B. "The Proper Study of Mankind." *Contemporary Review* 226 (1975): 221.
Belsey, A. "On Human Nature." *Times Higher Education Supplement* (London) (23 May 1975): 22. Gorman, J. L. [Comment on Belsey's review] 30 May 1975: 12.
*British Book News* (Sept. 1975): 625.
*Choice* 12 (1975): 858.
*Donizetti Society* (London) (Aug. 1975).
Forbes, D. *Historical Journal* 18 (1975): 894-96.
Haney, D. A. *Library Journal* 100 (1975): 1422.
Momigliano, A. "The One True History." *Times Literary Supplement* (London) (5 Sept. 1975): 982-93.
Stark, W. *Thought* 50 (1975): 456-57.
Bedani, G. L. C. *Italian Studies* 31 (1976): 116-17.
Gardiner, P. *History* 61 (1976): 72-73.

Perkins, R. L. *Review of Metaphysics* 29 (1976): 746.
Verene, D. P. *Philosophy and Rhetoric* 9 (1976): 59-61.
von Leyden, W. *Philosophical Books* 17 (1976): 20-22.
White, H. *History and Theory* 15 (1976): 186-202.
Morrison, J. C. "Three Interpretations of Vico." *Journal of the History of Ideas* 39 (1978): 511-18.
Haddock, B. A. *European Studies Review* 9 (1979): 273-75.
Schaeffer, John D. *Religious Studies Review* 13 (1987): 321-24.
Auxier, R. E. *New Vico Studies* 10 (1992): 88-91.

Pompa, Leon. *Human Nature and Historical Knowledge: Hume, Hegel, and Vico.* Cambridge: Cambridge University Press, 1990.
**Reviews:**
Gardiner, P. "Does History Have a Pattern?" *Times Literary Supplement* (London) (24 May 1991): 29.
Livingston, D. W. *American Historical Review* 91 (1991): 1497.
Auxier, R. E. *New Vico Studies* 10 (1992): 88-91.

Rossi, Paolo. *The Dark Abyss of Time: The History of the Earth and the History of Nations from Hooke to Vico,* trans. L. C. Cochrane. Chicago: University of Chicago Press, 1984.
**Reviews:**
Costa, Gustavo. *New Vico Studies* 3 (1985): 195-97.
Haber, Francis C. *American Historical Review* 90 (1985): 1187-88.
Laudan, R. *Philosophy of Science.* 52 (1985): 644-45.
Porter, Roy. *The Times Literary Supplement [London]* (27 Sept. 1985): 1077.
Secord, J. A. *Nature* 316 (1985): 686.
Cormier, R. *Seventeenth-Century News* 44 (1986): 73-74.
Rappaport, R. *British Journal for the History of Science* 19 (1986): 362-65.
Schaeffer, S. *Isis* 77 (1986): 320-23.
Westfall, R. *Journal of Modern History* 58 (1986): 883-84.
Schneer, C. J. *Annals of Science* 44 (1987): 314-16.

Schaeffer, John D. *Sensus communis: Vico, Rhetoric, and the Limits of Relativism.* Durham, NC: Duke University Press, 1990.
**Reviews:**
Struever, N. S. *New Vico Studies* 9 (1991): 68-76.
Danesi, M. "Common sense vs. communal sense: Vico's concept of *sensus communis.*" *Semiotica* 92 (1992): 359-69.
Hutton, Patrick H. *Journal of Modern History* 65 (1993): 878-89.

*Social Research* 43, nos. 3 and 4 (1976). *See below,* Tagliacozzo, Mooney, and Verene (1979).

Stephenson, Charles L. *Giambattista Vico and the Foundations of a Science of the Philosophy of History.* Albuquerque, NM: American Classical College Press, 1982.

Tagliacozzo, Giorgio, and Hayden V. White, co-eds. *Giambattista Vico: An International Symposium.* Baltimore: Johns Hopkins University Press, 1969. [Contents listed separately in Part I B.]

***Reviews:***
*School and Society* 97 (1969): 514.
Beitscher, H. *Review of Metaphysics* 24 (1970): 762.
Bobick, M. T. *American Sociological Review* 35 (1970): 926-27.
*Choice* 7 (1970): 240.
Collins, J. *Modern Schoolman* 48 (1970): 64-65.
Fox, J. "The Pedagogical Theory of Giambattista Vico: In Appreciation of an International Symposium." *Educational Theory* 20 (1970): 292-303.
Gianturco, E. *Italian Quarterly* 9 (1970): 108-11.
Grande, F. "Vico Without Hegel." *Review of National Literatures* 1 (1970): 293-99.
Gutmann, J. *Saturday Review* (18 April 1970): 41.
Harris, H. S. "Vico after Three Hundred Years." *Dialogue* 9 (1970): 410-14.
Henderson, J. L. *British Journal of Educational Studies* 18 (1970): 224-25.
Hershbell, J. P. *Library Journal* 95 (1970): 2485.
Nisbet, R. "Vico: The Anti-Descartes." *American Scholar* 39 (1970): 714, 716-18.
Robinson, D. S. *Journal of Philosophy and Phenomenological Research* 31 (1970): 133.
Schneider, H. W. *Journal of the History of Philosophy* 8 (1970): 467.
*Scientia* 105 (1970): 11-12.
Steiner, G. "Through Seas of Thought, Alone." *New Yorker* (9 May 1970): 154-56.
*Virginia Quarterly Review* 46 (1970): lxxvi.
Bevilacqua, V. M. *Quarterly Journal of Speech* 57 (1971): 124-25.
Brunius, T. *Journal of Aesthetics and Art Criticism* 30 (1971): 129-31.
Caponigri, A. R. *Philosophy and Rhetoric* 4 (1971): 135-36.
de Waal Malefijt, A. *Critical Anthropology* 2 (1971): 82-84.
_____. *Man* 6 (1971): 501-2.
Gardiner, P. "Sleeper Awake." *New York Review of Books* (20 May 1971): 35-39.
Gianturco, E. *Renaissance Quarterly* 24 (1971): 419-22.
Giorgi, A. P. *Journal of Phenomenological Psychology* 1 (1971): 253-64.
Goudge, T. A. *Philosophy of the Social Sciences* 1 (1971): 350-52.
McRae, D. G. "Vico in Our Time." *Times Literary Supplement* (London) (1 Oct. 1971): 1161-63.
Musto, D. F. *American Journal of Psychiatry* 127 (1971): 1710-11.
Noether, E. P. *American Historical Review* 76 (1971): 476-79.
Orsini, G. N. G. *Comparative Literature* 23 (1971): 365-66.
Palmer, L. *Studi internazionali di Filosofia* 3 (1971): 231-33.
Perkinson, H. J. *Main Currents of Modern Thought* 27 (1971): 167-68.
Shiner, L. E. *Journal of the American Academy of Religion* 39 (1971): 535, 538.
Stromberg, R. N. *Comparative Literature Studies* 8 (1971): 79-80.
Verene, D. P. *International Philosophical Quarterly* 11 (1971): 260-62.
_____. *Man and World* 4 (1971): 342-54.
Bergel, L. "Vico for Our Time." *Forum Italicum* 6 (1972): 575-83; also published in *Rivista di studi Crociani* 9 (1972): 135-42.
Casagrande, J. B. *American Anthropologist* 74 (1972): 11-12.
Costa, G. *Journal of the History of the Behavioral Sciences* 8 (1972): 441-43.

Dye, J. W. *Bibliography of Philosophy* 19 (1972): 76.
Fox, J. "Giambattista Vico's Theory of Pedagogy." *British Journal of Educational Studies* 20 (1972): 27-37.
Littleford, M. S. "Vico's Legacy to Contemporary Education." *Educational Forum* 36 (1972): 393-401.
McClintock, R. *Comparative Education Review* 16 (1972): 376-78.
Mora, G. *Psychoanalytic Quarterly* 41 (1972): 119-22.
Pasotti, R. *Journal of Value Inquiry* 6 (1972): 77-80.
Pompa, L. *Philosophy* 47 (1972): 162-69.
Di Pietro, R. J. *Foundations of Language* 9 (1973): 410-12.
Kelley, D. *Journal of Interdisciplinary History* 3 (1973): 772-75.
Mohan, R. P. *Catholic Historical Review* 59 (1973): 452.
Pompa, L. "Vico in Review." *Studi internazionali di Filosofia* 5 (1973): 215-19.
Struever, N. S. *Journal of Philosophy* 70 (1973): 801-4.
Rhea, B. *Contemporary Sociology* 10 (1981): 624-26.
Schaeffer, John D. *Religious Studies Review* 13 (1987): 321-24.

Tagliacozzo, Giorgio, and Donald Phillip Verene, eds. *Giambattista Vico's Science of Humanity*. Baltimore: Johns Hopkins University Press, 1976. [Contents listed separately in Part I B.]
**Reviews:**
Barnouw, J. *The 18th Century: A Current Bibliography*, n.s. 2 (1976): 395-97.
Belsey, A. "Vichian Themes." *Times Higher Education Supplement* (London) (29 Oct. 1976): 19.
*Choice* 13 (1976): 995.
Forbes, D. *Times Literary Supplement* (London) (10 Sept. 1976): 1101.
*Forum Italicum* 10 (1976): 151.
Haney, D. A. *Library Journal* 101 (1976): 818.
Krois, J. M. *Philosophy and Rhetoric* 9 (1976): 247-51.
Rome, H. P. *American Journal of Psychiatry* 133 (1976): 1357-58.
Barnouw, J. *Eighteenth-Century Studies* 10 (1977): 386-88.
Collins, J. *Modern Schoolman* 54 (1977): 312.
Gates, B. T. *Clio* 6 (1977): 351-54.
Luft, S. R. *Journal of the History of Philosophy* 15 (1977): 471-77.
*Manas* (12 Jan. 1977): 3, 4, 8; and (26 Jan. 1977): 5, 8.
Mohan, R. P. *Review of Metaphysics* 30 (1977): 536-37.
Morrison, J. *Philosophy and Phenomenological Research* 37 (1977): 569-70.
Berlin, I. "*Corsi e Ricorsi.*" *Journal of Modern History* 50 (1978): 480-89.
Cambon, G. *Renaissance Quarterly* 31 (1978): 368f.
Giorgi, A. *Journal of Phenomenological Psychology* 7 (1978): 227-29.
Krois, J. M. *Journal of the History of Behavioral Sciences* 14 (1978): 92-94.
Luft, S. R. *International Studies in Philosophy* 10 (1978): 149-62.
Valone, J. J. *International Philosophical Quarterly* 18 (1978): 101-3.
Luft, S. R. *Forum Italicum* 13 (1979): 258-65.
Rhea, B. *Contemporary Sociology* 10 (1981): 624-26.

Oliver, I. *British Journal of Sociology* 34 (1983): 519.
Schaeffer, John D. *Religious Studies Review* 13 (1987): 321-24.

Tagliacozzo, Giorgio, Michael Mooney, and Donald Phillip Verene, eds. *Vico and Contemporary Thought* (2 vols. in 1). Atlantic Highlands, NJ: Humanities Press, 1979. [Abstracts: *History and Theory* 19 (1980): 375; *New Vico Studies* 1 (1983): 121-25.] Reprinted from *Social Research* 43, nos. 3 and 4 (1976) (special issue in 2 nos.: *Vico and Contemporary Thought.*) [Contents listed separately in Part I B.]
**Reviews:**
Luft, Sandra Rudnick. "Vichian Studies," *International Studies in Philosophy* 10 (1978): 149-62.
Barnouw, Jeffrey. *The 18th Century: A Current Bibliography*, n.s. 2 (1976): 397-98.
Fulco, A. *Annals of Scholarship* 1 (1980): 118-23.
*Manas* 33 (1980): 1, 4, 8.
Nelson, R. S. *Ethics* 92 (1981): 149-52.
Rhea, B. *Contemporary Sociology* 10 (1981): 624-26.
Gellner, E. *Man* 17 (1982): 194-95.
Pennachetti, L. *Philosophy of the Social Sciences* 16 (1986): 274-81.
Schaeffer, John D. *Religious Studies Review* 13 (1987): 321-24.

Tagliacozzo, Giorgio, ed. *Vico: Past and Present*. Atlantic Highlands, NJ: Humanities Press, 1981 [Abstract: *New Vico Studies* 1 (1983): 123-24]. [Contents listed separately in Part I B.]
**Reviews:**
Rhea, B. *Contemporary Sociology* 10 (1981): 624-26.
*Choice* 19 (1982): 1475.
*Manas* 35 (1982): 3, 4, 8.
Schaeffer, J. D. *Religious Studies review* 9 (1983): 145.
Vasoli, C. *Journal of Modern History* 55 (1983): 500-2.
White, H. *Journal of the History of Philosophy* 2 (1983): 581-84.
Barnouw, J. *Journal of the History of the Behavioral Sciences* 20 (1984): 87-92.
de Waal Malefijt, A. *Man* (1984): 701-3.
Milbank, J. *History of European Ideas* 5 (1984): 99-103.
Bevilacqua, V. M. *Philosophy and Rhetoric* 18 (1985): 195-97.
Pennachetti, L. *Philosophy of the Social Sciences* 16 (1986): 274-81.
Schaeffer, John D. *Religious Studies Review* 13 (1987): 321-24.

Tagliacozzo, Giorgio, ed. *Vico and Marx: Affinities and Contrasts*. Atlantic Highlands, NJ: Humanities Press, 1983. [Contents listed separately in Part I B: Essays.]
**Reviews:**
Barnouw, Jeffrey. *The 18th Century: A Current Bibliography*, n.s. 9 (1983): 288.
*Choice* 21 (1984): 1021.
Kunze, D. E. Jr. *Environment and Planning: Society and Space* 2:3 (1984): 361-62.
Lachterman, D. *New Vico Studies* 2 (1984): 114-18.
*Manas* 37 (1984): 1-2, 7-8.
*Ethics* (D. I.) 95 (1985): 984.
Giddens, A. *Partisan Review* 2 (1985): 157-59.
Ingram, D. *Ethics* 95 (1985): 984.
Johnson, D. A. *History* (1985): 80-81.

Kellner, H. *Journal of Modern History* 57 (1985): 104-5.
Lubasz, H. *Italian Studies* 40 (1985); 139-41.
Minogue, K. "Marx and Vico." *Encounter* 66 (1986): 59-63.
Colbert, J. G. *Studies in Soviet Thought* 34 (1987): 286-88.
Kamenka, E. *Journal of the History of Philosophy* 25 (1987): 297-98.
Schaeffer, John D. *Religious Studies Review* 13 (1987): 321-24.

Tagliacozzo, Giorgio. *The Arbor scientiae Reconceived and the History of Vico's Resurrection.* Atlantic Highlands, NJ: Humanities Press for the Institute for Vico Studies, 1993. [Contents listed separately in Part I B.]

Vaughan, Frederick. *The Political Philosophy of Giambattista Vico: An Introduction to "La Scienza nuova."* The Hague: Martinus Nijhoff, 1972.
**Reviews:**
Goldstein, L. G. *International Studies in Philosophy* 4 (1974): 221-22.
Livingston, Donald W. *The 18th Century: A Current Bibliography* (1974): 1059.
Flanagan, T. E. *Canadian Journal of Political Science* 9 (1976): 158-59.

*Vera Lex* 5, no. 1 (1985). Special issue: *Giambattista Vico.* [Contents listed separately in Part I B.]

Verene, Donald Phillip. *Vico's Science of Imagination.* Ithaca, NY: Cornell University Press, 1981 (re-issue, paperback 1991) [Abstracts: *History and Theory* 21 (1982): 322; *New Vico Studies* 1 (1983): 122-23].
**Reviews:**
Armour, L. *Library Journal* 106 (1981): 887.
*Choice* 19 (1981): 226.
*Times Literary Supplement* (London) (6 Nov. 1981): 1309.
*Bibliographical Bulletin of Philosophy* 29 (1982): 112.
Cain, S. *Religious Studies Review* 8 (1982): 162.
Dupree, R. *Review of Metaphysics* 35 (1982): 916-17.
Evangeliou, C. *Philosophia* 12 (1982): 445-47.
Hemel, U. *Bijdragen Tijdschrift voor Filosofie en Theologie* 43 (1982): 456-67.
Nelson, R. Steven. *Ethics* 92 (1982): 792.
*Psychological Medicine* 12 (1982).
Walsh, W. H. *British Journal of Aesthetics* 22 (1982): 378-80.
Alberti, A. *Journal of Modern History* 55 (1983): 151-52.
Bevilacqua, V. M. *Quarterly Journal of Speech* 69 (1983): 444-47.
Blasi, A. *Journal of the History of the Behavioral Sciences* 19 (1983): 263-66.
Caponigri, A. R. *The Modern Schoolman* 60 (1983): 221-24.
Haddock, B. A. *Religious Studies* 19 (1983): 549-52.
Lovekin, D. *Philosophy and Rhetoric* 16 (1983): 55-60.
Milbank, J. *History of European Ideas* 4 (1983): 337-42.
Strong, E. F. *Journal of the History of Philosophy* 21 (1983): 273-75.
Munk, A. *Journal of Philosophy and Social Science* (1984): 356-57.

Pompa, L. *International Studies in Philosophy* 17 (1985): 101-3.
Pennachetti, L. *Philosophy of the Social Sciences* 16 (1986): 274-81.
Schaeffer, John D. *Religious Studies Review* 13 (1987): 321-24.
Gilman, Sander L. *Journal of the History of European Ideas* 17:1 (1993): 124-25.

Verene, Donald Phillip, ed. *Vico and Joyce.* Albany: State University of New York Press, 1987. [Contents listed separately in Part I B.]
**Reviews:**
Cook, P. *New Vico Studies* 5 (1987): 180-81.
Bishop, J. *New Vico Studies* 6 (1988): 133-42.
Herr, C. *Modern Fiction Studies* 34 (1988): 684-87.
Jacobik, G. *James Joyce Quarterly* 25 (1988): 392-94.
Janusko, R. *James Joyce Literary Supplement* 2 (1988): 10.
Rabate, J. M. *Clio: A Journal of Literature, History, and the Philosophy of History* 18 (1988): 91-94.
Schaeffer, J. *New Vico Studies* 6 (1988): 129-32.

Verene, Donald Phillip. *The New Art of Autobiography: An Essay on the 'Life of Giambattista Vico Written by Himself'*. Oxford: Clarendon Press, 1991.
**Reviews:**
Burke, P. "A Life Designed by Providence." *Times Higher Education Supplement* (London) (24 Jan. 1992).
Fletcher, A. *New Vico Studies* 10 (1992): 83-88.
Danesi, M. *Rivista di studi Italiani* 11 (1993): 180-89.
Olney, James. *Review of Metaphysics* 57 (1993): 393-94
Watson, Julia. *Philosophy and Literature* 17 (1993): 136-37.

Whittaker, Thomas. *Reason: A Philosophical Essay, with Historical Illustrations—Comte, Mill, Schopenhauer, Vico, Spinoza.* Cambridge: Cambridge University Press, 1934.

# Part I. Works on Vico

## B. Essays

Aarsleff, Hans. "Vico and Berlin." *London Review of Books* (Nov. 1981): 6-7.
_____. "Vico and Berlin." *London Review of Books* (June 1982): 4-5.

Abbott, D. P. "Croce and Vico." In "The Doctrine of Double Form: Benedetto Croce on Rhetoric and Poetics." *Philosophy and Rhetoric* 21 (1988): 10-15.

Adams, Henry Packwood. "Giambattista Vico." *Contemporary Review* 148 (1935): 79-85.

Alberti, A. "Primitive Language and Feudal Ideology: A Discovery of Vico." *European Institute Colloquium Papers* (28-30 Sept. 1983).

Alker, Hayward R. "Rescuing 'Reason' from the 'Rationalists': Reading Vico, Marx, and Weber as Reflective Institutionalists." *Millenium* 19 (1990): 161-84.

Amsler, Mark E. "Literary Onomastics and the Descent of Nations: The Example of Isidore and Vico." *Names: Journal of the American Name Society* 27 (1979): 106-16.

Arieti, Silvano. "Vico and Modern Psychiatry." *Social Research* 43 (1976): 739-52. Reprinted in *Vico and Contemporary Thought*, ed. G. Tagliacozzo, M. Mooney, and D. P. Verene. Atlantic Highlands, NJ: Humanities Press, 1979: 2: 81-94.

Aronovitch, Hilliard. "Vico and Verstehen." In *Vico: Past and Present*, ed. G. Tagliacozzo. Atlantic Highlands, NJ: Humanities Press, 1981: 1:216-25.
_____. "Vico and Marx on Human Nature and Historical Development." In *Vico: Past and Present*, ed. G. Tagliacozzo. Atlantic Highlands, NJ: Humanities Press, 1981: 2:45-47.
_____. "If a Science of Human Beings is Necessary, Can It Also Be Possible? A Paradox in Vico and Marx." In *Vico and Marx: Affinities and Contrasts*, ed. G. Tagliacozzo. Atlantic Highlands, NJ: Humanities Press; London: Macmillan, 1983: 163-77.

Auerbach, Erich. "Vico's Contribution to Literary Criticism." In *Studia philologica et litteraria in honorem L. Spitzer*. Bern: Franke, 1958: 31-37.
_____. "Vico and Aesthetic Historicism." *Journal of Aesthetics and Art Criticism* 8 (1949): 110-18. Reprinted in *Scenes from the Drama of European Literature*. New York: Meridian, 1959: 183-200.

Averill, James R. "Comments on 'A Sense of Vico's Place in the Social Production of Scientific Entities'." *British Journal of Social Psychology* 25 (1986): 212-14.

Badaloni, Nicola. "Ideality and Factuality in Vico's Thought." In *Giambattista Vico: An International Symposium*, ed. G. Tagliacozzo and H. White. Baltimore: Johns Hopkins University Press, 1969: 391-400.

Bahti, Timothy. "Vico, Auerbach, and Literary History." In *Vico: Past and Present*, ed. G. Tagliacozzo. Atlantic Highlands, NJ: Humanities Press, 1981: 2:97-114. Reprinted in *The Philological Quarterly* 60 (1981): 230-55.
———. "Vico and Frye: A Note." *New Vico Studies* 3 (1985): 119-29.

Ball, Terence. "On 'Making' History in Vico and Marx." In *Vico and Marx: Affinities and Contrasts*, ed. G. Tagliacozzo. Atlantic Highlands, NJ: Humanities Press; London: Macmillan Press, 1983: 78-93.

Barnard, F. M. "Natural Growth and Positive Development: Vico and Herder." *History and Theory* 18 (1979): 16-36 [Abstract in *The 18th Century: A Current Bibliography* n.s. 5 (1979): 588].

Barnouw, Jeffrey. "The Relation Between the Certain and the True in Vico's Pragmatist Construction of Human History." *Comparative Literature Studies* 15 (1978): 242-64 [Abstract in *The 18th Century: A Current Bibliography*, n.s. 4 (1978): 471].
———. "Vico and the Continuity of Science: The Relation of His Epistemology to Bacon and Hobbes." *Isis* 71 (1980): 609-20 [Abstract in *The 18th Century: A Current Bibliography* n.s. 6 (1980): 593].
———. "The Critique of Classical Republicanism and the Understanding of Modern Forms of Polity in Vico's *New Science*." *Clio* 9 (1980): 393-418 [Abstract in *The 18th Century: A Current Bibliography* n.s. 6 (1980): 593].
———. "Man Making History: The Role of the Plebians in Vico, the Proletariat in Marx." In *Vico and Marx: Affinities and Contrasts*, ed. G. Tagliacozzo. Atlantic Highlands, NJ: Humanities Press; London: Macmillan Press, 1983: 94-113.

Baron, Naomi S. "Writing and Vico's Functional Approach to Language Change." In *Vico: Past and Present*, ed. G. Tagliacozzo. Atlantic Highlands, NJ: Humanities Press, 1981: 2: 115-31.
———, and Nikhil Bhattacharya. "Vico and Joyce: The Limits of Language." In *Vico and Joyce*, ed. D. P. Verene. Albany: State University of New York Press, 1987: 175-95.

Bassett, Beth Dawkins. "The Resurrection and the Life of Giambattista Vico." *Emory Magazine* 61 (1985): 24-32.
———. "Welcome to the Museyroom." *Emory Magazine* 68 (1992): 2.

Battistini, Andrea. "Contemporary Trends in Vichian Studies." In *Vico: Past and Present*, ed. G. Tagliacozzo. Atlantic Highlands, NJ: Humanities Press, 1981: 1:1-42.
———. "Gian Battista Vico: Poesia, Logica, Religione." *New Vico Studies* 3 (1985): 234-35 [Report].
———. "Vico and the Passions." In *Teorie della Passioni*, ed. Elena Pulcini. Dordrecht: Kluwer, 1989: 113-28 [Abstract: *New Vico Studies* 9 (1991): 15-36].

Beckett, Samuel. "Dante...Bruno. Vico..Joyce." In *Our Exagmination Round His Factification for Incamination of Work in Progress*, ed. S. Beckett et al. Paris: Shakespeare and Co.; London: Faber and Faber, 1929; Norfolk, CT: New Directions, 1939: 1-22. Reprinted in *I can't go on, I'll go on*, ed. R. W. Seaver. New York: Grove Weidenfeld, 1976: 105-26.

Bedani, G. L. C. "The Poetic as an Aesthetic Category in Vico's *Scienza nuova.*" *Italian Studies* 31 (1976): 22-36.
**Review:**
Barnouw, Jeffrey. *The 18th Century: A Current Bibliography*, n.s. 2 (1976): 390.

Bedani, G. L. C. "A Neglected Problem in Contemporary Vico Studies: Intellectual Freedom and Religious Constraints in Vico's Naples." *New Vico Studies* 4 (1986): 57-72.
———. "The Origins of Vico's Epistemology and the Genesis of His New Science of Nations." *Italian Studies* 43 (1988): 75-87.

Behrenberg, Peter. "Vico, Cassirer, and Blumenberg." *New Vico Studies* 9 (1991): 17-28.

Belaval, Yvon. "Vico and Anti-Cartesianism." In *Giambattista Vico: An International Symposium*, ed. G. Tagliacozzo and H. White. Baltimore: Johns Hopkins University Press, 1969: 77-91.

Benstock, Bernard. "Vico...Joyce.Triv..Quad." In *Vico and Joyce*, ed. D. P. Verene. Albany: State University of New York Press, 1987: 59-67.

Bergel, Lienhart. "Vico and the Germany of Goethe." *Forum Italicum* 2 (1968): 566-88.

Berlin, Isaiah. "The Philosophical Ideas of Giambattista Vico." In *Art and Ideas in Eighteenth-Century Italy*. Rome: Edizioni di Storia e Letteratura, 1960: 156-223.
———. "A Note on Vico's Concept of Knowledge." In *Giambattista Vico: An International Symposium*, ed. G. Tagliacozzo and H. White. Baltimore: Johns Hopkins University Press, 1969: 371-77. Also published in *The New York Review of Books* (24 April 1969): 23-26.
———. "Vico, One of the Boldest Innovators in the History of Human Thought." *The New York Times Magazine* (23 Nov. 1969): 76-100. Reprinted in *Molders of Modern Thought*, ed. Ben B. Seligman. Chicago: Quadrangle Books, 1970: 41-56.
———. "Giambattista Vico." *The Listener* 88 (1972): 391-92, 394-98.
———. "Comment on Professor Verene's Paper." *Social Research* 43 (1976): 426-29. Reprinted in *Vico and Contemporary Thought* (ed. G. Tagliacozzo, M. Mooney, and D. P. Verene): 1: 36-39.
———. "Vico and the Ideal of the Enlightenment." *Social Research* 43 (1976): 640-53. Reprinted in *Vico and Contemporary Thought* (ed. G. Tagliacozzo, M. Mooney, and D. P. Verene): 1: 250-63.
———. "Corsi e Ricorsi." *Journal of Modern History* 50 (1978): 480-89.
———. "Professor Scouten on Herder and Vico." *Comparative Literature Studies* 16 (1979): 141-45.
———. "Isaiah Berlin Responds to the Foregoing Criticism of His Work." *London Review of Books* (5-18 Nov. 1981): 7-8.
———. [Reply to letter of H. Aarsleff titled "Vico and Berlin."] *London Review of Books* (3-16 June 1982): 5.
———. "Discussions on Vico." *The Philosophical Quarterly* 35 (1985): 281-90 [response to Zagorin, P. "Vico's Theory of Knowledge." Vol. 34 (1984): 15-30].

———. "Giambattista Vico and Cultural History." In *The Crooked Timber of Humanity*, ed. H. Hardy. London: John Murray, 1990; New York: Knopf, 1991: 49-72 [originally published in L. S. Cauman *et al*, eds. *How Many Questions? Essays in Honor of Sydney Morgenbesser*. Indianapolis: Hackett, 1983: 474-98].

———. "Letter to Antonio Verri." In *Vico e il pensiero contemporaneo*, ed. A. Verri. Lecce: Milella, 1991: vi-vii.

Betti, Emilio. "The Principles of New Science of G. B. Vico and the Theory of Historical Interpretation." *New Vico Studies* 6 (1988): 31-50.

Berrigan, Joseph R. "Vico and the Myth of Rome." *Classical Folia: Studies in the Christian Perpetuation of the Classics* 28 (1974): 191-205.

Bertolini, Andrea. "Vico on Etymology: Toward a Rhetorical Critique of Historical Genealogies." *Yale Italian Studies* 1 (1977): 93-106.

Bevilacqua, Vincent M. "Vico, Rhetorical Humanism, and the Study Methods of Our Time." *Quarterly Journal of Speech* 58 (1972): 70-83.

———. "Vico, 'Process', and the Nature of Rhetorical Investigation: An Epistemological Perspective." *Philosophy and Rhetoric* 7 (1974): 166-174 [Abstract in *The 18th Century: A Current Bibliography* (1974): 1059].

———. "Campbell, Vico, and the Rhetorical Science of Human Nature." *Rhetoric Society Quarterly* 13 (1983): 5-11 [Abstract in *The 18th Century: A Current Bibliography*, n.s. 11 (1985): 665].

———. "Campbell, Vico, and the Rhetorical Science of Human Nature." *Philosophy and Rhetoric* 18 (1985): 23-30.

Bhattacharya, Nikhil. "Knowledge 'Per Caussas': Vico's Theory of Natural Science." In *Vico: Past and Present*, ed. G. Tagliacozzo. Atlantic Highlands, NJ: Humanities Press, 1981: 1: 97-114.

———. "Scientific Knowledge in Vico and Marx." In *Vico and Marx: Affinities and Contrasts*, ed. G. Tagliacozzo. Atlantic Highlands, NJ: Humanities Press; London: Macmillan Press, 1983: 192-205.

Bidney, David. "Vico's New Science of Myth." In *Giambattista Vico: An International Symposium*, ed. G. Tagliacozzo and H. White. Baltimore: Johns Hopkins University Press, 1969: 259-77.

Birns, D. K. "Vico's 'De nostri temporis studiorum ratione' and Eighteenth-Century English Thought." *Carte italiane* 1 (1979-80): 37-47.

Bishop, John. "Vico's 'Night of Darkness': *The New Science* and *Finnegans Wake*." Ch. 7 in *Joyce's Book of the Dark, Finnegans Wake*. Madison: University of Wisconsin Press, 1986: 174-215 [et passim].

*Review:*
Norris, Margot. "As Through a Glass Darkly, Darkling." *James Joyce Literary Supplement* 1 (1987): 5-6.

Bishop, John. "*Vico and Joyce* and Joyce Scholarship." Review of *Vico and Joyce* (ed. D. P. Verene). *New Vico Studies* 6 (1988): 133-42.

Black, David W. "Vico, Education, and Childhood." *Educational Theory* 34 (1984): 103-12 [Abstract: *New Vico Studies* 2 (1984): 127].
_____. "The Vichian Element in Susanne Langer's Thought." *New Vico Studies* 3 (1985): 113-18.

Blasi, Augusto. "Vico, Developmental Psychology, and Human Nature." *Social Research* 43 (1976): 672-97. Reprinted in *Vico and Contemporary Thought*, ed. G. Tagliacozzo, M. Mooney, and D. P. Verene. Atlantic Highlands, NJ: Humanities Press, 1979: 2: 14-39.

Bonaparte, Felicia. "George Henry Lewes, George Eliot, and Vico: The Shaping of a Modern Creed." *New Vico Studies* 2 (1984): 93-102.

Bosinelli, Rosa Maria. "'I use his cycles as a trellis': Joyce's Treatment of Vico in *Finnegans Wake*." In *Vico and Joyce*, ed. D. P. Verene. Albany: State University of New York Press, 1987: 123-34.

Bowle, John. "Scientific Humanism: Spinoza: Vico." Ch. 7 in *Western Political Thought: A Historical Introduction from the Origins to Rousseau*. London: Jonathan Cape, 1947: 376-98.

Bray, Paul. *Ingens Sylva* [27-pg. poem]. New York: Chroma Press at Pelavin Editions, 1986.

Breisach, Ernst. "Giambattista Vico, God, and the Cultural Cycle" in *Historiography: Ancient and Modern*. Chicago: University of Chicago Press, 1983: 210-14; see also 201, 222, 241, 341.

Bryan, Ferald J. "Vico on Metaphor: Implications for Rhetorical Criticism." *Philosophy and Rhetoric* 19 (1986): 255-65 [Abstract in *The 18th Century: A Current Bibliography*, n.s. 12 (1986): 534].

Buford, Thomas O. "A Theater of Memory: Vico's View of Personal Identity." *Proceedings of the South Atlantic Philosophy of Education Society* 32 (1987): 69-76.
_____. "Knowing Conceptual Universals, Making Imaginative Universals." *Philosophy of Education: Proceedings* 44 (1988): 432-36.

Burke, Peter. "The Sage of Naples." *Times Literary Supplement* (London) (2 July 1993): 30.

Caesar, Michael. "Giambattista Vico, Dante's 'barbarousness'; three reasons for reading him." In Caesar, ed. *Dante: The Critical Heritage*. London and New York: Routledge, 1989: 346-48; see also 42-43, 45-50, 333, 337, 348-52, 452-55, 433, 448-49. [See Part II A for complete citations to M. Günsberg's translations, "To Gherardo degli Angioli" and "The discovery of the true Dante."]

*Review:*
Pietropaolo, Domenico. *New Vico Studies* 8 (1990): 149-53.

Cahnman, Werner J. "Vico and Historical Sociology." *Social Research* 43 (1976): 826-36. Reprinted in *Vico and Contemporary Thought*, ed. G. Tagliacozzo, M. Mooney, and D. P. Verene. Atlantic Highlands, NJ: Humanities Press, 1979: 2: 168-78.

———. "Hobbes, Toennies, and Vico." In *The Future of the Sociological Classics*, ed. B. Rhea. Winchester, MA: Allen and Unwin, 1981: 16-38.

Cairns, Grace E. "Giambattista Vico: The 'Science' of the Culture Cycle." In *Philosophies of History*, London: Peter Owen, 1963: 337-52.

Cambon, Glauco. "Vico and Dante." In *Dante's Craft*. Minneapolis: University of Minnesota Press, 1969: 146-60.

———. "Vico and Dante." In *Giambattista Vico: An International Symposium*, ed. G. Tagliacozzo and H. White. Baltimore: Johns Hopkins University Press, 1969: 15-28.

———. "Vico as Poet." *Forum Italicum* 2 (1968): 326-31.

———. "Vico and Wundt." *Italian Quarterly* 21 (1980): 55-63.

Campbell, Richard J. "Vico on Mathematical Truth"; "The True is the Made"; "Vico's New Science of History" "History and Providence." In Campbell, *Truth and Historicity*. Oxford: Clarendon Press, 1992: 251-68 *et passim*.

Campo, Vincent. "The Vico Connection to James Joyce's *Ulysses*." *The Newscribes* 2 (1977): 7-15.

Cantelli, Gianfranco. "Myth and Language in Vico." In *Giambattista Vico's Science of Humanity*, ed. G. Tagliacozzo and D. P. Verene. Baltimore: John Hopkins University Press, 1976: 47-63.

———. "Reflections on the Vichian Thesis That the Original Language of Humanity Was a Language Spoken by the Gods." *New Vico Studies* 11 (1993): 1-12.

Caponigri, A. Robert. "Vico and the Theory of History." *Giornale di metafisica* 9 (1954): 183-97.

———. "Giam Battista Vico." In A. R. Caponigri and R. M. McInery, eds., *A History of Western Philosophy*. Notre Dame, IN: University of Notre Dame Press, 1963-1971: 3:481-95.

———. "Umanità and Civiltà: Civil Education in Vico." *The Review of Politics* 31 (1969): 477-94.

———. "The Timelessness of the *Scienza nuova* of Giambattista Vico." In *Italian Literature: Roots and Branches*, ed. Giosé Rimanelli and K. J. Atchity. New Haven and London: Yale University Press, 1976: 309-32.

———. "Philosophy and Philology: The 'New Art of Criticism' of Giam Battista Vico." *The Modern Schoolman* (1982): 81-116.

Caramella, Santino. "Vico, Tacitus, and Reasons of State." In *Giambattista Vico: An International Symposium*, ed. G. Tagliacozzo and H. White. Baltimore: Johns Hopkins University Press, 1969: 29-37.

Carpanetto, Dino, and Giuseppe Ricuperati. "The *Veteres* against the *Moderni*: Paolo Mattia Doria (1662-1746) and Giambattista Vico (1668-1744)." In *Italy and the Age of Reason 1685-1789*. Longman History of Italy. London: Longman, 1987: 5:96-105.

Carravetta, Peter. "Toward a Study of Rhetorics and Hermeneutics in Vico and Heidegger." In *Prefaces to the Diaphora: Rhetoric, Allegory, and the Interpretation of Postmodernity* (P. Carravetta). West Lafayette, IN: Purdue University Press, 1991: 239-52 [see also 15, 25, 30, 94, 105, 164].
*Review:*
Jacobitti, Edmund. *New Vico Studies* 10 (1992): 124-26.

Caserta, Ernesto G. "From Machiavelli to Vico: Three Books by Rocco Montano." *Comparative Literature Studies* 19 (1982): 67-75.

Casserly, Julian Victor Langmead. "Vico." In *The Christian in Philosophy*. New York: Scribner's Sons, 1961: Ch. 3, sec. 6, 118-22; *see also* 46, 66-67, 123, 207-8, 237-38.

Cassirer, Ernst. "Descartes, Leibniz, and Vico." In *Symbol, Myth, and Culture: Essays and Lectures 1935-1945*, ed. Donald Phillip Verene. New Haven, CT: Yale University Press, 1979: 95-107 [see also 6, 13, 43-44].
*Review:*
Riley, Patrick. *American Political Science Review* 74 (1980): 1073-75.

Cellerino, Massimo. "A 'Vichian' Practical Philosophy?" Review of *Cosmopolis: The Hidden Agenda of Modernity* (S. Toulmin). *New Vico Studies* 9 (1991): 92-99.

Ceñal, Ramón. "Vico and Nineteenth Century Spanish Thought." In *Giambattista Vico: An International Symposium*, ed. G. Tagliacozzo and H. White. Baltimore: Johns Hopkins University Press, 1969: 187-201.

Chambliss, Joseph James. "Vico: Human Beings Make Themselves." In *Educational Theory as Theory of Conduct*. Albany: State University of New York Press, 1987: 87-99.
———. "Giambattista Vico's Imaginative Universals and Plato's Quest for the Good." *Educational Theory* 38 (1988): 311-20.
———. "Aristotle's Conception of Knowing and Vico's Imaginative Metaphysics." *Philosophy of Education: Proceedings* 44 (1988): 422-31.

Chambliss, Rollin. "Giambattista Vico." In *Social Thought: From Hammurabi to Comte*, 366-91. New York: Holt, Rinehart and Winston, 1954.

Cho, Hanook. "Vico Studies in Korea." *New Vico Studies* 8 (1990): 160-61 [Report].

Church, Margaret. "'Dubliners' and Vico." *James Joyce Quarterly* 5 (1968): 150-56.

———. "Joyce and Vico Panel." *James Joyce Quarterly* 9 (1972): 311-17.

———. "Vico and 'Ulysses'." In *Proceedings of the Third International James Joyce Symposium 14-18 June, 1971*, ed. Facoltà di Magistero, University of Trieste, 343-47. Trieste: La Editoriale Libraria, 1974.

———. "'A Portrait' and Giambattista Vico: A Source Study." In *Approaches to Joyce's "Portrait"*, ed. T. F. Staley and B. Benstock, 77-89. Pittsburgh: University of Pittsburgh Press, 1976.

———. "How the Vicocyclometer Works. The Fiction of James Joyce." In *Structure and Theme: Don Quixote to James Joyce*. Columbus: Ohio State University Press, 1983: 135-67.

Clark, M. A. "Rimbaud—Michelet—Vico." *Modern Language Review* 37 (1942): 50-55.

Clark, Robert T. Jr. "Herder, Cesarotti and Vico." *Studies in Philology* 44 (1947): 645-71.

Coers, Kathy Frashure. "Vico and MacIntyre." *New Vico Studies* 4 (1986): 131-33.

Collingwood, R. G. "Anti-Cartesianism: Vico." In *The Idea of History*. Oxford: Clarendon Press, 1946: 63-71.

Conte, Anthony. "The Use of Giambattista Vico in the Modern Tradition." *Literature and Ideology* 8 (1971): 31-42.

Copleston, Frederick. "Bossuet and Vico." *A History of Philosophy*. London: Burns and Oates, 1964: 6:150-63.

Corsano, Antonio. "Vico and Mathematics." In *Giambattista Vico: An International Symposium*, ed. G. Tagliacozzo and H. White. Baltimore: Johns Hopkins University Press, 1969: 425-37.

Costa, Gustavo. "Vico's Political Thought in His Time and Ours." *Social Research* 43 (1976): 612-24. Reprinted in *Vico and Contemporary Thought*, ed. G. Tagliacozzo, M. Mooney, and D. P. Verene. Atlantic Highlands, NJ: Humanities Press, 1979: 1:223-34.

———. "Vico's Influence on Eighteenth-Century European Culture: Footnote to Professor Nisbet's Paper." *Social Research* 43 (1976): 637-39. Reprinted in *Vico and Contemporary Thought*, ed. G. Tagliacozzo, M. Mooney, and D. P. Verene. Atlantic Highlands, NJ: Humanities Press, 1979: 1:247-49.

———. "Vico and Ancient Rhetoric." *Eighteenth Century Studies* 11 (1978): 247-62. Reprinted in *Classical Influences on Western Thought, A.D. 1650-1870*, ed. R. R. Bolgar. Cambridge: Cambridge University Press, 1979.

———. "An Enduring Venetian Accomplishment: The Autobiography of G. B. Vico." *Italian Quarterly* 21 (1980): 45-54.

———. "Melchiorre Cesarotti, Vico, and the Sublime." *Italica* 58 (1981): 3-15 [Abstract in *The 18th Century: A Current Bibliography*, n.s. 7 ((1981): 418].

———. "The Desert and the Rock: Giambattista Vico's *New Science* vis-à-vis Eighteenth-Century European Culture." In *Trans. Sixth International Congress on the Enlightenment*. Oxford: Voltaire Foundation, 1983: 450-51. Reprinted in *Quaderni d'italianistica* 6 (1985): 100-10.

———. "A Decade of Vichian Studies: Pietro Piovani's *Bollettino* (1971-1980)." In *New Vico Studies* 1 (1983): 77-83.

———. "Vico and Marx: Notes on the History of the Concept of Alienation." In *Vico and Marx: Affinities and Contrasts*, ed. G. Tagliacozzo. Atlantic Highlands, NJ: Humanities Press, 1983: 151-62.

———. "The Orpheus Myth in European Culture from Vossius to Vico." In *Selected Proceedings of the International Conference on "The Enlightenment in a Western Mediterranean Context,"* ed. F. Gerson, A. Percival, and D. Pietropaolo. Toronto: Benben/ Society for Mediterranean Studies, 1984: 53-60.

———. "Vico's 'Sali Nitri' and the Origins of Pagan Civilization: the Alchemical Dimension of the *New Science*," *Rivista di Studi Italiani* 10 (1992): 1-11.

Cotroneo, Girolamo. "A Renaissance Source of the *Scienza nuova*: Jean Bodin's *Methodus*." In *Giambattista Vico: An International Symposium*, ed. G. Tagliacozzo and H. White. Baltimore: Johns Hopkins University Press, 1969: 51-59.

Cousin, Victor. "Historians of Humanity." In *Course of the History of Modern Philosophy*, trans. O. W. Wright. New York: D. Appleton and Co., 1857: 211-27.

Craig, Robert Paul. "Comment on the 'Vico and Pedagogy' Session." *Social Research* 43 (1976): 802-6. Reprinted in *Vico and Contemporary Thought*, ed. G. Tagliacozzo, M. Mooney, and D. P. Verene. Atlantic Highlands, NJ: Humanities Press, 1979: 2:144-48.

Crease, Robert. "The Rediscovery of Vico." *International Daily News* (2 Sept. 1978): 13.

———. "Vico and the 'Cogito'." In *Vico: Past and Present*, ed. G. Tagliacozzo. Atlantic Highlands, NJ: Humanities Press, 1981: 1:171-81.

Cristofolini, Paolo. "Human Sciences and Philosophy of History between Vico and Marx, Croce, Labriola, Sorel, and 'Philosophy of History'." In *Vico and Marx: Affinities and Contrasts*, ed. G. Tagliacozzo. Atlantic Highlands, NJ: Humanities Press; London: Macmillan Press, 1983: 342-51.

Croce, Benedetto. "Giambattista Vico." In Croce, *Aesthetic as Science of Expression and General Linguistic*, trans. D. Ainslie. New York: Macmillan, 1922 (1909): pt. 2, ch. 5. Reprinted New York: Noonday, 1956.

———. "Machiavelli and Vico—Politics and Ethics." In Croce, *Politics and Morals*, trans. S. J. Castiglione. London: George Allen and Unwin, Ltd., 1946: 44-50.

———. "An Unknown Page from the Last Months of Hegel's Life," trans. J. W. Hillensheim and E. Caserta. *The Personalist* 45 (1964): 344-45, 351.

———. "Vico and the Subsequent Development of Philosophic and Historic Thought." In Croce, *Philosophy, Poetry, History: An Anthology of Essays*, trans. C. Sprigge. London: Oxford University Press, 1966: 138-44.

———. "Machiavelli and Vico." In Croce, *Philosophy, Poetry, History: An Anthology of Essays*, trans. C. Sprigge. London: Oxford University Press, 1966: 655-70.

Daffina, Paolo. "China in Giambattista Vico's Judgment." *Philosophy East and West* 9 (1958): 65-73.

Dallmayr, Fred R. "'Natural History' and Social Evolution: Reflections on Vico's *corsi e ricorsi*." *Social Research* 43 (1976): 857-73. Reprinted in *Vico and Contemporary Thought*, ed. G. Tagliacozzo, M. Mooney, and D. P. Verene. Atlantic Highlands, NJ: Humanities Press, 1979: 2:199-215.
———. "Hermeneutics and Historicism: Reflections on Winch, Apel, and Vico." *Review of Politics* 39 (1977): 60-81. Reprinted in Dallmayr, *Beyond Dogma and Despair*. Notre Dame, IN: University of Notre Dame Press, 1981: 139-55.
———. "Reading Horkheimer Reading Vico. An Introduction." *New Vico Studies* 5 (1987): 56-62.

Dane, Joseph A. "Viconian Ironies." In Dane, *The Critical Mythology of Irony*. Athens: University of Georgia Press, 1991: 159-171.

Danesi, Marcel. "Language and the Origin of Human Imagination: A Vichian Perspective." *New Vico Studies* 4 (1986): 45-56.
———. "Giambattista Vico in the Context of the Changing Coordinates of Anglo-American Science and Philosophy." *Rivista di Studi Italiani* 4-5 (Dec.1986-June 1987).
———. "Creativity in Language: Vico's Theory Comes of Age." *International Semiotic Spectrum* 9 (1987): 3.
———. "A Vichian Footnote to Nietzsche's Views of Metaphor: An Addendum to Schrift." *New Vico Studies* 5 (1987): 157-64.
———. "Vico and Chomsky: On the Nature of Creativity in Language." *New Vico Studies* 7 (1989): 28-42.
———, and Aldo D'Alfonso. "Creativity in the Language Classroom: Toward a 'Vichian' Approach in Second Language Teaching." *Italica* 66 (1989): 9-19.

Danesi, Marcel. "Semiosis, Cognition, and Reality: A Vichian Commentary on Krausz's Anthology on Relativism." Review of *Relativism: Interpretation and Confrontation* (M. Krausz). *New Vico Studies* 8 (1990): 71-78.
———. "Giambattista Vico and Semiotics." In *Recent Developments in Theory and History: The Semiotic Web 1990*, ed. T. A. Sebeok and J. U. Sebeok. Berlin, NY: Mouton de Gruyter, 1991: 89-109.
———. "Language and Myth: A Note on Cantelli's Study of Vico's Views on Language." *Rivista di Studi Italiani* 7 (1991): 39-46.
———. "International Conference on Vico in the Context of Anglo-American Science, Philosophy, and Aesthetics." *New Vico Studies* 9 (1991): 147-50 [Report].
———. "The Sapirean Paradigm in Linguistics: A Vichian Commentary." Review of *Edward Sapir: Linguist, Anthropologist, Humanist* (R. Darnell). Berkeley: University of California Press, 1990. *New Vico Studies* 10 (1992): 53-63.

_____. "Concepts and Emotions: A Vichian Perspective of Recent Work in Experientialist Cognitive Science." *New Vico Studies* 11 (1993): 77-87.

Daniel, Stephen H. "The Philosophy of Ingenuity: Vico on Proto-Philosophy," *Philosophy and Rhetoric* 18 (1985): 236-43.
_____. "Vico on Mythic Figuration as a Prerequisite for Philosophical Literacy," *New Vico Studies* 3 (1985): 61-72.
_____. "The Narrative Character of Myth and Philosophy in Vico." *International Studies in Philosophy* 20 (1988): 1-9.
_____. "Narrative and Mythic Figuration in Vico." In *Myth and Modern Philosophy*. Philadelphia: Temple University Press, 1990: 129-57 (ch. 5); see also xii, xiii, 19-21, 36, 64, 108, 178, 191, 206.

D'Arcy, Martin C. "The New Science of Vico." In *The Meaning and Matter of History: A Christian View*. New York: Farrar, Straus, and Cudahy, 1959: 122-32 (also published as *The Sense of History: Secular and Sacred*. London: Faber & Faber, 1959).

Dasenbrock, Reed Way. "Ulysses and Joyce's Discovery of Vico's 'True Homer'." *Eire-Ireland: A Journal of Irish Studies* 20 (1985): 96-108.
_____. "Homer, Dante, Vico, Croce, Joyce." In *Imitating the Italians: Wyatt, Spenser, Synge, Pound, Joyce*. Baltimore: Johns Hopkins University Press, 1991: 125-43.
**Reviews:**
Manglaviti, Leo M. *James Joyce Literary Supplement* (Fall, 1992): 26-27.
Herring, Phillip F. *Italica* 69 (1992): 248-49.

Day, Paul W. "Matthew Arnold and the Philosophy of Vico." *Proceedings of the Australasian Universities Language and Literature Association* 2 (1964: 26-27. Reprinted: Darby, PA: Darby Books, 1981.

De Gennaro, Angelo. "Croce and Vico." *Journal of Aesthetics and Art Criticism* 22 (1963): 43-46.
_____. "The Lasting Influence of Vico: On the Tercentenary of His Birth." *Italica* 45 (1968): 403-9.
_____. "The Relevance of Vico's Thought in the Tercentenary of His Birth." *Forum Italicum* 2 (1968): 299-304.
_____. "The Vico-Tercentenary, 1668-1744." *Personalist* 49 (1968): 453-57.
_____. "Vico and Croce: The Genesis of Croce's Aesthetics." *Personalist* 50 (1969): 508-25.

de La Roche, Michel. Book Notice of Vico's *De nostri temporis studiorum ratione*. *Memoirs of Literature*. London: J. Roberts (11 Dec. 1710): 160 (2d ed. *Memoirs of Literature, Containing a Large Account of Many Valuable Books, Letters, and Dissertations on Several Subjects*. London, 1722: 2:190-91).

De Mas, Enrico. "Vico's Four Authors." In *Giambattista Vico: An International Symposium*, ed. G. Tagliacozzo and H. White. Baltimore: Johns Hopkins University Press, 1969: 3-14.
_____. "Vico and Italian Thought." In *Giambattista Vico: An International Symposium*, ed. G. Tagliacozzo and H. White. Baltimore: Johns Hopkins University Press, 1969: 147-64.

_____. "On the New Method of a New Science: A Study of Giambattista Vico," trans. J. K. Houck. *Journal of the History of Ideas* 32 (1971): 85-94 [Abstract in *The 18th Century: A Current Bibliography* (1979): 778].

de Mauro, Tullio. "Giambattista Vico: From Rhetoric to Linguistic Historicism." In *Giambattista Vico: An International Symposium*, ed. G. Tagliacozzo and H. White. Baltimore: Johns Hopkins University Press, 1969: 279-95.

De Santillana, Giorgio. "Vico and Descartes." *Osiris* 9 (1950): 565-80. Reprinted in *Reflections on Men and Ideas*. Cambridge: Massachusetts Institute of Technology Press, 1968: 206-18.

Diamond, Stanley. "On Reading Vico." *Dialectical Anthropology* 2 (1977): 19-32.

Dieckman, Liselotte. "Giambattista Vico's Use of 'Renaissance Hieroglyphics'." *Forum Italicum* 2 (1968): 382-85.

Diefenbeck, James A. "Knowledge as What is Done: Vico." In Diefenbeck, *A Celebration of Subjective Thought*. Carbondale: Southern Illinois University Press, 1984: 116-21; *see also* 124-25.

Di Pietro, Robert. "Humanism in Linguistic Theory: A Lesson from Vico." In *Giambattista Vico's Science of Humanity*, ed. G. Tagliacozzo and D. P. Verene. Baltimore: Johns Hopkins University Press, 1976: 47-63.
_____. "Further Observations on the Symposium, 'Vico and Linguistics'." *Historiographia Linguistica* 3 (1976): 125-27.
_____. "Linguistic Creativity: A Vichian Key to Contemporary Humanism." In *Vico: Past and Present*, ed. G. Tagliacozzo. Atlantic Highlands, NJ: Humanities Press, 1981: 97-114.

Donagan, Alan, and Barbara Donagan. "Giambattista Vico: A New Conception of Historiography." In *Philosophy of History*. New York: Macmillan, 1965: 44-52.

Dorfles, Gillo. "Myth and Metaphor in Vico and in Contemporary Aesthetics." In *Giambattista Vico: An International Symposium*, ed. G. Tagliacozzo and H. White. Baltimore: Johns Hopkins University Press, 1969: 577-90.

Downs, Robert B. "Vico." In *Molders of the Modern Mind: 111 Books That Shaped Western Civilization*. New York: Barnes & Noble, 1961: 112-14.

Durant, Will, and Ariel Durant. "Giambattista Vico." In *The Story of Civilization*. Vol. 10: *Rousseau and Revolution*. New York: MJF Books, 1967 [1st ed. 1926]: 251-54.

Eberhard, John P. "A New Science Needed for Man." *Transactions of the New York Academy of Science* 32 (1970): 806.

Edie, James M. "Vico and Existential Philosophy." In *Giambattista Vico: An International Symposium*, ed. G. Tagliacozzo and H. White. Baltimore: Johns Hopkins University Press, 1969: 483-95.
_____. "Giambattista Vico's Theory of Metaphor." In *Speaking and Meaning: The Phenomenology of Language*. Bloomington: Indiana University Press, 1976: 166-71.

Eichhorn, Irma E., Joseph Cono, and Joan M. Todd. "'Heaven Is So Far Away': The Socio-Historical Role of Religion in Vico, Herder, and Wittram." *Journal of Baltic Studies* 8 (1977): 275-93.

Ellmann, Richard. "Yeats and Vico." *Irish Literary Supplement* 2 (1983): 1, 19.

Ellwood, Charles A. "Giambattista Vico and Social Evolution." In *A History of Social Philosophy*. New York: AMS Press, 1969: 138-47.

Engell, James. "Leading out into the World: Vico's New Education." *New Vico Studies* 3 (1985): 33-47.
———. "Bruner and Vico: Psychology and Pedagogy." Review of *Acts of Meaning* (J. Bruner); and Giambattista Vico, *On the Study Methods of Our Time*, trans. E. Gianturco (including Vico's "The Academies and the Relation between Philosophy and Eloquence," trans. D. P. Verene). *New Vico Studies* 10 (1992): 64-72. [See Part II A for full citation of these translations.]

Fáj, Attila. "Some Important, Hitherto Unnoticed Sources of *Finnegans Wake*." In *Proceedings of the Third International James Joyce Symposium, 14-18 June 1971*, ed. Facoltà di Magistero, University of Trieste. Trieste: La Editoriale Libraria, 1974: 358-74. Also published in *A Wake Newslitter* 10 (1973): 3-12; reprinted in *Neuphilologische Mitteilungen* 75 (1974): 650-62.
———. "Vico as Philosopher of *Metabasis*." In *Giambattista Vico's Science of Humanity*, ed. G. Tagliacozzo and D. P. Verene. Baltimore: John Hopkins University Press, 1976: 47-63.
———. "The Unorthodox Logic of Scientific Discovery in Vico." In *Vico: Past and Present*, ed. G. Tagliacozzo. Atlantic Highlands, NJ: Humanities Press, 1981: 198-205.
———. "Vico's Basic Law of History in *Finnegans Wake*." In *Vico and Joyce*, ed. D. P. Verene. Albany: State University of New York Press, 1987: 20-31.

Fassò, Guido. "The Problem of Law and the Historical Origin of the *New Science*." In *Giambattista Vico's Science of Humanity*, ed. G. Tagliacozzo and D. P. Verene. Baltimore: Johns Hopkins University Press, 1976: 3-14.

Faucci, Dario. "Vico and Grotius: Jurisconsults of Mankind." In *Giambattista Vico: An International Symposium*, ed. G. Tagliacozzo and H. White. Baltimore: Johns Hopkins University Press, 1969: 61-76.

Faur, José. "Vico, Religious Humanism and the Sephardic Tradition." *Judaism* 27 (1978): 63-71.
———. "The Splitting of the *Logos*: Some Remarks on Vico and Rabbinic Tradition." *New Vico Studies* 3 (1985): 85-103.
———. "Francisco Sanchez's Theory of Cognition and Vico's *verum/factum*." *New Vico Studies* 5 (1987): 131-46.
———. "Imagination and Religious Pluralism: Maimonides, ibn-Verga, and Vico." *New Vico Studies* 10 (1992): 36-52.

Feder, Lillian. "The Cyclic View: Giambattista Vico and Oswald Spengler." In *Ancient Myth in Modern Poetry*. Princeton, NJ: Princeton University Press, 1972: 270-76.

Feibleman, James K. "Toward the Recovery of Giambattista Vico." *Social Science* 14 (1939): 31-40.

Feldman, Burton, and R. D. Richardson. "Giambattista Vico (1668-1744)." In *The Rise of Modern Mythology 1680-1860*. Bloomington: Indiana University Press, 1972: 50-61.

Fisch, Max Harold. "The Coleridges, Dr. Prati, and Vico." *Modern Philology* 41 (1943): 111-22.
———. Introduction to *The Autobiography of Giambattista Vico*, trans. M. H. Fisch and T. G. Bergin. Ithaca, NY: Cornell University Press, 1944 (Reprinted 1963; 1975): 1-107. [See full citation to translation in Part II A].
———. "Vico on Roman Law." In *Essays in Political Theory Presented to George H. Sabine*, ed. M. R. Konvitz and A. E. Murphy. Ithaca, NY: Cornell University Press, 1948: 62-68.
———. Introduction to *The New Science of Giambattista Vico*, trans. T. G. Bergin and M. H. Fisch. Garden City, NY: Doubleday, Anchor, 1961. [Introduction first appears in this abridged trans. of the 2d rev. ed.] [See full citation to translation in Part II A].
———. "Vico and Pragmatism." In *Giambattista Vico: An International Symposium*, ed. G. Tagliacozzo and H. White. Baltimore: Johns Hopkins University Press, 1969: 401-24. Reprinted in *Peirce, Semiotic, and Pragmatism: Essays by M. H. Fisch*, ed. K. L. Ketner and C. J. W. Kloesel. Bloomington: Indiana University Press, 1986: 200-26.
———. "Croce and Vico." In *Thought, Action, and Intuition: A Symposium on the Philosophy of Benedetto Croce*, ed. L. M. Palmer and H. S. Harris. Hildesheim and New York: Georg Ohms Verlag, 1975: 184-233.
———. "Comment on Professor Pompa's Paper." *Social Research* 43 (1976): 445-47. Reprinted in *Vico and Contemporary Thought*, ed. G. Tagliacozzo, M. Mooney, and D. P. Verene. Atlantic Highlands, NJ: Humanities Press, 1979: 1:36-39.
———. "Preliminary Note" [to "Vico's *Pratica*"]. In *Giambattista Vico's Science of Humanity*, ed. G. Tagliacozzo and D. P. Verene. Baltimore: Johns Hopkins University Press, 1976: 423. [See full citation to trans. in Part II A: "English Translations of Vico's Works."]
———. "What Has Vico to Say to Philosophers of Today?" *Social Research* 43 (1976): 399-409. Reprinted in *Vico and Contemporary Thought*, ed. G. Tagliacozzo, M. Mooney, and D. P. Verene. Atlantic Highlands, NJ: Humanities Press, 1979: 1:9-19.

Fitzmorris, T. J. "Vico Adamant and Some Pillars of Salt: Neapolitan Philosopher of the Eighteenth Century." *Catholic World* 156 (1943): 568-77.

FitzPatrick, P. J. "Vieni, Viedi, Vico." *British Journal for Eighteenth Century Studies* 7 (1984): 77-85.

Fletcher, Angus. "On the Syncretic Allegory of the *New Science*." *New Vico Studies* 4 (1986): 25-43.

———. "*Dipintura*: The Visual Icon of Historicism in Vico." In Fletcher, *Colors of the Mind*. Cambridge, MA: Harvard University Press, 1991: 147-65.

Fox, June. "Giambattista Vico's Theory of Pedagogy." *British Journal of Educational Studies* 20 (1972): 27-37.

Franchini, Raffaello. "Vico, Historical Methodology, and the Future of Philosophy." In *Giambattista Vico: An International Symposium*, ed. G. Tagliacozzo and H. White. Baltimore: Johns Hopkins University Press, 1969: 543-52.

Frankel, Margherita. "The 'Dipintura' and the Structure of Vico's *New Science* as a Mirror of the World." In *Vico: Past and Present*, ed. G. Tagliacozzo. Atlantic Highlands, NJ: Humanities Press, 1981: 1:43-51.
———. "Vico and Rousseau through Derrida." *New Vico Studies* 1 (1983): 51-61.

Frye, Northrop. "Comment to Peter Hughes's Essay." *Yale Italian Studies* 1 (1977): 91-92.
———. "Cycle and Apocalypse in *Finnegans Wake*." In *Vico and Joyce*, ed. Donald Phillip Verene. Albany: State University of New York Press, 1987: 3-19.

Fulco, Adrienne. "Vico as a Political Theorist." *Annals of Scholarship* 1 (1980): 60-80.
———. "Vico and Political Science." In *Vico: Past and Present*, ed. G. Tagliacozzo. Atlantic Highlands, NJ: Humanities Press, 1981: 2:175-94.
———. "Vico and Marx: Human Consciousness and the Structure of Reality." In *Vico and Marx: Affinities and Contrasts*, ed. G. Tagliacozzo. Atlantic Highlands, NJ: Humanities Press; London: Macmillan Press, 1983.

Funkenstein, Amos. "Natural Science and Social Theory: Hobbes, Spinoza, and Vico." In *Giambattista Vico's Science of Humanity*, ed. G. Tagliacozzo and D. P. Verene. Baltimore: Johns Hopkins University Press, 1976: 187-212.
———. "Vico's Secularized Providence and His 'New Science'." In Funkenstein, *Theology and the Scientific Imagination from the Middle Ages to the Seventeenth Century*. Princeton, NJ: Princeton University Press, 1986: 279-89; see also 3, 24, 26, 202-3, 209n, 210-13, 327-28, 345.

Gadol, Eugene T. "The Idealistic Foundations of Cultural Anthropology: Vico, Kant, and Cassirer." *Journal of the History of Philosophy* 12 (1974): 207-25 [Abstract in *The 18th Century: A Current Bibliography* (1974): 795].

Gardiner-Janik, Linda. "G. B. Vico and the *Artes Historicae* of the Italian Renaissance." In *Vico: Past and Present*, ed. G. Tagliacozzo. Atlantic Highlands, NJ: Humanities Press, 1981: 89-98.
———. "A Renaissance Quarrel: The Origin of Vico's Anti-Cartesianism." *New Vico Studies* 1 (1983): 39-50.

Gardiner, Patrick. "Vico." In *Theories of History*. Glencoe, IL: The Free Press, 1959: 9-21.

Garin, Eugenio. "Vico and the Heritage of Renaissance Thought." In *Vico: Past and Present*, ed. G. Tagliacozzo. Atlantic Highlands, NJ: Humanities Press, 1981: 1:99-116.

Gash, Hugh. "Vico's Theory of Knowledge and Some Problems in Genetic Epistemology." *Human Development* 26 (1983): 1-10.
―――, and Ernst von Glaserfeld. "Vico (1668-1744): An Early Anticipator of Radical Constructivism." *Irish Journal of Psychology* 4 (1978): 22-32.

Gaukroger, Stephen. "Vico and the Maker's Knowledge Principle." *History of Philosophy Quarterly* 3 (1986): 29-44.

Gianturco, Elio. "Suarez and Vico: A Note on the Origin of the Vichian Formula." *Harvard Theological Review* 27 (1934): 207-10.
**Review:**
*Italica* 13 (1936): 132.

Gianturco, Elio. "Character, Essence, Origin, and Content of the *Jus Gentium* According to Vico and Suarez." *Revue de littérature comparée* 10 (1936): 167-72 [Abstract: "On Suarez and Vico." *Italica* 13 (1936): 116].
―――. "Bodin and Vico." *Revue de littérature comparée* 22 (1948): 272-90.
―――. "Words and Meaning in Vico." *Ethics* 61 (1951): 151-53.
―――. Introduction to Vico's *On the Study Methods of Our Time*, trans. E. Gianturco. Indianapolis, New York, Kansas City: Bobbs-Merrill Library of Liberal Arts, 1965: ix-xxxiii. Reprinted Ithaca: Cornell University Press, 1990: xxi-xlv. [See Part II A for complete citation to this translation.]
―――. "Giovanni Antonio Chiajese's Letter on the *De Uno*." *Forum Italicum* 2 (1968): 370-81 [for complete citation, see Part II A: "English Editions of Vico's Works"].
―――. "Vico's Commemoration at the Accademia dei Lincei." *Forum Italicum* 4 (1970): 421-34.
―――. "Vico's Significance in the History of Legal Thought." In *Giambattista Vico: An International Symposium*, ed. G. Tagliacozzo and H. White. Baltimore: Johns Hopkins University Press, 1969: 327-47.

Gilson, Étienne, and Thomas Langan. "Vico and the New Science." In *Modern Philosophy: Descartes to Kant*. New York: Random House, 1963: 341-49.

Giorgi, Amedeo. "Vico and Humanistic Psychology." *Social Research* 43 (1976): 727-36. Reprinted in *Vico and Contemporary Thought*, ed. G. Tagliacozzo, M. Mooney, and D. P. Verene. Atlantic Highlands, NJ: Humanities Press, 1979: 1:36-39.

Giuliani, Alessandro. "Vico's Rhetorical Philosophy and the New Rhetoric." In *Giambattista Vico's Science of Humanity*, ed. G. Tagliacozzo and D. P. Verene. Baltimore: Johns Hopkins University Press, 1976: 2:69-78.

Goretti, Maria. "Vico's Pedagogic Thought and That of Today." In *Giambattista Vico: An International Symposium*, ed. G. Tagliacozzo and H. White. Baltimore: Johns Hopkins University Press, 1969: 553-75.
_____. "The Heterogenesis of Ends in Vico's Thought: Premises for a Comparison of Ideas." In *Giambattista Vico's Science of Humanity*, ed. G. Tagliacozzo and D. P. Verene. Baltimore: Johns Hopkins University Press, 1976: 213-19.

Gorman, David. "Kelley on Vico and Renaissance Humanism." *New Vico Studies* 11 (1993): 53-60.

Gorman, Jonathan L. "Vico and a New Philosophy of History." In *Vico: Past and Present*, ed. G. Tagliacozzo. Atlantic Highlands, NJ: Humanities Press, 1981: 1:240-49.
_____. "A Neo-Vichian Conclusion." In *The Expression of Historical Knowledge*. Edinburgh: Edinburgh University Press, 1982: 105-13.

Grafton, Anthony. "Fear and Loathing in Naples." *The New Republic* 4105 & 4106 (20 & 27 Sept. 1993): 51-57.

Grassi, Ernesto. "Critical Philosophy or Topical Philosophy? Meditations on the *De nostri temporis studiorum ratione*." In *Giambattista Vico: An International Symposium*, eds. G. Tagliacozzo and H. White. Baltimore: Johns Hopkins University Press, 1969: 39-50.
_____. "Marxism, Humanism, and the Problem of Imagination in Vico's Works." In *Giambattista Vico's Science of Humanity*, ed. G. Tagliacozzo and D. P. Verene. Baltimore: Johns Hopkins University Press, 1976: 275-94.
_____. "The Priority of Common Sense and Imagination: Vico's Philosophical Relevance Today." *Social Research* 43 (1976): 553-75. Reprinted in *Vico and Contemporary Thought*, ed. G. Tagliacozzo, M. Mooney, and D. P. Verene. Atlantic Highlands, N.J.: Humanities Press, 1979: 1:36-39.
_____. "Response by the Author." *Social Research* 43 (1976): 577-80. Reprinted in *Vico and Contemporary Thought*, ed. Giorgio Tagliacozzo, M. Mooney, and D. P. Verene. Atlantic Highlands, NJ: Humanities Press, 1979: 1:187-90.
_____. "Vico versus Freud: Creativity and the Unconscious." In *Vico: Past and Present*, ed. G. Tagliacozzo. Atlantic Highlands, NJ: Humanities Press, 1981: 1:144-61.
_____. "Vico, Marx, and Heidegger." In *Vico and Marx: Affinities and Contrasts*, ed. G. Tagliacozzo. Atlantic Highlands, NJ: Humanities Press; London: Macmillan Press, 1983: 233-50.
_____. "Vico as Epochal Thinker." *Differentia* 1 (1986): 73-90.
_____. "Vico's Thought as the Highest Level of Philosophical Consciousness in the Latin Tradition," 4-8; "Vico's Characterization of Descartes' Philosophy," 37-39; "Vico's Affirmation of the Sphere of Pure Possibilities," 39-41. In Grassi, *Rhetoric as Philosophy: The Humanist Tradition*. University Park: Pennsylvania State University Press, 1980 [see also: 2, 10-13, 45-47, 66 (Vico quoted), 86].

**Reviews:**
Verene, Donald Phillip. *Philosophy and Rhetoric* 13 (1980): 279-82.
Dupree, Robert. *Review of Metaphysics* 35 (1981): 131-32.

Pennachetti, Leonard. *Renaissance and Reformation* 6 (1982): 211-15.
Black, David William. *New Vico Studies* 1 (1983): 83-86.
Gabin, Rosalind J. *Quarterly Journal of Speech* 69 (1983): 220-21.
Lorch, Maristella. *Italian Quarterly* 24 (1983): 118-19.
Perelman, Chaim H. *Journal of the History of Philosophy* 21 (1983): 256-57.
Schaeffer, John D. *Religious Studies Review* 13 (1987): 321-24.

Grassi, Ernesto. "Joyce and Vico: The Demythologization of the Real." In *Vico and Joyce*, ed. Donald Phillip Verene. Albany: State University of New York Press, 1987: 147-59.
──────. "The Originary Quality of the Poetical and Rhetorical Word: Heidegger, Ungaretti and Neruda." *Philosophy and Rhetoric* 20 (1987): 248-53.

Greenberg, Paul. "Heroic minds." *Charleston, South Carolina Post/Courier* (3 August 1993).

Griffin, Robert. "Vico, Joyce, and the Matrix of Worldly Appearance." *Rivista di Letterature moderne e comparate* 40 (1987): 123-38.

Gungov, Alexander. "Vico's Presence in the Intellectual World of Eastern Europe and Russia: An Overview of the Literature." *New Vico Studies* 10 (1992): 11-23.

Guzmán, Jorge. "The Concept of Letter in Vico's *Scienza nuova*." *Dispositio: Revista Hispánica de Semiòtica Literaria* 2 (1977): 140-59.

Haac, O. A. "Vico and Michelet." *Forum Italicum* 2 (1968): 483-93.

Haddad, Louis. "The Evolutionary Economics of Giambattista Vico." In *Altro Polo: Italian Economics Past and Present*, ed. P. Groenewegen and J. Halevi. (Frederick May Foundation for Italian Studies) Sydney: University of Sydney Press, 1983: 17-29.

Haddock, Bruce A. "Vico and the Problem of Historical Reconstruction." *Social Research* 43 (1976): 512-19. Reprinted in *Vico and Contemporary Thought*, ed. G. Tagliacozzo, M. Mooney, and D. P. Verene. Atlantic Highlands, NJ: Humanities Press, 1979: 1:122-29.
──────. "Vico: The Problem of Interpretation." *Social Research* 43 (1976): 535-52. Reprinted in *Vico and Contemporary Thought*, ed. G. Tagliacozzo, M. Mooney, and Donald Phillip Verene. Atlantic Highlands, NJ: Humanities Press, 1979: 1:145-62.
──────. "Vico and Anachronism." *Political Studies* 24 (1976): 483-87.
──────. "Vico on Political Wisdom." *European Studies Review* 8 (1978): 165-91.
──────. "Vico's '*Discovery of the True Homer*': A Case Study in Historical Reconstruction." *Journal of the History of Ideas* 40 (1979): 583-602.
**Review:**
Frankel, Margherita. *New Vico Studies* 1 (1983): 95-96.

Haddock, Bruce A. "A New Science." In *An Introduction to Historical Thought*. London: Edward Arnold, 1980: 60-72 (ch. 6) *et passim*.
──────. "Vico and the Methodology of the History of Ideas." In *Vico: Past and Present*, ed. G. Tagliacozzo. Atlantic Highlands, NJ: Humanities Press, 1981: 1:227-39.

Hall, Robert Anderson, Jr. "G. B. Vico and Linguistic Theory." *Italica* 18 (1941): 145-54.
_____. "Benedetto Croce and the Influence of G. B. Vico." In *Idealism in Romance Linguistics*. Ithaca: Cornell University Press, 1963: 21-36.

Hamlyn, D. W. "Vico." In *The Penguin History of Western Philosophy*. London: Penguin, 1987: 214-16; see also 206.

Hampshire, Stuart. "Vico and His 'New Science'." *The Listener* 44 (1949): 569-71.
_____. "Vico and Language." *New York Review of Books* (23 Feb. 1969): 19-22.
_____. "Vico and the Contemporary Philosophy of Language." In *Giambattista Vico: An International Symposium*, ed. G. Tagliacozzo and H. White. Baltimore: Johns Hopkins University Press, 1969: 475-81.
_____. "Joyce and Vico: The Middle Way." In *Giambattista Vico's Science of Humanity*, ed. G. Tagliacozzo and D. P. Verene. Baltimore: Johns Hopkins University Press, 1976: 321-32. Also published in *New York Review of Books* (18 Oct. 1973): 8, 9, 12, 14, 16, 18, 21.

Harris, H. S. "What is Mr. Ear-Vico Supposed to be 'Earing?" In *Vico and Joyce*, ed. D. P. Verene. Albany: State University of New York Press, 1987: 68-82.

't Hart, August C. "Hugo de Groot and Giambattista Vico." In *Netherlands International Law Review* 30 (1983): 5-41.
_____. "The Development of the Concept of Natural Law in Giambattista Vico." *Vera Lex* 5 (1985): 3-4.

Haskell, Robert E. "Giambattista Vico and the Discovery of Metaphor." In *Cognition and Symbolic Structures: The Psychology of Metaphoric Transformation*, ed. R. Haskell. Norwood, NJ: Ablex, 1987: 67-82.
_____. "Vico and Jaynes: Neurocultural and Cognitive Operations in the Origin of Consciousness." *New Vico Studies* 11 (1993): 24-51.

Heade, Michael F. "James Joyce's Italian Mentor: Giambattista Vico." *European Studies Journal* 3 (1986): 70-77.

Henderson, R. D. "Vico's View of History." *Philosophia Reformata* 49 (1984): 97-111.

Heron, Denis C. "Vico." In *An Introduction to the History of Jurisprudence*. London: Parker, 1860: 535-86.

Hersey, George L. "Ovid, Vico, and the Central Garden at Caserta." *Journal of Garden History* 1 (1981): 3-34 [Abstract in *The 18th Century: A Current Bibliography*, n.s. 7 (1981): 254].

Hershenson, D. B. "A Viconian Interpretation of Psychological Counseling." *Personnel and Guidance Journal* 62 (1983): 3-9.

Hesse, Mary B. "Vico's Heroic Metaphor." In *Metaphysics and Philosophy of Science in the Seventeenth and Eighteenth Centuries*, ed. R. S. Woolhouse. Norwell, MA: Kluwer, 1988: 185-212.

Hidalgo-Serna, Emilio. "Vico and the Spanish Rhetorical Tradition." *New Vico Studies* 8 (1990): 38-54.

Hillman, James. "Plotinus, Ficino, and Vico as Precursors of Archetypal Psychology." In *Jung e la cultura europea, Enciclopedia, 1974*. Rome: Istituto della Enciclopedia Italiana, 1974: 55-80. Reprinted in *Loose Ends: Primary Papers in Archetypal Psychology*. Zurich: Spring Publications, 1975: 149-69.

Hodgart, Matthew. "A Viconian Sentence in *Ulysses*." *Orbis Litterarum* 19 (1964): 201-4.

Hodges, Herbert A. "Vico and Dilthey." In *Giambattista Vico: An International Symposium*, ed. G. Tagliacozzo and H. White. Baltimore: Johns Hopkins University Press, 1969: 439-45.

Holmes, Stephen Taylor. "The Barbarism of Reflection." In *Vico: Past and Present*, ed. G. Tagliacozzo. Atlantic Highlands, NJ: Humanities Press, 1981: 2:213-22.

Horkheimer, Max. "Vico and Mythology," trans. Fred Dallmayr. *New Vico Studies* 5 (1987): 63-76.

Hornstein, Alan D. "From Oracle to Echo: The Development of Law and Justice in Vico's *Nuova Scienza*." *Law and History Review* 8 (1990): 129-37.

Hughes, H. Stuart. "Vico and Contemporary Social Theory and Social History." In *Giambattista Vico: An International Symposium*, ed. G. Tagliacozzo and H. White. Baltimore: Johns Hopkins University Press, 1969: 319-26.

Hughes, Peter. "Creativity and History in Vico and His Contemporaries." In *Giambattista Vico's Science of Humanity*, ed. G. Tagliacozzo and D. P. Verene. Baltimore: Johns Hopkins University Press, 1976: 155-69.
———. "Vico and Literary History." *Yale Italian Studies* 1 (1977): 83-90.
———. "From Allusion to Implosion: Vico. Michelet. Joyce. Beckett." In *Vico and Joyce*, ed. D. P. Verene. Albany: State University of New York Press, 1987: 83-99.

Hutton, Patrick H. "Vico's Theory of History and the French Revolutionary Tradition." *Journal of the History of Ideas* 37 (1976): 241-56.
———. "The New Science of Giambattista Vico: Historicism in Its Relation to Poetics." *Journal of Aesthetics and Art Criticism* 30 (1972): 359-67.
———. "Religion and the Civilizing Process in Vico and Marx." In *Vico and Marx: Affinities and Contrasts*, ed. G. Tagliacozzo. Atlantic Highlands, NJ: Humanities Press; London: Macmillan Press, 1983: 140-50.

————. "Vico's Significance for the New Cultural History." *New Vico Studies* 3 (1985): 73-84.

————. "The Problem of Oral Tradition in Vico's Historical Scholarship." *Journal of the History of Ideas* 53 (1992): 3-23.

————. "The Art of Memory Reconceived: From Renaissance Rhetoric to Giambattista Vico's Historicism." Ch. 2 in Hutton, *History as an Art of Memory*. Hanover, CT: University Press of New England, 1993: 27-51.

Jacobelli, Angela Maria. "The Role of the Intellectual in Giambattista Vico." In *Giambattista Vico's Science of Humanity*, ed. G. Tagliacozzo and D. P. Verene. Baltimore: Johns Hopkins University Press, 1976: 47-63.

Jacobitti, Edmund E. "From Vico's Common Sense to Gramsci's Hegemony." In *Vico and Marx: Affinities and Contrasts*, ed. G. Tagliacozzo. Atlantic Highlands, NJ: Humanities Press; London: Macmillan Press, 1983: 367-87.

————. "Political Thought and Rhetoric in Vico." *New Vico Studies* 4 (1986): 73-88.

————. "Croce, Vico and the Uses (and Misuses) of Historicism." Review of *Benedetto Croce and the Uses of Historicism* (D. Roberts). *New Vico Studies* 6 (1988): 113-27.

————. "The Middle Ground." Review of *New Vico Studies* 3 (1985); and *Bollettino del Centro di Studi Vichiani* 15 (1985). *Differentia* 2 (1988): 267-75.

————. "Between the *vita activa* and the *vita contemplativa*: Toulmin's *Cosmopolis* and the Return to (some) Vichian Concepts." Review of *Cosmopolis: The Hidden Agenda of Modernity* (S. Toulmin). *New Vico Studies* 9 (1991): 77-84.

Jay, Martin. "Vico and Western Marxism." In *Vico: Past and Present*, ed. G. Tagliacozzo. Atlantic Highlands, NJ: Humanities Press, 1981: 2:195-212.

Jennings, J. R. "Sorel, Vico, and Marx." In *Vico and Marx: Affinities and Contrasts*, ed. G. Tagliacozzo. Atlantic Highlands, NJ: Humanities Press; London: Macmillan Press, 1983: 326-41.

Johnston, William M. "The Influence of Croce, Gentile, and Vico on Collingwood during the Early 'Twenties." In *The Formative Years of R. G. Collingwood*. The Hague: Martinus Nijhoff, 1967: 81-90.

Jordan, Robert Welsh. "Vico and Husserl: History and Historical Science." In *Giambattista Vico's Science of Humanity*, ed. G. Tagliacozzo and D. P. Verene. Baltimore: Johns Hopkins University Press, 1976: 47-63.

————. "Vico and the Phenomenology of the Moral Sphere." *Social Research* 43 (1976): 520-31. Reprinted in *Vico and Contemporary Thought*, ed. G. Tagliacozzo, M. Mooney, and D. P. Verene. Atlantic Highlands, NJ: Humanities Press, 1979: 1:130-41.

Joseph, Roger. "Vico and Anthropological Knowledge." In *Vico: Past and Present*, ed. G. Tagliacozzo. Atlantic Highlands, NJ: Humanities Press, 1981: 2:157-64.

"Joyce and Vico." *Proceedings of the Third International James Joyce Symposium* (14-18 June, 1971), ed. Facoltà di Magistero, University of Trieste. Trieste: La Editoriale Libraria, 1974: 342-78. [Contents on Vico listed separately, herein.]

Jung, Hwa Yol. "Vico's Rhetoric: A Note on Verene's *Vico's Science of Imagination*." *Philosophy and Rhetoric* 15 (1982): 187-202 [Abstract in *The 18th Century: A Current Bibliography*, n.s. 8 (1982): 544].
———. "Vico and Bakhtin: A Prolegomenon to any Future Comparison." *New Vico Studies* 3 (1985): 157-65.
———. "The Anatomy of Language: Vico, Joyce, and Etymosinology." *Rivista di Studi Italiani* 4-5 (1986-87): 29-46. Reprinted in Jung, *The Question of Rationality and the Basic Grammar of Intellectual Texts*. Niigata: International University of Japan, 1989: 114-33.
———. "On Danesi's 'Vico and Chomsky'." *New Vico Studies* 9 (1991): 142-46 [Note].
———. "Vico and the Critical Genealogy of the Body Politic." *Rivista di Studi Italiani* 11 (1993): 39-66.

Kadir, Djelal. "The Architectonic Principle of *Cien Aos de Soledad* and the Vichian Theory of History." *Kentucky Romance Quarterly* 24 (1977): 251-61.

Kamenka, Eugene. "Vico and Marxism." In *Giambattista Vico: An International Symposium*, ed. G. Tagliacozzo and H. V. White. Baltimore: Johns Hopkins University Press, 1969: 137-43.

Kelley, Donald R. "In Vico Veritas: The True Philosophy and the New Science." *Social Research* 43 (1976): 601-11. Reprinted in *Vico and Contemporary Thought*, ed. G. Tagliacozzo, M. Mooney, and D. P. Verene. Atlantic Highlands, NJ: Humanities Press, 1979: 1:211-21.
———. "Vico's Road: From Philology to Jurisprudence and Back." In *Giambattista Vico's Science of Humanity*, ed. G. Tagliacozzo and D. P. Verene. Baltimore: Johns Hopkins University Press, 1976: 15-29.
———. "The Prehistory of Sociology: Montesquieu, Vico, and the Legal Tradition." *Journal of the History of the Behavioral Sciences* 16 (1980): 144-44 [Abstract: *New Vico Studies* 1 (1983): 104-5].
———. "Vico and Gaianism: Perspective on a Paradigm." In *Vico: Past and Present*, ed. G. Tagliacozzo. Atlantic Highlands, NJ: Humanities Press, 1981: 1:66-72.
———. "Giovanni Battista Vico." In *European Writers: The Age of Reason and Enlightenment*, ed. G. Stade. New York: Charles Scribner's Sons, 1984: 3:293-316.
———. "In Vico's Wake." In *Vico and Joyce*, ed. D. P. Verene. Albany: State University of New York Press, 1987: 135-46.

Kenner, Hugh. "Vico and History," 321-28; "Vico and the Analogy of Language," 329-36. In *Dublin's Joyce*. London: Chatto and Windus, 1955.

Kenrick, J. "Vico." *Philological Museum* 2 (1833): 626-44.

Kessler, Eckhard. "Vico's Attempt Toward a Humanistic Foundation of Science." In *Vico: Past and Present*, ed. G. Tagliacozzo. Atlantic Highlands, NJ: Humanities Press, 1981: 1:73-88.

Kiernan, Suzanne. "J. F. Lyotard's *The Postmodern Condition* and G. B. Vico's *De nostri temporis studiorum ratione*." *New Vico Studies* 4 (1986): 101-12.

Kline, George L. "Vico in Pre-Revolutionary Russia." In *Giambattista Vico: An International Symposium*, ed. G. Tagliacozzo and H. V. White. Baltimore: Johns Hopkins University Press, 1969: 203-13.
———. "The Question of Materialism in Vico and Marx." In *Vico and Marx: Affinities and Contrasts*, ed. G. Tagliacozzo. Atlantic Highlands, NJ: Humanities Press; London: Macmillan Press, 1983: 114-25.

Krois, John Michael. "Comment on Dr. Mora's Paper." *Social Research* 43 (1976): 712-14. Reprinted in *Vico and Contemporary Thought*, ed. G. Tagliacozzo, M. Mooney, and D. P. Verene. Atlantic Highlands, NJ: Humanities Press, 1979: 2:54-56.
———. "Comment on Professor Grassi's Paper." *Social Research* 43 (1976: 575-77. Reprinted In *Vico and Contemporary Thought*, ed. G. Tagliacozzo, M. Mooney, and D. P. Verene. Atlantic Highlands, NJ: Humanities Press, 1979: 1:185-87.
———. "Vico's and Peirce's '*Sensus communis*'." In *Vico: Past and Present*, ed. G. Tagliacozzo. Atlantic Highlands, NJ: Humanities Press, 1981: 2:58-71.

Kunze, Donald E. Jr. "Giambattista Vico as a Philosopher of Place: Comments on the Recent Article by Mills." *Transactions of the Institute of British Geographers*, n.s. 8 (1983): 237-48.
———. "Skiagraphy and the *Ipsum* of Architecture." *Via* 11 (1990): 62-76.

Labio, Catherine. Ch. 2: "Vico: 'Discovery of the True Homer' and *New Science*." In "Enlightenment and the Epistemology of Origins." Unpublished Ph.D. diss. New York University, 1992.

Lachterman, David R. "Vico and Marx: Notes on a Precursory Reading." In *Vico and Marx: Affinities and Contrasts*, ed. G. Tagliacozzo. Atlantic Highlands, NJ: Humanities Press; London: Macmillan Press, 1983: 38-61.
———. "Mathematics and Nominalism in Vico's *Liber Metaphysicus*." In *Sachkommentar zu Giambattista Vicos "Liber Metaphysicus*," ed. S. Otto and H. Viechtbauer. Munich: Fink, 1985: 47-75.

Lamparska, Rena A. "Descartes, Vico, Contextualism, and Social Psychology." In *Contextualism and Understanding in Behavioral Science*, ed. R. L. Rosnow and M. Georgudi. New York: Praeger, 1986: 67-85.
———. "A Polish Vichian: Stanislaw Brzozowski." *New Vico Studies* 1 (1983): 103-11.

Lana, Robert E. "Giambattista Vico and the History of Social Psychology." *Journal for the Theory of Social Behavior* 9 (1979): 251-63.
———. "Ibn-Khaldun and Vico: The Universality of Social History." *Journal of Mind and Behavior* 8 (1987): 153-65.

Land, Stephen K. "The Account of Language in Vico's *Scienza nuova*: A Critical Analysis." *Philological Quarterly* 55 (1976): 354-72.

Lansbury, Coral. "Marx and Vico at Finnegans Wake." *Meanjin* 34 (1975): 45-48.

Leach, Edmund. "Vico and Lévi-Strauss on the Origins of Humanity." In *Giambattista Vico: An International Symposium*, ed. G. Tagliacozzo and H. V. White. Baltimore: Johns Hopkins University Press, 1969: 309-18.
———. "Vico and the Future of Anthropology." *Social Research* 43 (1976) 807-17. Reprinted in *Vico and Contemporary Thought*, ed. G. Tagliacozzo, M. Mooney, and D. P. Verene. Atlantic Highlands, NJ: Humanities Press, 1979: 2:149-59.

Levin, Samuel R. "Catachresis: Vico and Joyce." *Philosophy and Rhetoric* 20 (1987): 94-105.
———. "Vico and the Language of the 'First Poets'." In *Metaphoric Worlds: Conceptions of a Romantic Nature*. New Haven: Yale University Press, 1988.

Levine, Joseph. "Collingwood, Vico, and the 'Autobiography'." *Clio* 9 (1980): 379-92.
———. "Collingwood and Vico." In *Vico: Past and Present*, ed. G. Tagliacozzo. Atlantic Highlands, NJ: Humanities Press, 1981: 2:72-84.
———. "Vico and the Quarrel between the Ancients and the Moderns." *Studies on Voltaire and the Eighteenth Century* 263 (1989): 564-65.
———. "Giambattista Vico and the Quarrel between the Ancients and the Moderns." *Journal of the History of Ideas* 52 (1991): 55-79 [Abstract in *New Vico Studies* 9 (1991): 118-19].

Levy, Ze'ev. "The Renaissance of Giambattista Vico: On Giorgio Tagliacozzo and the Modern Research on Vico's Thought," *International Problems, Society and Politics* 31, no. 58 (1992).

Lewis, Pericles. "The 'True' Homer: Myth and Enlightenment in Vico, Horkheimer, and Adorno." *New Vico Studies* 10 (1992): 24-35.

Liebel-Weckowicz, H. "Was Vico's Theory of History a True Social Science?" *Historian* 44 (1982): 466-82.

Lifshitz, Michail. "Giambattista Vico (1668-1744)." *Philosophy and Phenomenological Research* 8 (1948): 391-414.

Lilla, Mark. "Backing into Vico: Recent Trends in American Philosophy." *New Vico Studies* 4 (1986): 89-100.

Lion, Aline. "Giambattista Vico." In *The Pedigree of Fascism: A Popular Essay on the Western Philosophy of Politics*. London: Sheed & Ward, 1927: 125-36.

Littleford, Michael. "Vico's Legacy to Contemporary Education." *Educational Forum* 36 (1972): 393-401.

———. "Curriculum Implications of the Vichian 'Tree of Knowledge': An Appendix to Dr. Tagliacozzo's Paper." *Social Research* 43 (1976): 796-801. Reprinted In *Vico and Contemporary Thought*, ed. G. Tagliacozzo, M. Mooney, and D. P. Verene. Atlantic Highlands, NJ: Humanities Press, 1979: 1:36-39.

———. "Vico and Curriculum Studies." *Journal of Curriculum Theorizing* 1 (1979): 54-64.

———. "Vico and Dewey: Toward a Humanistic Foundation for Curriculum Studies." *Journal of Curriculum Theorizing* 2 (1979): 57-70.

———. "Vico and Dewey: Toward a Humanistic Foundation for Contemporary Education." In *Vico: Past and Present*, ed. G. Tagliacozzo. Atlantic Highlands, NJ: Humanities Press, 1981: 2:223-37.

———. "Giambattista Vico, Philosopher and Educator: Lessons for the Late Twentieth Century from an Eighteenth-Century Eccentric." *Teachers College Record* 85 (1983): 120-38 [Abstract: *New Vico Studies* 2 (1984): 127].

Litz, A. Walton. "Vico and Joyce." In *Giambattista Vico: An International Symposium*, ed. G. Tagliacozzo and H. V. White. Baltimore: Johns Hopkins University Press, 1969: 245-55.

Livingston, Donald W. "Hayek, Hume, and Vico" in "Hayek as Humean." *Critical Review* 5 (1991): 165-67; see also 175-76.

Lovekin, David. "Giambattista Vico and Jacques Ellul: The Intelligible Universal and the Technical Phenomenon." *Man and World* 15 (1982): 407-15.

———. "Artifacts, Politics, and Imagination: From Marx to Vico." *Research in Philosophy and Technology* 5 (1982): 65-75.

Löwith, Karl. "Vico." In *Meaning in History: The Theological Implications of the Philosophy of History*. Chicago: University of Chicago Press Phoenix Books, 1949: 115-36.

Lucente, Gregory L. "Vico's Notion of 'Divine Providence' and the Limits of Human Knowledge, Freedom, and Will." *Modern Language Notes* 97 (1982): 183-91.

———. "Vico, Hercules, and the Lion: Figure and Ideology in the *Scienza nuova*." *New Vico Studies* 6 (1988): 85-94.

Luft, Sandra Rudnick. "Creative Activity in Vico and the Secularization of Providence." In *Studies in Eighteenth-Century Culture*, ed. R. Rente. Madison: University of Wisconsin Press, 1979: 9:337-55.

———. "Giambattista Vico and Humanistic Knowledge." *Humanities 1980*. San Francisco, CA: San Francisco State University, 1980: 11-13.

———. "A Genetic Interpretation of Divine Providence in Vico's *New Science*." *Journal of the History of Philosophy* 20 (1982): 151-69.

———. "Hans Blumenberg's Use of *Verum/Factum*: A Vichian Perspective." *New Vico Studies* 5 (1987): 149-56.

———. "Funkenstein's Vichian Reassessment of *Verum/Factum* for the Modern Age." Review of *Theology and the Scientific Imagination from the Middle Ages to the Seventeenth Century* (A. Funkenstein). *New Vico Studies* 6 (1988): 105-12.

———. "Derrida, Vico, Genesis, and the Originary Power of Language." *The Eighteenth Century* 34 (1993): 65-84.

Lyons, Roger. "Vico: An Italian Renaissance." *Humanities* 7 (1977): 10-11.

McCalla, Arthur. "Pierre-Simon Ballanche as Reader of Vico." *New Vico Studies* 9 (1991): 43-59.

McCormick, John O. "Emerson, Vico, and History." In *The Rarer Action: Essays in Honor of Francis Fergusson*, ed. A. Cheuse and R. Koffler. New Brunswick, NJ: Rutgers University Press, 1971: 320-32.

MacIntyre, Alasdair. "Imaginative Universals and Historical Falsification: Rejoinder to Professor Verene." *New Vico Studies* 6 (1988): 21-30.

McMullin, Ernan. "Vico's Theory of Science." *Social Research* 43 (1976): 450-80. Reprinted In *Vico and Contemporary Thought*, ed. G. Tagliacozzo, M. Mooney, and D. P. Verene. Atlantic Highlands, NJ: Humanities Press, 1979: 1:60-90.

McReynolds, J. W. "Giambattista Vico on Education." *School and Society* 71 (1950): 159-51.

Madera, Romano. "Fetishism Theory. From Vico to Marx." *Review (Ferdinand Braudel Center)* 9 (1985): 241-56.

Maier, Joseph. "Vico and Critical Theory." *Social Research* 43 (1976): 845-56. Reprinted in *Vico and Contemporary Thought*, ed. G. Tagliacozzo, M. Mooney, and D. P. Verene. Atlantic Highlands, NJ: Humanities Press, 1979: 2:187-98.

———. "Vico's View of Jewish Exceptionalism." In *Ethnicity, Identity, and History: Essays in Memory of Werner J. Cahnman*, ed. J. Maier and C. I. Waxman. New Brunswick, NJ: Transaction, 1983: 81-92.

Makkreel, Rudolf A. "Vico and Some Kantian Reflections on Historical Judgment." *Man and World* 13 (1980): 99-120. Reprinted in *Vico: Past and Present*, ed. G. Tagliacozzo. Atlantic Highlands, NJ: Humanities Press, 1981: 2:15-34.

Mali, Joseph. "Mythology and Counter-History: The New Critical Art of Vico and Joyce." In *Vico and Joyce*, ed. Donald Phillip Verene. Albany: State University of New York Press, 1987: 32-47.

———. "The Public Grounds of Truth: The Critical Theory of Giambattista Vico." *New Vico Studies* 6 (1988): 59-83.

———. "Science, Tradition, and the Science of Tradition." *Science in Context* 3 (1989): 143-73.

———. "The Poetics of Politics: Vico's Philosophy of Authority." *History of Political Thought* 10 (1989): 41-69.

Manganiello, Dominic. "Vico's Ideal History and Joyce's Language." In *Vico and Joyce*, ed. D. P. Verene. Albany: State University of New York Press, 1987: 196-206.

Manuel, Frank. "Vico: The '*Giganti*' and Their Joves." In *The Eighteenth Century Confronts the Gods*. Cambridge, MA: Harvard University Press, 1959: 149-67.

Marengo Vaglio, Carla. "The 'Predicable' and the 'Practical': Language and History in Vico and Joyce." In *Vico and Joyce*, ed. D. P. Verene. Albany: State University of New York Press, 1987: 207-17.

Marias Aguilera, Julian. "Vico's Doctrine of History." In *History of Philosophy*, trans. S. Appelbaum and C. C. Strowbridge. New York: Dover Books, 1967: 268-70.

Mason, Ellsworth G. "Joyce and Vico—*Gemelli*." Proceedings of the Third International James Joyce Symposium (14-18 June 1971), ed. Facoltà di Magistero, University of Trieste. Trieste: La Editoriale Libraria, 1974: 353-57.

Mathieu, Vittorio. "Truth as the Mother of History." In *Giambattista Vico's Science of Humanity*, ed. G. Tagliacozzo and D. P. Verene. Baltimore: Johns Hopkins University Press, 1976: 113-24.

Matteo, Sante. "Language as 'Always Already' Metaphor: The Primacy of Writing in Vico, Derrida, and Said." *Proceedings of the Third Annual Symposium on the Deseret Language and Linguistic Society*. Provo, UT: Brigham Young University, 1986: 142-48 [Abstract: *New Vico Studies* 5 (1987): 205].
_____. "American Association for Italian Studies." *New Vico Studies* 5 (1987): 219-20 [Report].

Maurice, Frederick D. "Vico." In *Modern Philosophy; or, A Treatise of Moral and Metaphysical Philosophy from the Fourteenth Century to the French Revolution, with a Glimpse into the Nineteenth Century*. London: Griffin, Bohn, & Co., 1862: 500-4.

May, Rollo. "Comment on Professor Giorgi's Paper." *Social Research* 43 (1976): 737-38. Reprinted in *Vico and Contemporary Thought*, ed. G. Tagliacozzo, M. Mooney, and D. P. Verene. Atlantic Highlands, NJ: Humanities Press, 1979: 2:79-80.

Mayer, J. P. "The New Science of Giambattista Vico" [Preface to Robert Flint, *Vico*.] New York: Arno Press, 1979: v-vi.

Mazzarino, S. "Vico, Holland, and Modern Conceptions of History." *Quaderni Catanesi di Studi classici e medievali* 1 (1979): 335-72.

Mazzeo, Joseph A. "Genesis, Timaeus, and Vico's Conception of History." *Yale Italian Studies* 2 (1978): 169-81.

Mazzotta, Giuseppe. "Vico's Encyclopedia." *The Yale Journal of Criticism* 1 (1988): 65-79.

Megill, Allan. "Giambattista Vico and the Origin of Language." In "The Enlightenment Debate on the Origin of Language and Its Historical Background." Unpublished Ph.D. diss. Columbia University, 1975: 57-84.

———. "Vico and Marx after Nietzsche." In *Vico and Marx: Affinities and Contrasts*, ed. G. Tagliacozzo. Atlantic Highlands, NJ: Humanities Press; London: Macmillan Press, 1983: 388-400.

———. "The Identity of American Neo-Pragmatism: or, Why Vico Now?" *New Vico Studies* 5 (1987): 99-116.

———. "On Postmodernism." *New Vico Studies* 11 (1993): 67-76.

Meinecke, Friedrich. "Vico/Lafitau." In *Historism: The Rise of a New Historical Outlook*. New York: Herder and Herder, 1972: 37-53.

Melczer, William. "Relativity before Einstein: Leo Hebraeus and Giambattista Vico." In *Einstein and the Humanities*, ed. D. P. Ryan. New York: Greenwood Press, 1987: 99-103.

Merquior, J. G. "Defense of Vico against Some of His Admirers." In *Vico and Marx: Affinities and Contrasts*, ed. G. Tagliacozzo. Atlantic Highlands, NJ: Humanities Press; London: Macmillan Press, 1983: 401-26.

Milbank, A. J. "Theology and Philosophy in Vico's Account of Human Creativity." *History of European Ideas* 2 (1981): 229-314.

Mills, William J. "Positivism Reversed: The Relevance of Giambattista Vico." *Transactions of the Institute of British Geographers* 7 (1982): 1-14.

———. "Giambattista Vico as a Philosopher of Place—Reply." *Transactions of the Institute of British Geographers* 8 (1983): 249.

Minogue, Kenneth. "Marx and Vico," *Encounter* 66 (1986): 59-63.

Miuccio, Giuliana. "Heracles and the Passage from Nature to Culture in Giambattista Vico's *La Scienza nuova*." *Italian Journal* 4 (1990): 29-37. Also in *Diogenes* (Fall, 1990): 90-103.

Momigliano, Arnaldo. "Vico's *Scienza nuova*: Roman 'Bestioni' and Roman 'Eroi'." *History and Theory* 5 (1966): 3-23.

———. "Two English Books on Vico." In *Sesto contributo all storia degli studi classici e del mondo antico*. Roma: Edizioni di Storia e Letteratura, 1980: 200-30.

Monas, Sidney. "Did Bakhtin Read Vico?" *New Vico Studies* 8 (1990): 156-57.

Montano, Rocco. "Vico's Opposition to the Enlightenment," trans. O. Marrocco. *Italian Quarterly* 17 (1973): 3-34.

Montgomery, John W. "Vico and the Christian Faith." In *The Shape of the Past: An Introduction to Philosophical Historiography*. Ann Arbor, MI: Edwards Brothers, 1962: 187-216.

Montuori, Alfonso M. "Vico and Human Science." *Studi Filosofica* 8-9 (1985-86): 129-46.

Mooney, Michael. "The Primacy of Language in Vico." *Social Research* 43 (1976): 581-600. Reprinted in *Vico and Contemporary Thought*, ed. G. Tagliacozzo, M. Mooney, and D. P. Verene. Atlantic Highlands, NJ: Humanities Press, 1979: 1:191-210.
———. "Vico's Writings." In *Giambattista Vico's Science of Humanity*, ed. G. Tagliacozzo and D. P. Verene. Baltimore: Johns Hopkins University Press, 1976: xix-xxviii.
———. "Vico's Humanity." *Man and Nature* 9 (1990): 1-21.

Mora, George. "Vico and Piaget: Parallels and Differences." *Social Research* 43 (1976): 698-712. Reprinted in *Vico and Contemporary Thought*, ed. G. Tagliacozzo, M. Mooney, and D. P. Verene. Atlantic Highlands, NJ: Humanities Press, 1979: 2:40-54.
———. "Vico, Piaget, and Genetic Epistemology." In *Giambattista Vico's Science of Humanity*, ed. G. Tagliacozzo and D. P. Verene. Baltimore: Johns Hopkins University Press, 1976: 365-92.

Morrison, James. "Vico's Doctrine of the Natural Law of the Gentes." *Journal of the History of Philosophy* 16 (1978): 47-60 [Abstract in *The 18th Century: A Current Bibliography*, n.s. 4 (1978): 472].
———. "Three Interpretations of Vico." *Journal of the History of Ideas* 39 (1978): 511-18.
———. "Vico's Principle of *verum* is *factum* and the Problem of Historicism." *Journal of the History of Ideas* 39 (1978): 579-95 [Abstract in *The 18th Century: A Current Bibliography* n.s. 4 (1978): 472].
———. "How to Interpret the Idea of Divine Providence in Vico's *New Science*." *Philosophy and Rhetoric* 12 (1979): 256-61.
———. "Vico and Spinoza." *Journal of the History of Ideas* 41 (1980): 49-68.
———. "Vico and Machiavelli." In *Vico: Past and Present*, ed. G. Tagliacozzo. Atlantic Highlands, NJ: Humanities Press, 1981: 2:1-14.

Mosley, David L. "Giambattista Vico." In Mosley, *Gesture, Sign, and Song. An Interdisciplinary Approach to Schumann's "Liederkreis" Opus 39*. New York: Peter Lang, 1990: 181-83.

Muldoon, Paul. "[Vico]" [poem]. In *MADOC. A Mystery*. New York: Farrar Straus Giroux, 1991: 108-9.

Munz, Peter. "The Idea of 'New Science' in Vico and Marx." In *Vico and Marx: Affinities and Contrasts*, ed. G. Tagliacozzo. Atlantic Highlands, NJ: Humanities Press; London: Macmillan Press, 1983: 1-19.
———. "James Joyce, Myth-Maker at the End of Time." In *Vico and Joyce*, ed. D. P. Verene. Albany: State University of New York Press, 1987: 48-56.

Murrin, Michael. "Epilogue: The Disappearance of Homer and the End of Homeric Allegory: Vico and Wolf." In M. Murrin, *The Allegorical Epic: Essays in its Rise and Decline*. Chicago: University of Chicago Press, 1980.

Nash, Ronald H. "Giambattista Vico (1668-1744)." In *Ideas of History*, ed. Ronald H. Nash. New York: Dutton, 1969: 1:25-47.

Neff, Emery. "Gibbon, Vico, and the Masses." In *The Poetry of History*. New York: Columbia University Press, 1947: 79-89 *et passim*.

Nelson, Benjamin. "Vico and Comparative Historical Civilizational Sociology." *Social Research* 43 (1976): 874-81. Reprinted in *Vico and Contemporary Thought*, ed. G. Tagliacozzo, M. Mooney, and D. P. Verene. Atlantic Highlands, NJ: Humanities Press, 1979: 2:216-23.

"*The New Science*: by Vico. Translated by the Author [Princess Cristina Belgioioso] of the Essay on the Formation of Catholic Doctrine. With an Introduction on Vico and His Works." *Foreign Quarterly Review* 34 (1845): 289-303.

Nisbet, Robert. "Vico and the Idea of Progress." *Social Research* 43 (1976): 625-37. Reprinted in *Vico and Contemporary Thought*, ed. G. Tagliacozzo, M. Mooney, and D. P. Verene. Atlantic Highlands, NJ: Humanities Press, 1979: 1:235-47.

Noakes, Susan. "Emilio Betti's Debt to Vico." *New Vico Studies* 6 (1988): 51-57.

Noether, Emiliana P. "Giambattista Vico." In *Seeds of Italian Nationalism (1700-1815)*. New York Columbia University Press, 1951: 48-62.
_____. "Giambattista Vico and the Risorgimento." *Harvard Library Bulletin* 17 (1969): 309-18.

Norris, A. T. "Nietzsche and Vico on Irony and Cultural Dissolution." *Stanford Italian Review* 6 (1986): 313-32.

O'Neill, John. "On the History of the Human Senses in Vico and Marx." *Social Research* 43 (1976): 837-44. Reprinted in *Vico and Contemporary Thought*, ed. G. Tagliacozzo, M. Mooney, and D. P. Verene. Atlantic Highlands, NJ: Humanities Press, 1979: 2:179-86.
_____. "Time's Body: Vico on the Love of Language and Institution." In *Giambattista Vico's Science of Humanity*, ed. G. Tagliacozzo and D. P. Verene. Baltimore: Johns Hopkins University Press, 1976: 333-39.
_____. "Naturalism in Vico and Marx: A Theory of the Body Politic." In *Vico and Marx: Affinities and Contrasts*, ed. G. Tagliacozzo. Atlantic Highlands, NJ: Humanities Press; London: Macmillan Press, 1983: 277-89 [originally published in O'Neill, *For Marx against Althusser and Other Essays*. Washington, DC: Center for Advanced Research in Phenomenology and University Presses of America, 1982: 97-108].
_____. "Vico mit Freude ReJoyced." In *Vico and Joyce*, ed. D. P. Verene. Albany: State University of New York Press, 1987: 160-74.

Orelli, J. K. "Vico and Niebuhr." *Schweizerisches Museum* 1 (1916): 184f.

Orr, Leonard. "Vico's *Most Ancient Italian Wisdom* and the Epistemology of Joyce's *Finnegans Wake.*" *Neohelicon: Acta Comparationis Litterarum Universarum* 14 (1987): 21-37.

Osborne, Richard. "Giambattista Vico." In *Philosophy for Beginners*. New York: Writers and Readers Publishers, 1991: 80.

Paci, Enzo. "Vico and Cassirer." In *Giambattista Vico: An International Symposium*, ed. G. Tagliacozzo and H. White. Baltimore: Johns Hopkins University Press, 1969: 457-73.
_____. "Vico, Structuralism, and the Phenomenological Encyclopedia of the Sciences." In *Giambattista Vico: An International Symposium*, ed. G. Tagliacozzo and H. White. Baltimore: Johns Hopkins University Press, 1969: 497-515.

Palmer, Lucia M. "Reflections on M. Fisch's 'Croce and Vico'." In *Thought, Action, and Intuition: A Symposium on the Philosophy of Benedetto Croce*, ed. Lucia M. Palmer and H. S. Harris. Hildesheim and New York: Georg Ohms Verlag, 1975: 234-39].
_____. "Stephen Toulmin: Variations on Vichian Themes." *Science—International Review of Scientific Synthesis* 117 (1982): 91-96 [Abstract in *New Vico Studies* 2 (1984): 138-39].
_____. Introduction to *On the Most Ancient Wisdom of the Italians, Unearthed from the Origins of the Latin Language*. Including the disputations with the *Giornale de' Letterati d'Italia*, trans. L. M. Palmer. Ithaca, NY and London: Cornell University Press, 1988: 1-34. [See Part II A for full citation to this translation.]

Palmieri, Mario. "Two Forerunners of Fascism." In *The Philosophy of Fascism*. Chicago: Dante Alighieri Society, 1936: 191-200.

Paparella, Emanuel. "Vichian Themes in the Italian-American Saga: A Review Essay." Review of *Blood of My Blood* (R. Gambino). *Review Interamericana* 5 (1975): 197-206.

Papini, Mario. "A Graph for the *Dipintura*." *New Vico Studies* 9 (1991): 138-41.

Parry, David M. "Vico and Nietzsche." *New Vico Studies* 7 (1989): 59-75.
_____. "The Centrality of the Aesthetic in Vico and Nietzsche." *New Vico Studies* 9 (1991): 29-42.

Parsons, Talcott. "Vico and 'History'." *Social Research* 43 (1976): 881-85. Reprinted in *Vico and Contemporary Thought*, ed. G. Tagliacozzo, M. Mooney, and D. P. Verene. Atlantic Highlands, NJ: Humanities Press, 1979: 2:223-27.

Percival, W. Keith. "A Note on Thomas Hayne and His Relation to Leibniz and Vico." *New Vico Studies* 6 (1988): 97-101.

Perkinson, Henry J. "Giambattista Vico and 'The Method of Studies in Our Times': A Criticism of Descartes' Influence on Modern Education." *History of Education Quarterly* 2 (1962): 30-46.

―――. "Giambattista Vico: Philosopher of Education." *Pedagogica Historica* 14 (1974): 401-33.
―――. "Vico and the Methods of Study of *Our* Time." *Social Research* 43 (1976): 753-67. Reprinted in *Vico and Contemporary Thought*, ed. G. Tagliacozzo, M. Mooney, and D. P. Verene. Atlantic Highlands, NJ: Humanities Press, 1979: 2:95-109.

Perotta, P. C. "Giambattista Vico, Philosopher-Historian." *Catholic Historical Review* 20 (1934-35): 384-410.

Peterfreund, Stuart. "Shelley, Monboddo, Vico, and the Language of Poetry." *Style* 15 (1981): 382-400.

Piccolomini, Manfredi. "Vico, Sorel, and Modern Artistic Primitivism." *New Vico Studies* 4 (1986): 123-30.

Pietropaolo, Domenico. "Vico and Literary History in the Early Joyce." In *Vico and Joyce*, ed. D. P. Verene. Albany: State University of New York Press, 1987: 100-9.
―――. "Vico and the Language of Dante." *Italian Journal* 1 (1987): 70-74.
―――. "Giambattista Vico." In *Critical Survey of Literary Theory*, ed. F. N. Magill. Pasadena, CA: Salem, 1988: 1507-12.
―――. "McLuhan's Interpretation of Vico." *Scripta Mediterranea* 10-11 (1989-90): 63-70.
―――. "Frye, Vico, and the Grounding of Literature and Criticism." In *Ritratto di Northrop Frye*, ed. A. Lombardo. Rome: Bulzoni Editore, 1990.
―――. "Vico and Modern Thought: A Pedagogical Proposal." *Quaderni d'italianistica* 11 (1990).
―――. "Grassi, Vico, and the Defense of the Humanist Tradition." *New Vico Studies* 10 (1992): 1-10.

Piovani, Pietro. "Vico without Hegel." In *Giambattista Vico: An International Symposium*, ed. G. Tagliacozzo and H. White. Baltimore: Johns Hopkins University Press, 1969: 103-21.
―――. "Apoliticality and Politicality in Vico." In *Giambattista Vico's Science of Humanity*, ed. G. Tagliacozzo and D. P. Verene. Baltimore: Johns Hopkins University Press, 1976: 395-408.

Pipa, Arshi. "Economy in Vico's System." In *Vico: Past and Present*, ed. G. Tagliacozzo. Atlantic Highlands, NJ: Humanities Press, 1981: 2:144-56.
―――. "Marx's Relation to Vico: A Philological Approach." In *Giambattista Vico's Science of Humanity*, ed. G. Tagliacozzo and D. P. Verene. Baltimore: Johns Hopkins University Press, 1976: 290-325.

Pompa, Leon. "Vico's Science." *History and Theory* 10 (1971): 49-83.
―――. "Vico in Review." *Studi internazionali di Filosofia* 5 (1973): 215-19.
―――. "Comment on Professor McMullin's Paper." *Social Research* 43 (1976): 480-83. Reprinted in *Vico and Contemporary Thought*, ed. G. Tagliacozzo, M. Mooney, and D. P. Verene. Atlantic Highlands, NJ: Humanities Press, 1979: 1:90-93.

———. "Human Nature and the Concept of a Human Science." *Social Research* 43 (1976): 434-45. Reprinted in *Vico and Contemporary Thought*, ed. G. Tagliacozzo, M. Mooney, and D. P. Verene. Atlantic Highlands, NJ: Humanities Press, 1979: 1:44-55.

———. "Response by the Author." *Social Research* 43 (1976): 447-49. Reprinted in *Vico and Contemporary Thought*, ed. G. Tagliacozzo, M. Mooney, and D. P. Verene. Atlantic Highlands, NJ: Humanities Press, 1979: 1:57-59.

———. "Vico and the Presuppositions of Historical Knowledge." In *Giambattista Vico's Science of Humanity*, ed. G. Tagliacozzo and D. P. Verene. Baltimore: Johns Hopkins University Press, 1976: 125-40.

———. "Imagination in Vico." In *Vico: Past and Present*, ed. G. Tagliacozzo. Atlantic Highlands, NJ: Humanities Press, 1981: 1:162-70.

———. "Vico and Hegel: A Critical Assessment of Their Accounts of the Role of Ideas in History." In *Vico: Past and Present*, ed. G. Tagliacozzo. Atlantic Highlands, NJ: Humanities Press, 1981: 2:35-46.

———. "The Life and Works of Giambattista Vico." Introduction to Leon Pompa, ed. and trans. *Vico: Selected Writings*. Cambridge: Cambridge University Press, 1982: 1-29. [See complete citation of this translation in Part II A].

———. "Ontological and Historiographical Construction in Vico and Marx." In *Vico and Marx: Affinities and Contrasts*, ed. G. Tagliacozzo. Atlantic Highlands, NJ: Humanities Press; London: Macmillan Press, 1983: 62-77.

———. "Vico's Legislator: Between 'Positive' and Natural Law." *Vera Lex* 5 (1985): 1-2.

———. "The Function of the Legislator in Giambattista Vico." In *L'Educazione giuridica. Part 5: Modelli di legislatore e scienza della legislazione. Filosofia e scienze della legislazione*. Milan: Edizioni Scientifiche Italiane, 1987: 1:135-55.

Pons, Alain. "Vico and French Thought." In *Giambattista Vico: An International Symposium*, ed. G. Tagliacozzo and H. V. White. Baltimore: Johns Hopkins University Press, 1969: 165-85.

———. "Prudence and Providence: The *Pratica della Scienza nuova* and the Problem of Theory and Practice in Vico." In *Giambattista Vico's Science of Humanity*, ed. G. Tagliacozzo and D. P. Verene. Baltimore: Johns Hopkins University Press, 1976: 431-48.

———. "Vico and the *Nouveaux Philosophes*." *Annals of Scholarship* 1 (1980): 63-72.

———. "Vico, Marx, Utopia, and History." In *Vico and Marx: Affinities and Contrasts*, ed. G. Tagliacozzo. Atlantic Highlands, NJ: Humanities Press; London: Macmillan Press, 1983: 20-37.

———. "Vico Between the Ancients and the Moderns." *New Vico Studies* 11 (1993): 13-23.

Popkin, Richard H. "Isaac La Peyrère and Vico." *New Vico Studies* 7 (1989): 79-81.

Poviliunas, A. "The world outlook of the Renaissance and Vico's philosophy of history" [English summary of article in Lithuanian: *Problemos 37 Sociolinie Pazenemo aspektai* (1987): 14-22].

Preus, J. Samuel. "A 'New Science' of Providence: Giambattista Vico." In Preus, *Explaining Religion: Criticism and Theory from Bodin to Freud*. New Haven, CT: Yale University Press, 1987: (ch. 4) 59-83; see also 20, 54.

*Reviews:*
Ausmus, Henry J. *American Historical Review* 93 (1988): 1293-94.
Bird, Laura J., and John D. Schaeffer. *New Vico Studies* 7 (1989): 106-8.

Preus, J. Samuel. "Spinoza, Vico, and the Imagination of Religion." *Journal of the History of Ideas* 50 (1989): 71-93.
*Review:*
Bird, Laura J., and John D. Schaeffer. *New Vico Studies* 7 (1989): 106-8.

Prezzolini, Giuseppe. "Vico: The Discovery of Poetry." In Prezzolini, *The Legacy of Italy.* New York: Vanni, 1948: 169-76.

Purdy, Strother B. "Vico's *verum-factum*, and the Status of the Object in *Finnegans Wake*." *James Joyce Quarterly* 26 (1989): 367-78.

"Radio Programs in France on Vico," trans. Erik Nordenhaug. *New Vico Studies* 6 (1988): 185-86 [Report].

Rafferty, Michael. "Giovanni Battista Vico." In *Great Jurists of the World*, ed. J. MacDonnell and E. Manson. Boston: Little, Brown, 1914: 345-89.

Randall, John Herman, Jr. "The Science of Society: Montesquieu, Vico, the Physiocrats, and Rousseau." In Randall, *The Career of Philosophy*. New York: Columbia University Press, 1962: 1:940-83.

Read, Herbert. "Vico and the Rise of the Genetic Concept of Art." In Read, *Art Now: An Introduction to the Theory of Modern Painting and Sculpture*. London: Harcourt, Brace & Co., 1933: 32-34. Rev. eds. London: Pitman, 1948: 35-37; London: Faber & Faber, 1960: 24-26.
———. "Vico and the Genetic Theory of Poetry." In *Giambattista Vico: An International Symposium*, ed. G. Tagliacozzo and H. V. White. Baltimore: Johns Hopkins University Press, 1969: 591-97.

Reichert, Klaus. "Vico's Method and Its Relation to Joyce's." In *Finnegans Wake: Fifty Years*, ed. G. Lernout. *European Joyce Studies*, ed. Fritz Senn. Amsterdam and Atlanta: Editions Rodopi B. V., 1990: 3:47-60.

Rella, Franco. "Fabula." In *Recoding Metaphysics: The New Italian Philosophy*, ed. G. Borradori. Evanston: Northwestern University Press, 1988: 147-53 [see also 5-8, 9, 11-14, 16, 19, 25, 202].
*Review:*
Struever, Nancy S. *New Vico Studies* 8 (1990): 56-61.

Renaldo, John J. "Antecedents of Vico: The Jesuit Historians." *Archivium Historicum Societatis Jesu* 39 (1970): 349-55.

Reynolds, Mary T. "The City in Vico, Dante, and Joyce." In *Vico and Joyce*, ed. D. P. Verene. Albany: State University of New York Press, 1987: 110-22.

Rhea, Buford. "Vico and the Future of Sociology." In *Vico: Past and Present*, ed. G. Tagliacozzo. Atlantic Highlands, NJ: Humanities Press, 1981: 2:165-74.
_____. "Vico Again." *Contemporary Sociology* 10 (1981): 624-26.

Rickman, H. P. "Vico and Dilthey's Methodology of the Human Studies." In *Giambattista Vico: An International Symposium*, ed. G. Tagliacozzo and H. V. White. Baltimore: Johns Hopkins University Press, 1969: 447-56.
_____. "Vico's First Principle and the Critique of Historical Reason." In *Vico: Past and Present*, ed. G. Tagliacozzo. Atlantic Highlands, NJ: Humanities Press, 1981: 1:206-15.
_____. "Vico and Hermeneutics." *International Studies in Philosophy* 20 (1988): 43-52.

Riverso, Emanuele. "Vico and Wittgenstein." In *Giambattista Vico's Science of Humanity*, ed. G. Tagliacozzo and Donald P. Verene. Baltimore: Johns Hopkins University Press, 1976: 263-73.
_____. "Vico and the Humanistic Concept of *Prisca Theologia*." In *Vico: Past and Present*, ed. G. Tagliacozzo. Atlantic Highlands, NJ: Humanities Press, 1981: 1:52-65.
_____. "Marx and Vico on the Oriental Mode of Production." In *Vico and Marx: Affinities and Contrasts*, ed. G. Tagliacozzo. Atlantic Highlands, NJ: Humanities Press; London: Macmillan Press, 1983: 263-76.
_____. "History as Metascience: A Vichian Cue to the Understanding of the Nature and Development of Sciences." *New Vico Studies* 3 (1985): 49-59.

Roberts, David D. "Straight Stories, Crooked Histories, and Vichian Possibilities." Review of *Language and Historical Representation: Getting the Story Crooked* (H. Kellner). *New Vico Studies* 8 (1990): 77-88.

Robertson, J. G. "Giambattista Vico." In Robertson, *Studies in the Genesis of Romantic Theory in the Eighteenth Century*. Cambridge: Cambridge University Press, 1923: 179-94.

Rockmore, Tom. "Vico, Marx, and Anti-Cartesian Theory of Knowledge." In *Vico and Marx: Affinities and Contrasts*, ed. G. Tagliacozzo. Atlantic Highlands, NJ: Humanities Press; London: Macmillan Press, 1983: 163-76.
_____. "A Note on Vico and Antifoundationalism." *New Vico Studies* 7 (1989): 18-27.

Romano, Carlin. "Viva Vico!" *The Village Voice Literary Supplement* 27 (1982): 17-18.

Rosnow, Ralph L. "The Prophetic Vision of Giambattista Vico: Implications for the State of Social Psychological Theory." *Journal of Personality and Social Psychology* 36 (1978): 1322-31.
_____. "Shotter, Vico, and Fallibilistic Indeterminacy." *British Journal of Social Psychology* 25 (1986): 215-16.

Rossides, Daniel W. "The New Sciences of History: Vico (1668-1774)." In Rossides, *The History and Nature of Sociological Theory*. Boston: Houghton Mifflin, 1978: 65-82.

Rotenstreich, Nathan. "Vico and Kant." In *Giambattista Vico's Science of Humanity*, ed. G. Tagliacozzo and D. P. Verene. Baltimore: Johns Hopkins University Press, 1976: 221-40.
———. "On Cyclical Patterns and Their Interpretation. The Interpretation of Judaism in the Wake of Vico and Hegel." *Hegel-Studien* 11 (1976): 181-204.

Rubinoff, Lionel. "Vico and the Verification of Historical Interpretation." *Social Research* 43 (1976): 484-511. In *Vico and Contemporary Thought*, ed. G. Tagliacozzo, M. Mooney, and D. P. Verene. Atlantic Highlands, NJ: Humanities Press, 1979: 1:94-121.

Said, Edward. "Vico: Autodidact and Humanist." *Centennial Review* 11 (1967): 336-52.
———. "Vico on the Discipline of Bodies and Texts." *Modern Language Notes* 91 (1976): 817-26.
———. "Conclusion: Vico in His Work and in This." In Said, *Beginnings. Intention and Method*. New York: Basic Books, 1975.
**Reviews:**
*Diacritics* 6 (1976): 2, 47.
Ilie, Paul. *Eighteenth Century Studies* 10 (1976-77): 282-83.
*Times Literary Supplement* [London] (20 Aug. 1976): 1026-27.

Saisselin, R. G. "Vichian Architecture." *Eighteenth Century: Theory and Interpretation* 26 (1985): 178-86.

Salamone, William. "Pluralism and Universality in Vico's *Scienza nuova*." In *Giambattista Vico: An International Symposium*, ed. G. Tagliacozzo and H. V. White. Baltimore: Johns Hopkins University Press, 1969: 517-41.

Salstrom, Paul. "Vico, Newton, and Leibniz: The Frustration of the Goals of Three Contemporaries." *Journal of the West Virginia Philosophical Society* 16 (1979): 17-18.

Samuels, Marilyn Schauer. "Is Technical Communication 'Literature'? Current Writing Scholarship and Vico's Cycles of Knowledge." *Iowa State Journal of Business and Technical Literature* 1 (1987): 48-67.

Sandulescu, C. George. "Joyce and Vico and Linguistic Theory." Princess Grace Irish Library Lecture 8. Gerrards Cross: Colin Smythe, 1991: 32-42.
**Review:**
Verene, D. P. *James Joyce Literary Supplement* (27 Sept. 1992): 28.

Saunders, J. J. "Giambattista Vico, 1744-1944." *Dublin Review* 214 (1944): 137-44.

Schaeffer, John D. "Vico's Rhetorical Model of the Mind: *Sensus communis* in the *De nostri temporis studiorum ratione*." *Philosophy and Rhetoric* 14 (1981): 152-67 [Abstract in *The 18th Century: A Current Bibliography*, n.s. 7 (1981): 595].
———. "From Wit to Narration: Vico's Theory of Metaphor in Its Rhetorical Context." *New Vico Studies* 2 (1984): 71-74.
———. "*Sensus Communis* in Vico and Gadamer." *New Vico Studies* 5 (1987): 117-30.
———. "Vico and Religion." *Religious Studies Review* 13 (1987): 321-24 [review of 10 books].

———. "*Vico and Joyce* and Vico Scholarship." Review of *Vico and Joyce* (ed. D. P. Verene). *New Vico Studies* 6 (1988): 129-32.
———. "The Use and Misuse of Giambattista Vico: Rhetoric, Orality, and Theories of Discourse." In *The New Historian*, ed. H. A. Vesser. New York: Routledge, 1989: 89-101.
———. "Vico and MacIntyre's *Whose Justice? Which Rationality?*" *New Vico Studies* 7 (1989): 85-98 [Review].
———. "Vico and Rorty." Review of *Contingency, Irony, and, Solidarity* (R. Rorty). *New Vico Studies* 9 (1991):100-110.
———. "Eco and Vico." Review of *The Limits of Interpretation* (U. Eco). *New Vico Studies* 10 (1992): 73-77.

Sewell, Elizabeth. "Bacon, Vico, Coleridge, and the Poetic Method." In *Giambattista Vico: An International Symposium*, ed. G. Tagliacozzo and H. V. White. Baltimore: Johns Hopkins University Press, 1969: 125-36. Reprinted in *To Be a True Poem: Essays by Elizabeth Sewell*, ed. W. R. Ray. Winston-Salem, NC: Hunter Publisheng Co., 1979: 68-79.

Shenker, Israel. "Tricentennial-Plus-8 Sunders A Savant's Veil of Obscurity." *New York Times* (30 Jan. 1976): 31, 47.
———. "Wiring the Lectern for Giambattista Vico." *International Herald Tribune* (4 Feb. 1976): 5.

Shin, Sachiko, and Tadao Uemura. "Vico Studies in Japan." *New Vico Studies* 5 (1987): 215-18 [Report].

Shotter, John. "Vico, Social Worlds, Personhood and Accountability." In *Indigenous Psychologies: The Anthropology of the Self*, ed. P. Heelas and A. Lock. London: Academic, 1981: 266-84.
———. "A Sense of Place: Vico and the Social Production of Social Identities." *British Journal of Social Psychology* 2 (1986): 199-211 [Abstract: *New Vico Studies* 5 (1987): 186-87].
———. "Vico and Psychology as a History of the Present: A Reply to Averill and Rosnow." *British Journal of Social Psychology* 2 (1986): 217-18.
———. "Vico and the 'Conceits of Knowledge'"; and "Vico and 'Sensory Topics.'" In Shotter, "A Poetics of Relational Terms: The Sociality of Everyday Social Life," *Cultural Dynamics* 4 (1991): 383-87.
———. "Vico and the Poetics of Practical Sociology." In *Cultural Politics of Everyday Life. Social Constructionism, Rhetoric, and Knowing of the Third Kind*. Toronto: University of Toronto Press, 1993: (ch.3) 57-72. See also 1, 3, 6-7, 135-38, 203-7, 222, 232.

Simon, Lawrence H. "Vico and Marx: Perspectives on Historical Development." *Journal of the History of Ideas* 42 (1981): 317-31.
———. "Vico and Marx and the Problem of Moral Relativism." In *Vico and Marx: Affinities and Contrasts*, ed. G. Tagliacozzo. Atlantic Highlands, NJ: Humanities Press; London: Macmillan Press, 1983: 206-32.
———. "Vico and the Problem of Other Cultures." *The Philosophical Forum* 25, No. 1 (1993): 33-54.

Simonsuuri, Kirsti. "Vico's Discovery of the True Homer." In Simonsuuri, *Homer's Original Genius: Eighteenth-Century Notions of the Early Greek Epic (1688-1798)*. Cambridge: Cambridge University Press, 1979: 90-98 (ch. 7).

Singer, Jerome L. "Vico's Insight and the Scientific Study of the Stream of Consciousness." *Social Research* 43 (1976): 715-26. Reprinted in *Vico and Contemporary Thought*, ed. G. Tagliacozzo, M. Mooney, and D. P. Verene. Atlantic Highlands, NJ: Humanities Press, 1979: 2:57-68.

Skagestad, Peter. "The Problem of Vico." Review of *The Expression of Historical Knowledge* (J. L. Gorman). *History and Theory* 23 (1984): 127-31.

Sorensen, Dolf. "Vico." In Sorenson, *James Joyce's Aesthetic Theory*. Amsterdam: Rodopi, 1977: 29-35.

Stadelmann, R. "Giam Battista Vico's Philosophy of History, *Scienza nuova*." *Tübingen University Lecture Series*, nos. 3-4 [n.d.]: 72-75.

Stam, James H. "Prospects of a New Science"; "Man the Language Maker"; "A New Homer... and a New Moses." In Stam, *Inquiries into the Origin of Language: The Fate of a Question*. New York: Harper & Row, 1976, 9-19; 65-71.

Stark, Werner. "Giambattista Vico's Sociology of Knowledge." In *Giambattista Vico: An International Symposium*, ed. G. Tagliacozzo and H. V. White. Baltimore: Johns Hopkins University Press, 1969: 297-307.
———. "The Theoretical and Practical Relevance of Vico's Sociology for Today." *Social Research* 43 (1976): 818-25. Reprinted in *Vico and Contemporary Thought*, ed. G. Tagliacozzo, M. Mooney, and D. P. Verene. Atlantic Highlands, NJ: Humanities Press, 1979: 2:160-67.

Steinke, Horst. "Hintikka and Vico: An Update on Contemporary Logic." *New Vico Studies* 3 (1985): 147-55.

Stevenson, David R. "Vico's *Scienza nuova*: An Alternative to the Enlightenment Mainstream." In *The Quest for the New Science: Language and Thought in Eighteenth-Century Science*, ed. K. J. Fink and J. W. Marchand. London: Feffer & Simons; Carbondale: Southern Illinois University Press, 1979: 6-16, 69-71.

Stevenson, W. Taylor. "Giambattista Vico and the Modern Historical Consciousness." In Stevenson, *History as Myth: The Import for Contemporary Theology*. New York: Seabury Press, 1969: 33-57, 94-107 *passim*.

Stone, Harold. "The Scientific Basis of Vico's *Scienza nuova*." In *Vico: Past and Present*, ed. G. Tagliacozzo. Atlantic Highlands, NJ: Humanities Press, 1981: 1:117-26.
———. "A Note on Vico Studies Today: Toulmin and the Development of Academic Disciplines." *New Vico Studies* 1 (1983): 69-75.

———. "Vico and Doria: The Beginnings of Their Friendship." *New Vico Studies* 2 (1984): 83-92.

Struever, Nancy S. "Vico, Valla, and the Logic of Humanist Inquiry." In *Giambattista Vico's Science of Humanity*, ed. G. Tagliacozzo and D. P. Verene. Baltimore: Johns Hopkins University Press, 1976: 173-85.
———. "Vico, Foucault, and the Strategy of Intimate Investigation." *New Vico Studies* 2 (1984): 41-70.
———. "Rhetoric and Philosophy in Vichian Inquiry." *New Vico Studies* 3 (1985): 131-45.
———. "Vico in Post-Modern Philosophy." Review of *Recoding Metaphysics: The New Italian Philosophy* (ed. G. Borradori). *New Vico Studies* 8 (1990): 56-61.
———. "Giambattista Vico (1668-1744)." In *Philosophy of Language*, ed. M. Dascal *et al.* Berlin: de Gruyter, 1992: 1:330-38.
———. "Afterword I: Purity as Danger; Gramsci's Machiavelli, Croce's Vico." In *Theory as Practice: Ethical Inquiry in the Renaissance*. Chicago: University of Chicago Press, 1992: 210-24; see also 93, 151, 128, 225, 231-32.
———. "Humanism and Science in the Context of Vichian Inquiry." *New Vico Studies* 11 (1993): 61-66.

Sumberg, Theodore A. "Reading Vico Three Times." *Interpretation* 17 (1990): 347-53.

Swinny, S. H. "Giambattista Vico." *Sociological Review* 7 (1914): 50-57.

Syska-Lamparska, Rena Anna. "A Polish Vichian: Stanislaw Brzozowski." *New Vico Studies* 2 (1984): 103-11.

Tagliacozzo, Giorgio. "Economic Vichianism: Vico, Galiani, Croce—Economics, Economic Liberalism," *Quarterly Review of the Banca Nazionale del Lavoro* 85 (1968): 95-119. Reprinted in *Giambattista Vico: An International Symposium*, ed. G. Tagliacozzo and H. V. White. Baltimore: Johns Hopkins University Press, 1969: 215-23.
———. "Epilogue" and "Tree of Knowledge." In *Giambattista Vico: An International Symposium*, ed. G. Tagliacozzo and H. V. White. Baltimore: Johns Hopkins University Press, 1969: 599-613.
———. "Vico and Joyce." *Proceedings of the Third International James Joyce Symposium (14-18 June 1971)*, ed. Facoltà di Magistero, Università di Trieste. Trieste: La Editoriale Libraria, 1974: 374-78.
———. "Introductory Remarks ["Vico and Contemporary Thought" Conference 27-31 Jan. 1976]. *Social Research* 43 (1976): 391-98 Reprinted in *Vico and Contemporary Thought*, ed. G. Tagliacozzo, M. Mooney, and D. P. Verene. Atlantic Highlands, NJ: Humanities Press, 1979: 1:1-8.
———. "General Education as Unity of Knowledge: A Theory Based on Vichian Principles." *Social Research* 43 (1975): 768-96. Reprinted in *Vico and Contemporary Thought*, ed. G. Tagliacozzo, M. Mooney, and D. P. Verene. Atlantic Highlands, NJ: Humanities Press, 1979: 2:110-38.

———, and Margherita Frankel. "Progress in Art? A Vichian Answer." In *Vico: Past and Present*, ed. Giorgio Tagliacozzo. Atlantic Highlands, NJ: Humanities Press, 1981: 2:238-51.

Tagliacozzo, Giorgio. "Vico: A Philosopher of the Eighteenth—and Twentieth—Centuries." *Italica* 59 (1982): 93-108 [Abstract: *New Vico Studies* 2 (1984): 161].

———. "Vico and Marx. One Hundred Years after Marx's Death." *Rivista di Studi Italiani* 1 (1983): 98-121 [Abstract: *New Vico Studies* 2 (1984): 160-61].

———. "Toward a History of Recent Anglo-American Vico Scholarship: Part 1: 1944-1969." *New Vico Studies* 1 (1983): 1-19.

———. "Part 2: 1969-1973." *New Vico Studies* 2 (1984): 1-40.

———. "Part 3: 1974-1977." *New Vico Studies* 3 (1985): 1-32.

———. "Part 4: The Vico/Venezia Conference (1978) and its Bountiful Aftermath." *New Vico Studies* 4 (1986): 1-24. Parts 1-4 reprinted in Tagliacozzo, *The Arbor Scientiae Reconceived and the History of Vico's Resurrection*. Atlantic Highlands, NJ: Humanities Press for The Institute for Vico Studies, 1993: 46-154.

———. "Part 5: 'Toward a History of Recent Vico Scholarship in English.' After Vico/Venezia (1978-1987)." *New Vico Studies* 5 (1987): 1-56.

———. "Vico, the Counter-Enlightenment, and Advanced Contemporary Thought." In *Man, God and Nature in the Enlightenment*, ed. T. E. D. Braun, D. C. Mell, and L. Palmer. East Lansing, MI: Colleagues, 1988: 13-24.

———. "Giambattista Vico: Neglect and Resurrection." *New Vico Studies* 7 (1989): 1-17. Reprinted in Tagliacozzo, *The Arbor Scientiae Reconceived and the History of Vico's Resurrection*. Atlantic Highlands, NJ: Humanities Press for The Institute for Vico Studies, 1993: 29-45.

———. "The Study of Vico Worldwide and the Future of Vico Studies." *New Vico Studies* 8 (1990): 20-37. Reprinted in Tagliacozzo, *The Arbor Scientiae Reconceived and the History of Vico's Resurrection*. Atlantic Highlands, NJ: Humanities Press for The Institute for Vico Studies, 1993: 172-89.

———. "The *Arbor Scientiae* Reconceived: A Modern Vichian Tree of Knowledge." In Tagliacozzo, *The Arbor Scientiae Reconceived and the History of Vico's Resurrection*. Atlantic Highlands, NJ: Humanities Press for The Institute for Vico Studies, 1993: 1-28.

Titone, Renzo. "From Images to Words: Language Education in a 'Vichian' Perspective." *Rassegna Italiane di Linguistica Applicata* 23 (1991): 201-14.

Todd, Joan, and Joseph Cono. "Vico and Collingwood on the 'Conceit of Scholars'." *History of European Ideas* 6 (1985): 59-69.

Tokarczyk, Roman. "The Reception of Vico's Thought in Poland." *Vera Lex* 5 (1985): 19-20.

Toulmin, Stephen, and June Goodfield. "Vico: The Mendel of History." In Toulmin and Goodfield, *The Discovery of Time*, New York: Harper & Row, 1965: 125-29.

Trabant, Jürgen. "*Parlare scrivendo*: Deconstructive Remarks on Derrida's Reading of Vico." *New Vico Studies* 7 (1989): 43-58.
_____. "*Parlare cantando*: Language Singing in Vico and Herder." *New Vico Studies* 9 (1991): 1-16.

Tristram, R. J. "Explanation in the *New Science*: On Vico's Contribution to Scientific Sociohistorical Thought." *History and Theory* 21 (1983): 146-77.
_____. "Vico on the Production and Assessment of Knowledge." *Philosophy and Phenomenological Research* 48 (1988): 355-88.

Tuttle, Howard N. "Comment on Professor Jordan's Paper." *Social Research* 43 (1976): 531-34. Reprinted in *Vico and Contemporary Thought*, ed. G. Tagliacozzo, M. Mooney, and D. P. Verene. Atlantic Highlands, NJ: Humanities Press, 1979: 1:141-44.
_____. "The Epistemological Status of the Cultural World in Vico and Dilthey." In *Giambattista Vico's Science of Humanity*, ed. G. Tagliacozzo and D. P. Verene. Baltimore: Johns Hopkins University Press, 1976: 241-50.

Uemura, Tadao. "In the Beginning There Was Fear: Vico and the Dialectic of Foundation, II." *Area and Culture Studies* 36 (1986): 231-48.

Valdès, Mario J. "Giambattista Vico at the Crossroads between Literary Theory and Comparative Literature; *Festschrift* for Henry Remak." In *Sensus Communis: Contemporary Trends in Comparative Literature/Panorama de la situation actuelle en litterature comparée*, ed. J. Riesz, P. Boerner, and B. Scholz. Tubigen: Narr, 1986: 441-52.
_____. "Relational Theory from Vico to Reader-Reception Aesthetics." In *Phenomenological Hermeneutics and the Study of Literature*. Toronto: University of Toronto Press, 1987: 5-26 (ch. 1); see also 67.

Valone, James J. "Vico's Human Science: The Paradox of Consciousness and Access to the Social." *Southern Journal of Philosophy* 18 (1980): 371-92 [Abstract in *The 18th Century: A Current Bibliography*, n.s. 6 (1980): 593].
_____. "Why Vico Today?" In *Philosophy and Culture: Proceedings of the 17th World Congress of Philosophy*, ed. V. Cauchy. Montreal: Montmorency, 1988: 2:953-58.

Vaughan, Charles E. "Giambattista Vico, An Eighteenth-Century Pioneer." *John Rylands Library Bulletin* (Deansgate, Manchester) 6 (1921): 3.
_____. "The Eclipse of Contract: Vico,, Montesquieu." In *Studies in the History of Political Philosophy before and after Rousseau*, ed. A. G. Little. Manchester: The University Press, 1925: 1:204-302.

Vaughan, Frederick. "*La Scienza Nuova*: Orthodoxy and the Art of Writing." *Forum Italicum* 2 (1968): 332-58.

Verdicchio, Massimo. "The Rhetoric of Epistemology in Giambattista Vico." *Philosophy and Rhetoric* 19 (1986): 178-93 [Abstract in *The 18th Century: A Current Bibliography*, n.s. 12 (1986): 534].

_____. "Croce: Reader of Vico." *Italian Quarterly* 29 (1988): 41-55.
_____. "Exagmination Round the Fictification of Vico and Joyce." *James Joyce Quarterly* 28 (1989): 531-39.
_____. "Papers on Vico at the American Association of Italian Studies." *New Vico Studies* 7 (1989): 155 [Report].

Verene, Donald Phillip. "Vico's Science of Imaginative Universals and the Philosophy of Symbolic Forms." In *Giambattista Vico's Science of Humanity*, ed. G. Tagliacozzo and D. P. Verene. Baltimore: Johns Hopkins University Press, 1976: 295-317.
_____. "Vico's Philosophy of Imagination." *Social Research* 43 (1976): 410-26. Reprinted in *Vico and Contemporary Thought*, ed. G. Tagliacozzo, M. Mooney, and D. P. Verene. Atlantic Highlands, NJ: Humanities Press, 1979: 1:20-36.
_____. "Response by the Author." *Social Research* 43 (1976): 429-33. Reprinted in *Vico and Contemporary Thought*, ed. G. Tagliacozzo, M. Mooney, and D. P. Verene. Atlantic Highlands, NJ: Humanities Press, 1979: 1:39-43.
_____. "Vico's Humanity." *Humanitas* 15 (1979): 227-40.
_____. "Vico's Philosophical Originality." In *Vico: Past and Present*, ed. G. Tagliacozzo. Atlantic Highlands, NJ: Humanities Press, 1981: 1:127-43.
_____. "Vico's Place: A Response to Professor Hwa Yol Jung." *Philosophy and Rhetoric* 15 (1982): 203-6 [Abstract in *The 18th Century: A Current Bibliography*, n.s. 8 (1982): 544-45].
_____. "The New Art of Narration: Vico and the Muses." *New Vico Studies* 1 (1983): 21-38.
_____. "Vico and Marx on Poetic Wisdom and Barbarism." In *Vico and Marx: Affinities and Contrasts*, ed. G. Tagliacozzo. Atlantic Highlands, NJ: Humanities Press; London: Macmillan Press, 1983.
_____. "Philosophical Laughter: Vichian Remarks on Umberto Eco's *The Name of the Rose*." *New Vico Studies* 2 (1984): 75-82.
_____. "A Vichian Understanding of Custom, Rights, and the Origin of Society." *Vera Lex* 5 (1985): 5-6, 27.
_____. "Vico's Influence on Cassirer." *New Vico Studies* 3 (1985): 105-11.
_____. "Eliade's Vichianism: The Regeneration of Time and the Terror of History." *New Vico Studies* 4 (1986): 115-22.
_____. "Vico as Reader of Joyce." In *Vico and Joyce*, ed. D. P. Verene. Albany: State University of New York Press, 1987: 221-31.
_____. "Vico's 'Ignota latebat'." *New Vico Studies* 5 (1987): 77-98.
_____. "Imaginative Universals and Narrative Truth." *New Vico Studies* 6 (1988): 1-19.
_____. "International James Joyce Symposium: Session on Joyce and Vico—June 1988." *New Vico Studies* 6 (1988): 184-85 [Report].
_____. "Vico's Frontispiece and the Tablet of Cebes." In *Man, God, and Nature in the Enlightenment: Proceedings of the 14th Annual Meeting of the East-Central American Society for 18th-Century Studies*, ed. T. E. D. Braun, D. C. Mell, and L. M. Palmer. East Lansing, MI: Colleagues Press, 1988: 3-11.
_____. "Vico's Imaginative Universals and the Origin of Culture." In *Philosophy and Culture: Proceedings of the 17th World Congress of Philosophy*, ed. V. Cauchy. Montreal: Montmorency, 1988: 2:109-13.
_____. "Vico's New Critical Art and the Authority of the Noble Lie." In *Discourse of Authority in Medieval and Renaissance Literature*, ed. K. Brownlee and W. Stephens. Hanover, NH: University Press of New England for Dartmouth, 1989: 47-59.

———. "Giambattista Vico's 'Reprehension of the Metaphysics of René Descartes, Benedict Spinoza, and John Locke': An Addition to the *New Science* (Translation and Commentary)." *New Vico Studies* 8 (1990): 2-18. [See complete citation to translation in Part II A.]

———. "Vico's Road and Hegel's Owl as Historiographies of Renaissance Philosophy." *Clio* 21 (1992): 329-43.

———. "Introduction: On Humanistic Education" to Giambattista Vico, *On Humanistic Education: Six Inaugural Orations, 1699-1707*, trans. G. A. Pinton and A. W. Shippee. Ithaca, NY: Cornell University Press, 1993: 1-27. [See Part II A for complete citation to translation.]

———. "Two Sources of Philosophical Memory: Vico versus Hegel." In *Philosophical Imagination and Cultural Memory*, ed. Patricia Cook. Durham, NC: Duke University Press, 1993: 40-58. See also 5-6, 9.

———. "Metaphysical Narration, Science, and Symbolic Form." *Review of Metaphysics* 47 (1993): 115-32.

Vickers, B. "The Atrophy of Modern Rhetoric, Vico to De Man." *Rhetorica—A Journal of the History of Rhetoric* 6 (1988): 21-56.

"Vico's *New Science* and the *Ancient Wisdom of the Italians*," *Foreign Review* 5 (1830): 380-91.

Viechtbauer, Helmut. "Giambattista Vico and the Foundation of Science." In *The Philosophy of Order: Essays on History, Consciousness, and Politics*, ed. P. J. Opitz and G. Sebba. Stuttgart: Klett-Cotta, 1981: 406-15.

Vittorini, D. "Giambattista Vico and Reality: An Evaluation of the '*De nostri temporis studiorum ratione*' (1708)." *Modern Language Quarterly* 13 (1952): 90-98.

Wainwright, E. H. "The Historical Thought of Giambattista Vico." *Kleio* 9 (1977): 1-21.

Walsh, W. H. "The Logical Status of Vico's Ideal Eternal History." In *Giambattista Vico's Science of Humanity*, ed. G. Tagliacozzo and D. P. Verene. Baltimore: Johns Hopkins University Press, 1976: 141-53.

Walton, Craig. "*Corsi, ricorsi*, and the Way out of Modern Barbarism in Vico's *New Science*." In *Kant und sein Jahrhundert-Gedenkschrift für Giorgio Tonelli*, ed. C. Cesa and N. Hinske. Bern: Peter Lang, 1993: 5-27.

Ward, Patricia A. "Joubert and Vico." *Revue de Littérature Comparée* 55 (1981): 226-31.

Ward, Robert Stafford. "The Influence of Vico upon Longfellow." *Emerson Society Quarterly: Journal of the American Renaissance* 58 (1970): 57-62.

Weintraub, Karl Joachim. "Vico and Gibbon: The Historical Mode of Understanding Self-Development." In Weintraub, *The Value of the Individual: Self and Circumstance in Autobiography*. Chicago and London: University of Chicago Press, 1978: 261-93.

Weir, Lorraine. "*Laws of Media*: Vico and McLuhan on the New Science." *Signature—A Journal of Theory and Canadian Literature* 2 (1989): 60-70.

———. "Performing the Dreamwork: *Finnegans Wake* as Vichian Morphogenesis." In *Writing Joyce: A Semiotics of the Joyce System*. Bloomington: Indiana University Press, 1989: 54-81.

———. "Auerbach and Vico." *Lettere Italiane* 30 (1978): 456-69. Reprinted in *Vico: Past and Present*, ed. G. Tagliacozzo. Atlantic Highlands, NJ: Humanities Press, 1981: 1:85-96.

Wells, George A. "Vico and Herder." In *Giambattista Vico: An International Symposium*, ed. G. Tagliacozzo and H. V. White. Baltimore: Johns Hopkins University Press, 1969: 93-102.

———. "Religion in Vico and Hume." *Trivium* 11 (1976): 12-20.

Wescott, Roger W. "Giambattista Vico as a Philologist." *Historiographia Linguistica* 3 (1976): 123-25.

Wesseley, Anna. "The Frontispiece of Vico's *New Science*." *Studies on Voltaire and the Eighteenth Century* 263 (1989): 565-68.

Whalley, George. "Coleridge and Vico." In *Giambattista Vico: An International Symposium*, ed. G. Tagliacozzo and H. V. White. Baltimore: Johns Hopkins University Press, 1969: 225-44.

White, Hayden. "What is Living and What is Dead in Croce's Criticism of Vico." In *Giambattista Vico: An International Symposium*, ed. G. Tagliacozzo and H. V. White. Baltimore: Johns Hopkins University Press, 1969: 379-89. Reprinted in White, *Tropics of Discourse*. Baltimore: Johns Hopkins University Press, 1978: 218-29.

———. "Croce contra Vico." In White, *Metahistory: The Historical Imagination in Nineteenth-Century Europe*. Baltimore: Johns Hopkins University Press, 1973: 415-22.

———. "The Tropics of History: The Deep Structure of the *New Science*." In *Giambattista Vico's Science of Humanity*, ed. G. Tagliacozzo and D. P. Verene. Baltimore: Johns Hopkins University Press, 1976: 65-85. Reprinted in White, *Tropics of Discourse*. Baltimore: Johns Hopkins University Press, 1978: 197-217.

———. "Vico and the Radical Wing of Structuralist/Poststructuralist Thought Today." *New Vico Studies* 1 (1983): 63-68.

———. "Vattimo's 'Weak' Thought and Vico's 'New' Science." *New Vico Studies* 9 (1991): 61-67 [review of *The End of Modernity* (G. Vattimo)].

White, Patrick T. "Vico's Institution of Burial in '*Ulysses*'." *Ball State University Forum* 14 (1973): 59-68.

———. "'*Ulysses*' and Vico's 'Principles of Humanity'." *Proceedings of the Third International James Joyce Symposium (14-18 June 1971)*, ed. Facoltà di Magistero, University of Trieste. Trieste: La Editoriale Libraria, 1974: 348-54.

White, Sheldon H. "Developmental Psychology and Vico's Concept of Universal History." *Social Research* 43 (1976): 659-71. Reprinted in *Vico and Contemporary Thought*, ed. G. Tagliacozzo, M. Mooney, and D. P. Verene. Atlantic Highlands, NJ: Humanities Press, 1979: 2:1-13.

Whittaker, Thomas. "Vico's New Science of Humanity." *Mind* 35 (1926): 59-71, 204-21, 319-36. Reprinted in Whittaker, *Reason: A Philosophical Essay, with Historical Illustrations —Comte, Mill, Schopenhauer, Vico, Spinoza*. Cambridge: Cambridge University Press, 1934.

Wilcox, Donald J. "Vico and the Critique of Absolute Destiny" In Wilcox, *The Measure of Times Past*. Chicago: University of Chicago Press, 1987: 214-20 [see also 261, 269].

Zagorin, Perez. "Vico's Theory of Knowledge: A Critique." *The Philosophical Quarterly* 34 (1984): 15-30.
*Review:*
Palmer, Lucia M. *New Vico Studies* 2 (1984): 155-58.

Zagorin, Perez. "Berlin on Vico." *The Philosophical Quarterly* 35 (1985): 290-96 [response to Berlin, Isaiah, "Discussions on Vico": 281-90]. [Abstract in *The 18th Century: A Current Bibliography*, n.s. 10 (1984): 308.]

Zamora, Lois Parkinson. "Magic Realism and Fantastic History: Carlos Fuentes's *Terra Nostra* and Giambattista Vico's *The New Science*." *Review of Contemporary Fiction* 8 (1988): 249-56.

Zhang, Longxi. "The *New Science* in Chinese." *New Vico Studies* 5 (1987): 218-19 [Report].
_____. "Vico Studies in China." *New Vico Studies* 3 (1985): 236-39 [Report].

Zhu Guangqian. "Postscript, by the Chinese translator of Vico's *New Science* and *Autobiography*." *New Vico Studies* 6 (1988): 186-88.

# Part I. Works on Vico

## C. Dissertations and Theses

Accomando, John Andrew. "The *New Science as Metaphor of History.*" University of California (Los Angeles), 1991.

Albano, Maeve Edith. "Providence as a Principle of Teleological Explanation in the Philosophy of G. B. Vico." University of Southern California, 1982.

Allen, Robert van Roden. "The Political Common Place: The Convertibility of True and Made in Vico and Rousseau." The Pennsylvania State University, 1983.

Amari, Vincenzo Maria. "Vico, Leopardi, Nietzsche: A Comparative Study of the Problem of Nihilism." Columbia University, 1979.

Bank, Bruce H. "Where Terms Begin: Giambattista Vico and the Natural Law." Harvard University, 1966.

Bedani, G. L. C. "A Reappraisal of Vico's '*Scienza nuova*' in the Light of the Study of the Religious, Epistemological, and General Theoretical Undercurrents, Ambiguities, and Limitations of the Work." University of Wales, 1981.

Bertolini, Andrea. "The Logic of Representation in Vico and Nietzsche." Yale University, 1976.

Cho, Hanook. "For Michelet's Vico: An Interpretation of Michelet's Translation of Vico's *Scienza nuova.*" University of Texas (Austin), 1991.

Connelly, Frances Susan. "The Origins and Development of Primitivism in Eighteenth and Nineteenth-Century European Art and Aesthetics (Gauguin, Vico)." University of Pittsburgh, 1987.

Cornecelli, George M. "Truth and Certainty in History: An Analysis of the Concepts 'Maker's Knowledge' and 'Teleology' in the Philosophies of History of Giambattista Vico and Immanuel Kant." University of Oklahoma, 1977.

Dismukes, W. P. "Michelet and Vico: A Study of Michelet's Use of Vichian Principles." University of Illinois, 1936.

Failla, Dominic Salvatore. "Providence as a Category of Social Ordering and Social Preservation in the Thought of Giambattista Vico (1668-1744)." Florida State University, 1984.

Finkel, Candida A. "Reason and Rhetoric: The Influence upon Rhetoric of Major Philosophical Changes in the Concept of Reason (Aristotle, Plato, Vico)." Northwestern University, 1984.

Fulco, Adrienne. "A Study of the Political Ideas of Giambattista Vico's *New Science.*" City University of New York, 1981.

Gianturco, Elio. "Joseph de Maistre and Giambattista Vico." Columbia University, 1937.

Goetsch, James Robert, Jr. "Vico's Axioms: A Study of the Methodology of the *Scienza nuova* in the Light of Aristotle's *Rhetoric.*" Emory University, 1993.

Grimaldi, Alfonsina Albini. "The Universal Humanity of Giambattista Vico." Columbia University, 1957.

Haddock, Bruce A. "Vico and Idealism." Oxford University, 1977.

Henseler, Donna Leah. "Vico's Doctrine of *ricorso* in James Joyce's *Finnegans Wake.*" Michigan State University, 1970.

Holub, Renate. "Problematics of Giambattista Vico's Theory of Poetics and Aesthetics." University of Wisconsin, 1983.

Kunze, Donald E. "Thought and Place: The Imagination and Memory of Eternal Places in the Philosophy of Giambattista Vico." The Pennsylvania State University, 1983.

Lilla, Mark. "A Preface to Vico: Skepticism, Politics, Theodicy." Harvard University, 1990.

Mason, Ellsworth G. "James Joyce's 'Ulysses' and Vico's Cycle." Yale University, 1948.

Meskill, Michael Francis. "Holistic Educational Theory in Vico, Joyce, and McLuhan, Applied to American Higher Education." Claremont College, 1979.

Mestastasio, Arthur Paul. "Vico and French Romanticism." Boston University, 1963.

Miller, Cecilia DesBrisay. "Giambattista Vico: Imagination and Historical Knowledge." Balliol College, Oxford University, 1988 [Abstract in *New Vico Studies* 7 (1989): 133-34].

Mooney, Michael. "Wisdom Speaking: Language and Society in Vico." Columbia University, 1982.

Negro, Sergio P. "G. B. Vico and Contemporary Theology: A Study of the Thought of Giambattista Vico in the Light of Some Contemporary Theological Developments." Graduate Theological Union (Berkeley), 1974.

Nutkiewicz, Micheal Eli. "The Impact of Mechanical Philosophy on Early Modern Political Theory: Hobbes, Spinoza, Pufendorf, and Vico." University of California (Los Angeles), 1978.

Paparella, Emanuel Louis. "The Paradox of Transcendence and Immanence in Vico's Concept of Providence." Yale University, 1991.

Pasotti, Robert N. "Giambattista Vico and the Psychology of History." Columbia University, 1963.

Peaden, Catherine Lynn Hobbs. "Language and Rhetoric in Locke, Condillac, and Vico." Purdue University, 1989.

Pennachetti, Leonard. "From Ancient Wisdom to New Science: An Essay on Vico's Development." York University (Toronto), 1984.

Perkinson, Henry J. "Giambattista Vico: Philosopher of Education." Harvard University, 1959.

Pietropaolo, Domenico. "Italian Dante Studies in the Age of Vico." University of Toronto, 1980.

Pinton, Giorgio A. "Emilio Betti's (1890-1969) Theory of General Interpretation: Its Genesis in Giambattista Vico (1668-1744) with Its Relevance to Contemporary Dialogue on Hermeneutic." Hartford Seminary Foundation, 1972.

Rockey, Palmer. "The Moral Philosophy of Giambattista Vico." St. Louis University, 1955.

Rosolowski, Tacey A. "Shapes of Indeterminacy: Analogy and Sequence in Vico's *New Science* and Rousseau's *Reveries* and *Emile*." State University of New York (Buffalo), 1992.

Simon, Lawrence H. "The Problem of Historical Knowledge: Epistemology in the *New Science* of Giambattista Vico." Boston University, 1980.

Slomich, Sidney J. "Studies in Eschatological Politics: Reason, Fact, Value, and Law in the Historical Political Theories of Vico, Marx, Hegel, Mazzini, and Kant." Harvard University, 1951.

Stone, Harold. "Epicureanism and Historical Writing: A Study of Vico and Giannone." University of Chicago, 1981.

Skotnicki, Theodore Peter. "The Idea of Punishment in the 'New Science' of Giambattista Vico." Unpublished M.A. thesis, University of Chicago, 1983.

Syska-Lamparska, Rena Anna. "Giambattista Vico's Thought in Stanislaw Brzozowski's Work." Harvard University, 1983.

Tubino, F. "The Articulation of Philosophy and the Human Sciences in the 'New Science' of Giambattista Vico." 1983 [*Dissertation Abstract International* 48 (1987): 1083].

Van Nostrand, C. Alexandra. "A Vichian Theory of Making and Knowing: Imagination and Consciousness in Human and Organization Development." The Fielding Institute, 1993.

Verdicchio, Massimo. "Reading and Epistemology in Vico and Croce." Yale University, 1980.

Weatley, Owen K. "Giambattista Vico: A Forgotten Eighteenth-Century Student of Early Man." Unpublished M. A. thesis, Australian National University (Canberra), 1984.

White, Patrick T. "James Joyce's 'Ulysses' and Vico's 'Principles of Humanity'." University of Michigan, 1963.

# Part I. Works on Vico

### D. Reviews in English of Works on Vico in Other Languages

Agrimi, Mario. *Ricerche e discussioni vichiane*. Lanciano: Editrice Intinerari, 1984.
*Review:*
Costa, Gustavo. *New Vico Studies* 4 (1986): 145-48.

Americo, R. et al. *Campanella e Vico*. In *Archivio di Filosofia*. Padova: CEDAM, 1969.
*Review:*
Schneider, Herbert W. *Journal of the History of Philosophy,* 9 (1971): 253.

*Atti del convegno internazionale sul tema: "Campanella e Vico." Problemi attuali di scienza e cultura*, no. 126. Rome: Accademia Nazionale dei Lincei, 1969.
*Review:*
Gianturco, Elio. *Forum Italicum* 4 (1970): 421-34.

Badaloni, Nicola, ed. *Un vichiano in Messico: Lorenzo Boturini Benaduci*. Lucca: Maria Pacini Fazzi, 1990.
*Review:*
Costa, Gustavo. *New Vico Studies* 11 (1993).

Badaloni, Nicola, ed. *Introduzione a Vico*. I filosofi, 39. Rome/Bari: Laterza, 1984.
*Review:*
Costa, Gustavo. *New Vico Studies* 3 (1985): 173-75.

Battafarano, Italo Michele. *Von Andrea zu Vico: Untersuchungen zur Beziehung zwischen deutscher und italienischer Literatur im 17. Jahrundert*. Stuttgart: H. D. Heinz, 1979.
*Review:*
Marigold, W. G. *Germanic Notes* 17 (1986): 62-63.

Battistini, Andrea. "Vico, Joyce, e il romanzo dell'etimologia." *Lingua e stile* 21 (1986): 137-48 [Abstract in *The 18th Century: A Current Bibliography*, n.s. 12 (1986): 534].

*Bollettino del Centro di Studi Vichiani* 11-13 (1981-83).
*Review:*
Syska-Lamparska, Rena A. *New Vico Studies* 2 (1984): 161-64.

*Bollettino del Centro di Studi Vichiani* 14-15 (1984-85).
*Reviews:*
Costa, Gustavo. *New Vico Studies* 4 (1986): 138-45.
Jacobitti, Edmund E. *Differentia* 2 (1988): 267-75.

*Bollettino del Centro di Studi Vichiani* 16 (1986), ed. M. Sanna.
*Review:*
Costa, Gustavo. *New Vico Studies* 5 (1987): 182-85.

*Bollettino del Centro di Studi Vichiani* 17-18 (1987-88), ed. R. Mazzola.
*Review:*
Costa, Gustavo. *New Vico Studies* 7 (1989): 114-18.

*Bollettino del Centro di Studi Vichiani* 19 (1989). Naples: Bibliopolis, 1989; and *Contributo al catalogo vichiano nazionale: Supplemento*, eds. R. Mazzola and M. Sanna.
*Review:*
Costa, Gustavo. *New Vico Studies* 8 (1990): 95-99.

*Bollettino del Centro di Studi Vichiani* 20 (1990), ed.
G. Giarrizzo and F. Tessitore; and *Indice generale della seconda serie* 11-20 (1981-90), eds. R. Mazzola and M. Sanna.
*Review:*
Costa, Gustavo. *New Vico Studies* 9 (1991): 119-25.

*Bollettino del Centro di Studi Vichiani* 21 (1991), eds. G. Giarrizzo and F. Tessitore.
*Review:*
Costa, Gustavo. *New Vico Studies* 11 (1993).

Bonfante, Giuliano. "Vico e la linguistica." *Bollettino del Centro di Studi Vichiani* 10 (1980): 134-38 [Abstract in *The 18th Century: A Current Bibliography*, n.s. 7 (1981): 589].

Brown, John L. "Bodin précurseur de Giambattista Vico." In *Jean Bodin: Actes du Colloque Interdisciplinaire d'Angers*, vol. 1. Angers: Presses de l'Université d'Angers, 1985: 147-54.
*Review:*
Costa, Gustavo. *New Vico Studies* 4 (1986): 148-51.

Cantelli, Gianfranco. *Mente corpo linguaggio: Saggio sull' interpretazione vichiana del mito*. Florence: Sansoni, 1987.
*Reviews:*
Costa, Gustavo. *New Vico Studies* 5 (1987): 169-72.
Danesi, Marcel. *Rivista di Studi Italiani* 7 (1989): 39-46.

Costa, Gustavo. "Vico e il Settecento." *Forum Italicum* 10 (1976): 10-30.
*Review:*
*The 18th Century. A Current Bibliography*, n.s. 2 (1976): 393-94.

Costa, Gustavo. *Le antichità germaniche nella cultura italiana da Machiavelli a Vico*. Naples: Bibliopolis, 1977.
*Reviews:*
Kelley, Donald R. *American Historical Review* 84 (1979): 731-32.
Rolfs, Daniel. *Forum Italicum* 13 (1979): 417-22.

Schellhase, K. *Journal of Modern History* 51 (1979): 317-18.
Tagliacozzo, Giorgio. *Renaissance Quarterly* 32 (1980): 609-11.
Moss, Myra. *Journal of the History of Philosophy* 19 (1981): 112-14.

*Cuadernos sobre Vico* 1 (1991), ed. J. M. Sevilla. Seville: University of Seville, Spain.
*Review:*
Lucente, Gregory L. *New Vico Studies* 10 (1992): 97-100.

*Cuadernos sobre Vico* 2 (1992), ed. J. M. Sevilla.
*Review:*
Lucente, Gregory L. *New Vico Studies* 11 (1993): 98-99.

Cruz, Juan Cruz. *Hombre e Historia en Vico*. Pamplona: Ediciones Universidad de Navarra, 1982 [Abstract: *New Vico Studies* 2 (1984): 140].

Daus, H. J. *Selbstverständnis und Menschenbild in den Selbstdarstellungen Giambattista Vicos und Pietro Giannones: Ein Beitrag zur Geschichte der Italienischen Autobiographie*. Geneva: Librarie E. Droz; Paris: L. Minard, Kolner Romanistische Arbeiten, Neue Folge, 1962.
*Review:*
Scott, J.A. *Modern Language Quarterly* 25 (1964): 365-67.

De Michelis, Cesare, and Gilberto Pizzamiglio, eds. *Vico e Venezia*. Florence: L.S. Olschki, 1982.
*Review:*
Costa, Gustavo. *New Vico Studies* 2 (1984): 120-24.

Donati, Benvenuto. *Nuovi studi sulla filosofia civile di G. B. Vico*. Florence: Le Monnier, 1937.
*Review:*
Gianturco, Elio. *Journal of Modern History* 9 (1937): 414-16.

Duro, Aldo. *Concordanze e Indici di frequenza dei "Principj di una scienza nuova" (1725) di Giambattista Vico*. Lessico Intellettuale Europeo, 25. Rome: Edizioni dell' Ateneo, 1981.
*Review:*
Costa, Gustavo. *Philosophy and Rhetoric* 16 (1983): 140-42.

Fáj, Attila. "Vico, il filosofo della metabasi." *Rivista Critica di Storia della filosofia* 31 (1976): 251-78 [Abstract in *The 18th Century: A Current Bibliography*, n.s. 2 (1976): 394].
_____. *I Karamazov tra Poe e Vico. Genere poliziesco e concezione ciclica della storia nell'ultimo Dostoevskij*. Studi vichiani 15. Naples: Guida, 1984 [Abstract: *New Vico Studies* 2 (1984): 152-54].
*Reviews:*
Terras, V. *Slavic and East European Journal* 29 (1985): 475-76.

Kline, George. *New Vico Studies* 5 (1987): 165-66 [Comment].
Lamparska, Rena. *Slavic Review* 46 (1987): 162-63.

Fellmann, Ferdinand. *Das Vico-Axiom: Der Mensch Macht die Geschichte.* Freiburg/Munich: Karl Alber, 1976 [Abstract: *History and Theory* 16 (1977): 369-70].
**Reviews:**
Morrison, J. C. *Journal of the History of Ideas* 39 (1978): 511-18.
Barnouw, Jeffrey. *The 18th Century: A Current Bibliography*, n.s. 5 (1979): 589-90.
Verene, Donald Phillip. *Journal of the History of Philosophy* 17 (1979): 471-74.

Fellmann, Ferdinand. "Vicos Theorem der Gleichursprünglichheit von Theorie und Praxis und die dogmatische denkform." *Philosophischer Jahrbuch* 85 (1978): 259-73 [Abstract in *The 18th Century: A Current Bibliography*, n.s. 4 (1978): 471].

t' Hart, A. C. *Recht en Staat in het denken van Giambattista Vico.* Alphen: H. D. Tjeenk Willink, 1979 [Abstract: *New Vico Studies* 2 (1984): 118-20].
**Reviews:**
Crease, Robert P. *Review of Metaphysics* 33 (1990): 806-7.
_____. *Philosophy and Rhetoric* 14 (1981): 133-35.

Jacobelli Isoldi, A. M. *G. B. Vico: Per una "Scienza della Storia."* Rome: Armando, 1985.
**Review:**
Palmer, L. M. *New Vico Studies* 3 (1985): 179-81.

Löwith, K. *Gott, Mensch und Welt in der Philosophie der Neuzeit: G. B. Vico—Paul Valery.* Stuttgart: J. B. Metzlersche Verlagsbuchhandlung: 1986.
**Review:**
Wolfgazo, E. *Philosophy and History* 23 (1990): 33.

Mainberger, G. K. *Rhetorica II: Spiegelungen des Geistes: Sprachfiguren bei Vico und Lévi-Strauss.* Stuttgart-Bad Cannstatt: Frommann-Holzboog, 1988.
**Review:**
Rutherford, I. *Classical Review* 90 (1990): 495-96.

Mendlewitsch, Doris. *Die Menschen Machen die Geschichte. Das Verständnis des Politischen in der Scienza Nuova von G. B. Vico.* Cologne: E. J. Brill, 1983.
**Review:**
Krois, John Michael. *New Vico Studies* 2 (1984): 159-60.

Modica, Giuseppe. *La filosofia del "senso comune" in Giambattista Vico* [Abstract: *New Vico Studies* 2 (1984): 124-25.

Nakamura, Yûjirô. *Kyôtsû-kankaku-ron* (Reflections on "sensus communis"). Tokyo: Iwanami-shoten, 1979: ch. 3 *et passim* [Abstract: *New Vico Studies* 3 (1985): 203-4].

Nicolini, Fausto. *Uomini di spada, di chiesa, di toga, di studio ai tempi di Giambattista Vico.* Milan: Hoepli, 1942.
*Review:*
Fisch, Max H. *Philosophical Review* 58 (1949): 528-29.

Nicolini, Fausto. *La religiosità di Giambattista Vico: quattro saggi.* Bari: Laterza, 1949.
*Review:*
Gianturco, Elio. *Journal of Philosophy* 48 (1951): 153-57.

Nicolini, Fausto. *Commento storico alla seconda Scienza nuova.* Storia e Letteratura. Raccolta di Studi e Testi, 24-35. 2 vols. Rome: Edizioni di Storia e Letteratura, 1978 (originally published 1949-50).
*Review:*
Costa, Gustavo. *New Vico Studies* 1 (1983): 128.

Nuzzo, Enrico. *Vico.* (Sintesi Vallecchi: I Filosofi, 4.) Florence: Vallecchi, 1974.
*Review:*
Pipa, Arshi. *The 18th Century: A Current Bibliography*, n.s. 1 (1975): 388-89.

Papini, Mario. *Il Geroglifico della storia. Significato e funzione della dipintura nella "Scienza nuova" di G. B. Vico.* Universale Il Portolano 15. Bologna: Cappelli, 1984.
*Review:*
Costa, Gustavo. *New Vico Studies* 3 (1985): 168-72.

Papini, Mario. *Arbor Humanae Linguae. L'etimologico di G. B. Vico come chiave ermeneutica della storia del mondo.* Universale il Portolano 16. Bologna: Cappelli, 1984.
*Review:*
Costa, Gustavo. *New Vico Studies* 3 (1985): 168-72.

Papini, Mario. "'Ignota latebat.' L'impresa negletta della *Scienza nuova*." *Bollettino del Centro di Studi Vichiani* 14-15 (1984-85): 179-214 [Abstract: *New Vico Studies* 3 (1985): 193-95.
_____. "Uomini di sterco e di nitro." *Bollettino del Centro di Studi Vichiani* 20 (1990): 9-76 [Abstract: *New Vico Studies* 9 (1991): 116-17].

Pennisi, Antonio. *La linguistica dei mercatanti: Filosofia linguistica e filosofia civile da Vico a Cuoco.* Studi vichiani 17. Naples: Guida, 1987.
*Review:*
Costa, Gustavo. *New Vico Studies* 8 (1990): 100-4.

*Per il secondo Centenario della "Scienza Nuova" di G. B. Vico (1725-1925)* [Sixteen studies]. Rome: A cura di *Rivista internazionale di filosofia del diritto*, 1925.
*Review:*
Whittaker, Thomas. *Mind* 36 (1926): 519-20.

Piccolomini, Manfredi. "Gravina e Vico." In *Il pensiero estetico di Gianvincenzo Gravina*. Revenna: Longo, 1984: ch. 4 [Abstract: *New Vico Studies* 2 (1984): 142].

Piovani, Pietro. *Introducion al pensamiento de Vico*. Caracas: Ediciones de la Universidad Central de Venezuela, 1987.
*Review:*
Tessitore, Fulvio. *Differentia* 2 (1988): 309-10.

Piovani, Pietro. *La filosofia nuova di Vico*, ed. Fulvio Tessitore. Collana di Filosofia, n.s. 4. Naples: Morano, 1990.
*Review:*
Costa, Gustavo. *New Vico Studies* 11 (1993).

Pons, Alain. "*De Inventione*. L'invention chez Vico." In *La sexualité: D'où vient l'Orient? Où va l'Occident? Documents du Congrès de Tokio, "La Deuxième Renaissance,"* ed. A. Verdiglione. Paris: Belfond, 1984: 159-69 [Abstract: *New Vico Studies* 3 (1985): 182-84].

Rigol, Monserrat Negre. *Poiesis y Verdad en Giambattista Vico*. Sevilla: Publicaciones de la Universidad de Sevilla, 1986.
*Review:*
Bergstrom, Timothy. *New Vico Studies* 7 (1989): 119-21.

Riverso, Emanuele, ed. *Leggere Vico*. Milan: Spirali Edizioni, 1982 [Abstract: *New Vico Studies* 1 (1983): 125-26].

Rossi, Paolo. *I segni del tempo. Storia della terra e storia delle nazioni da Hooke a Vico*. Milan: Feltrinelli, 1979.
*Reviews:*
Tagliagambe, S. *Scientia* 116 (1981): 129.
Porter, R. *Isis* 73 (1982): 140-41.

Rossi, Paolo. "Giambattista Vico: arcaico e moderno." In *Scienza e filosofia: Saggi in onore di Ludovico Geymonat*, ed. C. Mangione. Milan: Garzanti, 1985: 787-95.
*Review:*
Costa, Gustavo. *New Vico Studies* 4 (1986): 151-54.

Salamone, Rosario. *Lingua e linguaggio nella filosofia di Giambattista Vico*. Rome: Edizioni dell'Ateneo, 1984.
*Review:*
Costa, Gustavo. *New Vico Studies* 4 (1986): 165-67.

Schmidt, Richard Wilhelm. *Die Geschichtsphilosophie G. B. Vicos. Mit einem Anhang zu Hegel*. Würzburg: Königshausen und Neumann, 1982 [Abstract: *History and Theory* 24 (1985): 111-12].
*Reviews:*
Korte, P. *Argument* 25 (1983) 277-78.

Krois, John Michael. *New Vico Studies* 2 (1984): 158-59.

Sevilla, Jose Manuel. *Giambattista Vico: metafisica de la mente e historicismo antropologico.* Sevilla: Servicio de Publicaciones de la Universidad de Sevilla, 1988.
**Review:**
Munn, Edward C. *New Vico Studies* 8 (1990): 94-95.

Tessitore, Fulvio. "Vico nelle origini dello storicismo tedesco." *Bollettino del Centro di Studi Vichiani* 9 (1979): 5-34.
**Review:**
Frankel, Margherita. *New Vico Studies* 1 (1983): 96-97.

Verri, Antonio. *Vico e Herder nella Francia della Restaurazione. Agorà*, 10. Ravenna: Longo Editore, 1984.
**Reviews:**
Costa, Gustavo. *New Vico Studies* 3 (1985): 190-93.
Haac, Oscar A. *Gradiva*, n.s. 2-3 (1984-85): 176-79.

Verri, Antonio. *Cicli e rivoluzioni da Vico a Rousseau.* Università degli Studi di Lecce: Congedo Editore, 1990.
**Review:**
Haac, Oscar A. *New Vico Studies* 10 (1992): 92-93.

Viechtbauer, Helmut. *Transcendentale Einsicht und Theorie der Geschichte: Überlegungen zu G. Vicos "Liber Metaphysicus."* Munich: Fink, 1977.
**Review:**
Herkless, John L. *History and Theory* 18 (1979): 435.

Wohlfhart, Günter. *Denken der Sprache: Sprache und Kunst bei Vico. Hamann, Humbolt und Hegel.* Freiburg: K. Alber, 1984.
**Review:**
Leinfellnerrupertsberger, E. *Literature, Music, Fine Arts* 20 (1987): 27-29.

# Part I. Works on Vico

## E. Entries in Reference Works

Bartlett, John. *[Bartlett's] Familiar Quotations*, ed. E. M. Beck (16th ed.). Boston: Little, Brown and Co., 1992: "Vico, Giovanni Battista (Giambattista)": 290 [3 quotes from the *New Science*].

Bergel, Lienhart. "Giambattista Vico." In *Collier's Encyclopedia*, 1974.

Bergin, Thomas G. "Vico: Giambattista." In *Dictionary of Italian Literature*, ed. P. Bondanella and J. Bondanella. Westport, CT: Greenwood, 1979: 539-42.

Cook, Patricia. "Vico." In *Great Lives from History*, ed. F. Magill. Pasadena, CA: Salem Press, 1989: 2435-39.

Cosford, R. H. "Vico, Giambattista." In *The Penguin Companion to European Literature*, ed. A. Thorlby. Harmondsworth: Penguin, 1969: 802.

Croce, Benedetto. "Vico." In *Encyclopedia of the Social Sciences*. New York: Macmillan, 1935: 15:249-50 [reprinted 1962].

David, Zdenek V., and Robert Strassfeld eds. *Bibliography of Works in the Philosophy of History*. Middletown, CT: Wesleyan University Press, 1984: 129.

*The Eighteenth Century: A Current Bibliography.* Iowa City: University of Iowa, 1970-1974; n.s. 1 (1975)—. [Under the heading "Giambattista Vico (1668-1743)" lists recent publications on Vico (in English and various languages), frequently with annotation or an abstract, occasionally with lists of reviews; also publishes reviews (such reviews and abstracts are listed herein with individual works). Also lists publications with essays, chapters, or sections on Vico.] (1970): 584, 778-79; (1972): 360, 426, 427, 588-89; (1973): 809; (1974): 781-82, 795, 1059-60. n.s. 1 (1975): 388-90; n.s. 2 (1976): 304, 390-98; n.s. 3 (1977): 288; n.s. 4 (1978): 192, 275, 471-72; n.s. 5 (1979): 167, 588-91; n.s. 6 (1980): 245, 593; n.s. 7 (1981): 211, 254, 354, 358, 418, 587, 588-97; n.s. 8 (1982): 223, 544-45; n.s. 9 (1983): 288, 294, 342, 721-23; n.s. 10 (1984): 156, 301, 308, 424, 476, 730-31; n.s. 11 (1985): 96, 293, 665-67; n.s. 12 (1986): 148, 197, 413, 534-35.

*Encyclopedia of World Art.* New York and London: McGraw-Hill, 1959-1968: 5:42-43, 45, 49-50; 7:518; 11:706; 13:797-98.

Flew, Anthony. "Vico." In *A Dictionary of Philosophy*. New York: St. Martin's Press, 1979: 342; London: Macmillan Press, 1979: 369 (rev. 2d ed. 1984: 369).

Gardiner, Patrick. "Vico." In *The Encyclopedia of Philosophy*. New York: Collier-Macmillan, 1967: 8:247-51.

"Giambattista Vico." *History of Philosophy*. Chicago: University of Chicago Press, 1971: 5:54-59; see also 68, 92.

"Giambattista Vico." *Encyclopedia Brittanica,* Macropedia (11th ed.), 1974: 19:103-5.

Guerry, Herbert, ed. *A Bibliography of Philosophical Bibliographies*. Westport, CT: Greenwood Press, 1977: 168-69.

Harris, Henry S. "Vico." In *Encyclopedia Americana* (1956): 28:65-66; reprinted 1980: 28:82-83.
⎯⎯⎯. "Vico"; "Vico's 'new science'"; "Historical cycles"; "Grace and Providence." *Encyclopaedia of Philosophy*. New York: Collier-Macmillan, 1967: 4:228-29 [see also 2:264; 5:545; 6:247; 7:475].

Hayes, Carlton H. "Giambattista Vico." In *Encyclopedia Brittanica* (11th ed.), 1911: 28:23-25; see also 13:532; 14:909; 23:659.

Iggers, Georg G. "Vico." In *Academic American Encyclopedia*. Danbury, CT: Grolier Inc., 1980: 19:572.

Knox, Thomas M. "Vico." In *Chamber's Encyclopaedia*, 1966.

Lacey, A. R. "Vico." In *A Dictionary of Philosophy*. London: Routledge & Kegan Paul, 1976: 234.

Novikov, N. V. "Vico." In *Great Soviet Encyclopedia* (trans. of 3d ed.). New York and London: Macmillan-Collier, 1974: 5:421.

*Oxford Companion to the Mind*. Oxford and New York: Oxford University Press, 1987: 786.

Reese, W. L. "G. B. Vico." In *Dictionary of Philosophy and Religion*. Atlantic Highlands, NJ: Humanities Press, 1991 (1980): 612.

Reynolds, Barbara, ed. *The Cambridge Italian Dictionary*, vol. 1. Cambridge: At the University Press, 1981: 219 see degnità.

Verene, Donald Phillip. "Vico." In *Encyclopëdic Dictionary of Semiotics*, ed. T. Sebeok. The Hague: de Gruyer, 1987: 2:1149.
⎯⎯⎯. "Giovanni Battista Vico." In *The Encyclopaedia of Religion*, ed. M. Eliade *et al.* New York: Macmillan, 1987: 16.

———. "Vico." *The Johns Hopkins Guide to Literary Theory and Criticism,* ed. M. Groden and M. Kreiswirth. Baltimore: The Johns Hopkins University Press, 1993: 722-25.

"Vico." *The New Catholic Encyclopedia.* New York: McGraw Hill, 1967: 14:644-45.

"Vico, Giambattista." *The Cassell Encyclopaedia Dictionary.* London: Cassell, 1991: 1569.

"Vico, Giovanni Battista." *Webster's Biographical Dictionary.* Springfield, MA: Merriam, 1980: 1519.

"Vico, Giovanni Battista." *International Encyclopedia of the Social Sciences,* Vol. 19, *Social Science Quotations.* New York: Macmillan, 1991: 242-43.

"Vico, Giovanni Battista or Giambattista." *Concise Columbia Encyclopedia.* Irvington, NY: Columbia University Press, 1983: 893; Reprinted 1993: 2882.

White, Hayden V. "Vico, Giovanni Battista." In *International Encyclopedia of the Social Sciences.* New York: Macmillan, 1968: 313-26.

# Part II. Vico's Works

## A. English Editions of Vico's Works
(In chronological order)

Vico, Giambattista. "The Third Book of Vico's *Scienza nuova* [1744]: On the Discovery of the True Homer," trans. Henry Nelson Coleridge. In Coleridge, *Introductions to the Study of the Greek Classic Poets: Designed Principally for the Use of Young Persons at School and College*. 2d ed. London: Murray, 1834: 73-98; 3d ed. (1846): 63-84.

Vico, Giambattista. "[Selections from] the *Scienza nuova* [1744]," trans. E. F. Carritt. In Carritt, *Philosophies of Beauty from Socrates to Robert Bridges: Being the Sources of Aesthetic Theory*. Oxford: Clarendon Press, 1931: 73-74.

Vico, Giambattista. "Affetti di un disperato" [poem], trans. H. P. Adams. In Adams, *The Life and Writings of Giambattista Vico*. London: Allen & Unwin, 1935: 223-26. 2d ed. New York: Russell & Russell, 1970.

Vico, Giambattista. *The Autobiography of Giambattista Vico*, trans. Max Harold Fisch and Thomas Goddard Bergin. Introduction and notes by M. H. Fisch. Ithaca, NY: Cornell University Press, 1944. Reprinted, with corrections and supplementary notes: Cornell University Press, Great Seal Books, 1963; reprinted, Cornell Paperbacks, 1975.

Vico, Giambattista. "Letter of 25 October 1725 to Fr. Bernardo Maria Giacco," trans. Max Harold Fisch. In *The Autobiography of Giambattista Vico* (trans. Fisch and Bergin). Ithaca, NY: Cornell University Press, 1944 and subsequent editions.

Vico, Giambattista. *The New Science of Giambattista Vico*, trans. from the 3d (1744) edition by Thomas G. Bergin and Max H. Fisch. Ithaca, NY: Cornell University Press, 1948.
_____. Abridged edition of the 1st rev. edition, Garden City, NY: Doubleday, Anchor Books, 1961; reprinted, Ithaca, NY: Cornell University Press, Cornell Paperbacks, 1970.
_____. 2d rev. ed., with introduction by M. H. Fisch, 1968; reprinted with corrections, 1976.
_____. Unabridged edition of the 1976 corrected revised ed., including Vico's "Practic of the New Science," trans. T.G. Bergin and M.H. Fisch. Ithaca, NY: Cornell University Press, Cornell Paperbacks, 1984 [Abstract: *New Vico Studies* 2 (1984): 164].

*Reviews of the Various Editions:*
Auerbach, Eric. *Modern Language Notes* 64 (1949): 196-97.
Voegelin, Eric. *Catholic Historical Review* 35 (1949-50): 75-76.
Gianturco, Elio. *Ethics* 60 (1950): 140-41; [Response] Arthur Child, "Vico in Translation," 292-93; [Reply] "Words and Meaning in Vico," *Ethics* 61 (1951): 151-53.
Edie, James M. *Italica* 39 (1962): 147-49.
*Choice* 6 (1969): 68.
*Choice* 8 (1971): 815-16.

Verene, Donald Phillip. *Review of Metaphysics* 39 (1985): 378-79.

Vico, Giambattista. "Discovery of the True Dante," trans. Irma Brandeis. In Brandeis, ed. *Discussions of the Divine Comedy*. Boston: Heath, 1961: 11-12.

Vico, Giambattista. *The New Science, Selections*. Vol. 5, no. 4 of *The Ninth Year Course*. Chicago: Great Books Foundation, 1962: 1-101 [reprinted from *The New Science (1744)*, trans. T. G. Bergin and M. H. Fisch. Ithaca: Cornell University Press].

Vico, Giambattista. *On the Study Methods of Our Time*, trans. Elio Gianturco. Indianapolis: Bobbs-Merrill, Library of the Liberal Arts, 1965. Reissued: Ithaca, NY: Cornell University Press, 1990.
**Reviews:**
Mascioli, Fredrick P. *Italica* 43 (1966): 443-45.
Bergin, Thomas Goddard. *Journal of Modern History* 30 (1968): 691-92.

Vico, Giambattista. "Gli affetti di un disperato" [poem], trans. Thomas Goddard Bergin. *Forum Italicum* 2 (1968): 305-9.

Vico, Giambattista. "A Factual Digression on Human Genius, Sharp, Witty Remarks, and Laughter" [from *Vici vindiciae*], trans. A. Illiano, J. D. Tedder, and P. Treves. *Forum Italicum* 2 (1968): 310-14.

Vico, Giambattista. [Selections from *The New Science* (1744), books 1 and 2, pars. 338-68, trans. T. G. Bergin and M. H. Fisch. Ithaca, NY: Cornell University Press] "Vico: The New Science of Poetry." In *Man and Culture: A Philosophical Anthology*, ed. Donald Phillip Verene. New York: Dell Laurel, 1970: 63-75.

Vico, Giambattista. "Practic of the New Science" (from the unpublished 1731 edition of the conclusion of the *Scienza nuova*), trans. Thomas Goddard Bergin and Max Harold Fisch. In G. Tagliacozzo and D. P. Verene, eds., *Giambattista Vico's Science of Humanity*. Baltimore, MD: Johns Hopkins University Press, 1976: 451-54. Reprinted as Appendix in *The New Science of Giambattista Vico*. Ithaca, NY: Cornell University Press, Cornell Paperbacks, 1984: 427-30.

Vico, Giambattista. "On the Heroic Mind," trans. Elizabeth Sewell and Anthony C. Sirignano. *Social Research* 43 (1976): 886-903. Reprinted in G. Tagliacozzo, M. Mooney, and D. P. Verene, eds., *Vico and Contemporary Thought*. Atlantic Highlands, NJ: Humanities Press, 1979: 2:228-45.

Vico, Giambattista. [Selections from *De nostri temporis studiorum*; *De antiquissima Italorum sapientia ex linguae latinae originibus eruenda*; and from two editions of the *Scienza nuova* (1725; 1744)]. In *Vico: Selected Writings*, trans. and ed. by Leon Pompa. Cambridge: Cambridge University Press, 1982 [Abstract: *New Vico Studies* 1 (1983): 129].

*Reviews:*
Choice 20 (1982): 104.
Bedani, G. L. C. *British Journal of Aesthetics* 123 (1983): 169-71.
Haddock, Bruce A. *Bulletin of the Hegel Society of Great Britain* 7 (1983): 45-47.
Jones, Verina. *Italian Studies* 38 (1983): 110-12.
Leach, Edmund. *Man* 18 (1983): 228-29.
Verene, D. P. *Review of Metaphysics* 38 (1985): 678-79.

Vico, Giambattista. "Juno to Apollo" ("Giunone in danza," ll. 195-299) [poem], trans. Joseph Tusiani. *Rivista di Studi Italiani* 1 (1983): 106-9.

Vico, Giambattista. *The Course of Nations and the Historical Future of Mankind* (illus.). Albuquerque, NM: Institute for Economic and Political World Strategic Studies (affiliate of American Classical College), 1985 [Selected translations from the *New Science*].

Vico, Giambattista. *On the Most Ancient Wisdom of the Italians, Unearthed from the Origins of the Latin Language*. Including the Disputations with the *Giornale de' Letterati d'Italia*, trans. L. M. Palmer. Ithaca, NY and London: Cornell University Press, 1988.
*Review:*
Costa, Gustavo. *New Vico Studies* 7 (1989): 99-100.

Vico, Giambattista. "To Gherardo degli Angeli: On Dante and on the Nature of True Poetry" [letter]; and "'The discovery of the true Dante' or 'New principles in Dante criticism'. Concerning the commentary of an anonymous writer on the *Comedy*," trans. Maggie Günsberg. In M. Caesar, *Dante: The Critical Heritage*. London and New York: Routledge, 1989: 348-55.
*Review:*
Pietropaolo, Domenico. *New Vico Studies* 8 (1990): 149-53.

Vico, Giambattista. "The Academies and the Relation between Philosophy and Eloquence," trans. Donald Phillip Verene. In Giambattista Vico, *On the Study Methods of Our Time*, trans. Elio Gianturco. Reissued with a preface by Donald Phillip Verene. Ithaca, NY: Cornell University Press, 1990: 85-90.
*Review:*
Engell, James. *New Vico Studies* 10 (1992): 64-72.

Vico, Giambattista. "Reprehension of the Metaphysics of René Descartes, Benedict Spinoza, and John Locke: An Addition to the *New Science* (Translation and Commentary)," trans. Donald Phillip Verene. *New Vico Studies* 8 (1990): 2-18.

Vico, Giambattista. *Tropes, Monsters, and Poetic Transformations* [chapbook] [pars. 400-11, *New Science*], trans. Pasquale Verdicchio (illus.). LaJolla, CA: Parentheses Writing Series, 1990.

Vico, Giambattista. *On Humanistic Education: Six Inaugural Orations (1699-1707)*, trans. Giorgio A. Pinton and Arthur W. Shippee, from the definitive Latin text, introduction, and notes of Gian Galeazzo Visconti. Preface by Donald Phillip Verene. Ithaca, NY: Cornell University Press, 1993.

# Part II. Vico's Works

**B. Reviews in English of Editions of Vico's Works in Foreign Languages**
(In chronological order)

Veneziani, Marco, ed. *Indici e concordanze delle "Orazioni inaugurali" di Giambattista Vico.* Lessico Intellettuale Europeo, LV: Lessico filosofico dei secoli XVII e XVIII: Strumenti critici, 3. Rome: Edizioni dell'Ateneo, 1991.
*Review:*
Costa, Gustavo. *New Vico Studies* 11 (1993): 91-93.

Vico, Giambattista. *Oeuvres choisies de Vico, contenant ses memoires, écrits par lui-même, La Science Nouvelle, &c. Précédées d'une introduction sur sa vie et ses ouvrages,* trans. Jules Michelet. Paris: Hachette, 1835.
*Review:*
Walker, James M. *Southern Quarterly Review* 1 (1842): 404-16.

Vico, Giambattista. *La Science Nouvelle,* trans. Cristina [Trivulzio] Belgioioso. Paris, 1844.
*Review:*
*Foreign Quarterly Review* 34 (1845): 289-303.

Vico, Giambattista. *Autobiografia di Giambattista Vico (1725-1728),* ed. Fausto Nicolini. Milan: Bompiani, 1947.
*Review:*
Fisch, Max Harold. *Philosophical Review* 58 (1949): 528-29.

Vico, Giambattista. *Atarashii-Gaku* [*The New Science*]. Japanese trans. Ikutaro Shimizu, Junichi Shimizu, and Yoshiaki Yoneyama. Tokyo: Chuo-Koron Publishing Co., 1974 [Abstract: *New Vico Studies* 1 (1983): 133-35].

Vico, Giambattista. *Liber Metaphysicus,* eds. and trans. Stephan Otto and Helmut Viechtbauer. Munich: Fink Verlag, 1979.
*Review:*
Kessler, Eckhard. *New Vico Studies* 1 (1983): 132-33.

Vico, Giambattista. *Principj di una Scienza nuova d'intorno alla comune natura delle nazioni,* ed. Tullio Gregory. Rome: Edizioni dell'Ateneo e Bizzarri, 1979.
*Review:*
Costa, Gustavo. *New Vico Studies* 1 (1983): 131-32.

Vico, Giambattista. *Die neue Wissenschaft von der gemeinschaftlichen Natur der Nationen,* trans. Ferdinand Fellmann. Frankfurt am Main: Vittorio Klostermann, 1981.

*Review:*
Verene, Donald Phillip. *New Vico Studies* 1 (1983): 129-30.

Vico, Giambattista. *Vie de Giambattista Vico écrite par lui-même, Lettres, La méthode des études de notre temps*, ed. Alain Pons. Paris: Bernard Grasset, 1981.
*Reviews:*
Costa, Gustavo. *Philosophy and Rhetoric* 16 (1983): 143-45.
Tagliacozzo, Giorgio, and Donald Phillip Verene. *New Vico Studies* 1 (1983): 130-31.

Vico, Giambattista. *Le orazioni inaugurali, I-VI*, trans. Galeazzo Visconti. *Opere di Giambattista Vico*, vol. 1. Bologna: Il Mulino, 1982.
*Review:*
Costa, Gustavo. *New Vico Studies* 2 (1984): 169-71.

Vico, Giambattista. *Origine de la poésie et du droit: De Constantia jurisprudentis*, trans. Catherine Henri and Annie Henry. Introduction by Jean Louis Schefer. Langres: Clima Editeur, 1983.
*Review:*
Costa, Gustavo. *New Vico Studies* 2 (1984): 167-69.

Vico, Giambattista. "Sentiments d'un désespéré" (poem), trans. Alain Pons. *Poésie* 27 (1983): 3-14.
*Review:*
Costa, G. *New Vico Studies* 2 (1984): 164-66.

Vico, Giambattista. [*New Science* and *Autobiography*]. Chinese trans. Zhu Guangqian. Peking: Commercial Press of Peking, 1986 [See "Postscript," *New Vico Studies* 6 (1988): 186-88].

Vico, Giambattista. *Prinzipien einer neuen Wissenschaft über die gemeinsame Natur der Völker*, trans. Vittorio Hösle and Christoph Jermann. 2 vols. Hamburg: Felix Meiner, 1990.
*Review:*
Verene, Donald Phillip. *New Vico Studies* 8 (1990): 92-94.

Vico, Giambattista. *Institutiones oratoriae*. Testo critico, versione e commento di Giuliano Crifò. Naples: Istituto Suor Orsola Benincasa, 1989.
*Reviews:*
Patella, Giuseppe. *Differentia* 5 (1991).
Costa, Gustavo. *New Vico Studies* 9 (1991): 130-34.

Vico, Giambattista. *Opere di G. B. Vico*, ed. Andrea Battistini. I Meridiani: Collezione diretta da Luciano De Maria. Milan: Mondadori, 1990 [Abstract: *Journal of the History of Ideas* 52 (1991): 351].

***Review:***
Costa, Gustavo. *New Vico Studies* 9 (1991): 125-29.

Vico, Giambattista. *Principj d'una Scienza nuova d'intorno all comune natura delle nazioni (1730)*, ed. Manuela Sanna and Fulvio Tessitore. Fondazione Pietro Piovani per gli Studi Vichiani: Serie testi, I. Naples: Morano, 1991.
***Review:***
Costa, Gustavo. *New Vico Studies* 11 (1993): 89-91.

# Part III. Works Citing Vico

Abbagnano, Nicola. "Philosophy in Italy." *Philosophy* 25 (1950): 172-73.

Abbs, Peter. *Reclamations: Essays on Culture, Mass Culture, and the Curriculum.* London: Heineman, 1979: 37n.

———. *A is for Aesthetics. Essays on Creative and Aesthetic Education.* Philadelphia: Falmer Press of Taylor & Francis, 1989: 109-11.

Adair-Toteff, Stephanie. "Historical Perspectives on the Theory of Linguistic Relativity." Ph.D. diss. University of Virginia, 1985 [Ann Arbor, MI: University Microfilms].

Adams, Brooks. *The Law of Civilization and Decay.* New York: Knopf, 1943: 31.

Adams, Hazard. *Philosophy of the Literary Symbolic.* Gainesville: University Presses of Florida, 1983: 7-12 *et passim* [Abstract: *New Vico Studies* 3 (1985): 203].
**Review:**
Bickman, Martin. *Philosophy and Literature* 8 (1984): 143.

Adams, Hazard. "Synecdoche and Method." In *Critical Paths: Blake and the Argument of Method*, ed. D. Miller, M. Bracher, and D. Ault. Durham, NC: Duke University Press, 1987: 41-71.

Adams, Robert M. *James Joyce: Common Sense and Beyond.* New York: Random House, 1966: 181, 185, 207n.

Adamson, Walter L. "Modernism and Fascism: The Politics in Italy, 1903-22." *The American Historical Review* 95 (1990): 359-90.

Adorno, T. W. *Aesthetic Theory*, trans. C. Lenhardt. London: Routledge & Kegan Paul, 1984: 360.

Alleman, Beda. "Metaphor and Antimetaphor." In *Interpretation: The Poetry of Meaning*, ed. S. R. Hopper and D. L. Miller. New York: Harcourt, Brace and World, 1967: 105.

Altieri, C. "*Finnegans Wake* as Modernist Historiography." *Novel* 21 (1988): 238-50.

Althusser, Louis. *Essays in Self-Criticism*, trans. G. Lock. London: Low and Brydone, 1976: 41, 55.

*American (Whig) Review* 6, no. 4 (1847): 390.

Anderle, Othmar F. "A Plea for Theoretical History." *History and Theory* 4 (1964): 39, 48, 49.

Angelil, Marc M. "Technique and the Metaphysics of Science—the Rational Irrational Element of Science-Technology within the Making of Architecture." *Harvard Architecture Review* 7 (1989): 62-75 *passim*.

Apel, Karl-Otto. *Toward a Transformation of Philosophy*, trans. D. Frisby and G. Adey. Boston: Routledge & Kegan Paul, 1980: 38, 164, 166.
**Review:**
Struever, Nancy. *New Vico Studies* 1 (1983): 91-95.

Apel, Karl-Otto. *Charles S. Peirce: From Pragmatism to Pragmaticism*, trans. J. M. Krois. Amherst: University of Massachusetts Press, 1981: 212, 215, 217, 228 [Abstract: *New Vico Studies* 1 (1983): 90-91.
_____. *Understanding and Explanation: A Transcendental-Pragmatic Perspective*, trans. G. Warnke. Cambridge: MIT Press, 1984: 6, 59.

Arendt, Hannah. "History and Immortality." *Partisan Review* 24 (1957): 23-24.
_____. *The Human Condition.* Chicago: University of Chicago Press, 1958: 232, 283n, 298.
_____. *Between Past and Future.* New York: Viking Press, 1961: 50, 57-58, 77, 82, 84.
_____. *The Life of the Mind.* New York: Harcourt Brace Jovanovich, 1971: 154-55.
_____. "On Hannah Arendt." In *Hannah Arendt: The Recovery of the Public World*, ed. M. A. Hill. New York: St. Martins Press, 1979: 33.

Arias, Judith Hepler. "Toward a Theory of the Don Juan Myth." Unpublished Ph.D. diss. University of North Carolina, 1987.

Arieti, Silvano. *Interpretation of Schizophrenia.* New York: Basic Books, 1974 (1955): *passim*.
_____. *The Intrapsychic Self.* New York: Basic Books, 1967: *passim*.
_____. *Creativity: The Magic Synthesis.* New York: Basic Books, 1976: *passim*.
_____. *Abraham and the Contemporary Mind.* New York: Basic Books, 1981: 7, 21.

Arnheim, Rudolf. "The Double-Edged Mind: Intuition and Intellect." In *New Essays on the Psychology of Art.* Berkeley: University of California Press, 1986: 16.

Atherton, James S. *The Books at the Wake: A Study of Literary Allusions in James Joyce's "Finnegans Wake."* New York: Viking Press, 1960: *passim*.

Auber, Jacques. *The Aesthetics of James Joyce.* Baltimore: Johns Hopkins University Press, 1992: 130.

Auerbach, Eric. *Mimesis: The Representation of Reality in Western Literature*, trans. W. R. Trask. Princeton, NJ: Princeton University Press, 1953: 34, 38n.
_____. *Dante: Poet of the Secular World*, trans. R. Manheim. Chicago: University of Chicago Press, 1961: 25n, 188.
_____. *Literary Language and Its Public in Late Latin Antiquity and in the Middle Ages*, trans. R. Manheim. New York: Pantheon Books, 1965: 7-24, 122.

Ausubel, Herman. *Historians and Their Craft: A Study of Presidential Addresses of the American Historical Association, 1884-1945*. New York: Columbia University Press, 1950: 202, 229.

Avineri, Shlomo. *The Social and Political Thought of Karl Marx*. Cambridge: Cambridge University Press, 1968: 77.

Bagby, Philip. *Culture and History*. Berkeley: University of California Press, 1963: 12-13, 65, 158, 203.

Bahti, Timothy. Review of *Redrawing the Lines: Analytic Philosophy, Deconstruction, and Literary Theory* (ed. R. W. Dasenbrock). *New Vico Studies* 8 (1990): 122-26.
_____. *Allegories of History—Literary Historiography after Hegel*. Baltimore and London: Johns Hopkins University Press, 1992: 141-42.

Bair, Dierdre. *Samuel Beckett: A Biography*. New York: Harcourt Brace Jovanovich, 1978: 76, 90.

Barbi, Michele. *Life of Dante*. Berkeley and Los Angeles: University of California Press, 1966: 113.

Bardis, Panos D. "The School and International Cooperation: An Interdisciplinary Essay." In *Información, Educación y Progreso Politico*. Barcelona: Instituto de Ciencias Sociales. Diputación Prov. de Barcelone, 1967: 273-75.
_____. "Student Attitudes toward World Government, Universal Peace, and International Law." *Sociologia Internationalis* 21 (1983): 261-74.

Barnard, F. M. *Herder's Social and Political Thought*. Oxford: Clarendon Press, 1965: 110n.

Barnes, H. E. *A History of Historical Writing*. Norman: University of Oklahoma Press, 1938: 80-81, 108, 240.

Baron, Naomi S. Review of *Metaphors We Live By* (ed. G. Lakoff and M. Johnson). *New Vico Studies* 9 (1983): 118-22.
_____. Review of *The Roots of Language* (ed. D. Bickerton). *New Vico Studies* 3 (1985): 220-26.

Barzar, Jacques, and Henry F. Graff. *The Modern Researcher: The Classic Work on Research and Writing* (5th rev. ed.). Boston: Houghton Mifflin, 1992: 194, 197.

Bass, T. A. "Fiction and History: Essays on the Novels of Flaubert, Marquez, Coover, and Pynchon." Unpublished Ph.D. diss. University of California (Santa Cruz), 1980: ch. 3.

Baum, R. F. *Doctors of Modernity*. Peru, IL: Sherwood, Sugden, 1988: 50, 125.

Bazargan, Susan. "Myth and Narration in James Joyce's *Ulysses*." Unpublished Ph.D. diss. University of Washington, 1984.

_____. "Monologue as Dialogue: Molly Bloom's 'History' as Myriorama." *Works and Days: Essays in the Socio-Historical Dimensions of Literature and the Arts* 5 (1987): 63-77.

Bear, Greg. "A Martian *Ricorso*." In *Tangents: Nine Tales of the Imagination*. New York: Warner Books, 1989: 105.

Beardsley, Monroe. *Aesthetics from Classical Greece to the Present: A Short History*. New York: Macmillan, 1966: 259n.

Becker, Ernest. *Beyond Alienation: A Philosophy of Education for the Crisis of Democracy*. New York: Braziller, 1967: *passim*.

_____. *The Structure of Evil: An Essay on the Unification of the Science of Man*. New York: Braziller, 1968: 27-28 *et passim*.

Begnal, Michael H., and G. Eckley. *Narrator and Character in "Finnegans Wake."* Lewisburg: Bucknell University Press; London: Associated University Press, 1974: 83-86 *et passim*.

Beiner, Ronald. *Political Judgment*. Chicago: University of Chicago Press, 1983: 4, 21, 22, 84-85, 105.

Bell, Daniel. "Toward the Great Instauration: Reflections on Culture and Religion in a Post-Industrial Age." *Social Research* 42 (1975): 382-84.

Bender, John, and David E. Wellbery, eds. *The Ends of Rhetoric: History, Theory, Practice*. Stanford, CA: Stanford University Press, 1990: 211.
**Review:**
Struever, Nancy S. *New Vico Studies* 11 (1993): 119-20.

Benin, Stephen D. "The 'Cunning of God' and Divine Accommodation: The History of an Idea." *Journal of the History of Ideas* 15 (1984): 179-92.

Benstock, Bernard. *Joyce-Again's Wake: An Analysis of "Finnegans Wake."* Seattle: University of Washington Press, 1965: *passim*.

_____. *James Joyce: The Undiscovered Country*. Dublin: Gill and Macmillan; New York: Barnes and Noble Books, 1977: 99.

Bentley, Jerry H. *Politics and Culture in Renaissance Naples*. Princeton, NJ: Princeton University Press, 1987: 286.

Benvenuto, Bice, and Roger Kennedy. *The Works of Jacques Lacan—An Introduction*. New York: St. Martin's, 1986: 166.

Berenson, Bernard. *Rumor and Reflection*. New York: Simon & Schuster, 1952: 110.

Bergin, Thomas Goddard. *Perspectives on the Divine Comedy*. New Brunswick, NJ: Rutgers University Press, 1967: 89, 103.

Berlin, Isaiah, ed. *The Age of Enlightenment*. New York: New American Library of Mentor Books, 1956: 273-75.

Berlin, Isaiah. "History and Theory: The Concept of Scientific History." *History and Theory* 1 (1960): 6, 24, 26, 28, 30. Reprinted in *Concepts and Categories*, ed. H. Hardy. New York: Viking Press, 1979: *passim*.
_____. *Karl Marx: His Life and Environment*. London: Oxford University Press, 1963: 156 [originally published 1939].
_____. "Herder and the Enlightenment." In *Aspects of the Eighteenth Century*, ed. E. R. Wasserman. Baltimore: Johns Hopkins University Press, 1965: *passim*.
_____. "The Concept of Scientific History." In *Philosophical Analysis and History*, ed. W. H. Dray. New York: Harper & Row, 1966: 7, 12, 40, 43, 46, 48.
_____. "Historical Inevitability." In *Four Essays on Liberty*. New York: Oxford University Press, 1969: 42, 90 n. 1.
_____. "Georges Sorel." *London Times Literary Supplement* (31 Dec. 1971): 1617-22.
_____. *Russian Thinkers*, ed. H. Hardy and Aileen Kelly. New York: Penguin, 1979: *xvi*, 140.
_____. *Against the Current*, ed. H. Hardy. New York: Viking Press, 1980: 93-129 *et passim* [see also Roger Hausheer, Introduction: *xx, xxv, xxix-xxxii*].

**Reviews:**
Clemons, Walter. "Prince of Foxes." *Newsweek* (3 March 1980): 74, 76.
Rosen, Stanley. *Journal of Modern History* 53 (1981): 309-11.

Berlin, Isaiah.. "Notes on Alleged Relativism in Eighteenth-Century European Thought." *British Journal of Eighteenth Century Studies* 3 (1980): 89-104. Rev. ed. in *Substance and Form in History*, ed. L. Pompa and W. H. Dray. Edinburgh: University of Edinburgh Press, 1981: 3-8. 10-12.
_____. "On the Pursuit of the Ideal." *New York Review of Books* (17 March 1988): 11-18.
_____. "Joseph de Maistre and the Origins of Fascism." Part 1: *New York Review of Books* (11 Oct. 1990): 54, 55, 57; Part 2: (25 Oct. 1990): 61-65 [also published in *The Crooked Timber of Humanity* (*q.v.*)].
_____. *The Crooked Timber of Humanity: Chapters in the History of Ideas*, ed. H. Hardy. London: John Murray, 1990; New York: Knopf, 1991: 8-10, 59-62, 65-68, 74-76, 80-89, 141-42.

**Reviews:**
Dunn, John. "Our Insecure Tradition." *Times Literary Supplement*, 5-11 Oct. 1990: 1053-54.
Anderson, Perry. "England's Isaiah." *London Review of Books* 12, no. 24 (20 Dec. 1990): 3-7.
Himmelfarb, Gertrude. *New York Times Book Review* (24 March 1991): 1, 30-31.
O'Brien, Conor Cruise. "Paradise Lost." *New York Times Review of Books* (25 April 1991): 52, 54, 55.
Hutton, Patrick H. *New Vico Studies* 10 (1992): 120-23.

Berlin, Isaiah. "Philosophy and Life" (Interview). *New York Review of Books* (28 May 1992): 50-52.
_____, and Nathan Gardels. "The Concepts of Nationalism: An Interview with Isaiah Berlin." *New York Review of Books* 38, no. 19 (21 Nov. 1991): 20, 22.

Bernardo, Aldo. "Dante, Petrarca, Boccaccio." In *Italian Poets and English Critics, 1755-1859*, ed. B. Corrigan. Chicago: University of Chicago Press, 1969: 201-2.

Bernstein, Richard J. *Beyond Objectivism and Relativism*. Philadelphia: University of Pennsylvania Press, 1983: 48, 113.
_____. "Why Hegel Now?" In *Philosophical Profiles*. Philadelphia: University of Pennsylvania Press, 1986: 141-75 [originally published in *Review of Metaphysics* 31 (1977): 29-60].

Berrone, Louis. "Some Thoughts on Dickensian Correspondences in the First Chapter of Joyce's *Ulysses*." *Trinity Reporter* 7 (19 Nov. 1976): 1-8 *passim*.
_____. *James Joyce in Padua*. New York: Random House, 1978: 16-18, 21f., 67, 81-96, 98n., 100n., 116f.

Bertalanffy, Ludwig von. *General Systems Theory*. New York: Braziller, 1969: 11, 110, 117, 198, 199.

Betti, Emilio. "Hermeneutics as the General Methodology of the *Geisteswissenschaften*." In *Contemporary Hermeneutics*, ed. J. Bleicher. Boston: Routledge & Kegan Paul, 1980: 87.
_____. "The Epistemological Problem of Understanding as an Aspect of the General Problem of Knowing." In *Hermeneutics: Questions and Prospects*, ed. G. Shapiro and A. Sica. Amherst: University of Massachusetts Press, 1984: 25.

Bhattacharya, Nikhil. Review of *On Language: The Diversity of Human Language-Structure and Its Influence on the Mental Development of Mankind* (W. von Humboldt). *New Vico Studies* 7 (1989): 142-45.

Biasin, Gian Paolo. *Italian Literary Icons*. Princeton, NJ: Princeton University Press, 1985: 5.

Bidney, David. *Theoretical Anthropology*. 2d ed. New York: Schoken, 1967: 287, 306-7, 361.

Billigheimer, Rachel C. *Wheels of Eternity: A Comparative Study of William Blake and William Butler Yeats*. Dublin: Gill and Macmillan, 1990: 171.

Bishop, John Michael. "The End: An Introductory Study of *Finnegans Wake*." Unpublished Ph.D. diss. Stanford University, 1981: ch. 6.

Black, David W. "Pedagogical Places." In *Commonplaces: Essays on the Nature of Place*, ed. D. W. Black, D. Kunze, and J. Pickles. Lanham, MD: University Press of America, 1989: 56-65; see also 3 [Book abstract: *New Vico Studies* 8 (1990): 108-9].

Black, Virginia. "How Variable Is Natural Law?" *Vera Lex* 5 (1985): 11-12.

Blakey, Robert. *History of the Philosophy of Mind*. London: Longmans, Green, 1850: 3:212, 219.
_____. *Historical Sketch of Logic*. London: H. Bailliere, 1851: 331-34.

Blanchard, Paul. *Blue Guide to Southern Italy*, 6th ed. Condon: A. C. Black, 1986: 108, 134.

Blanchard, Wells Scott. "Poetry and the Encyclopedia: Studies in the Iconology of the Liberal Arts in Renaissance Humanism." Unpublished Ph.D. diss. Columbia University, 1987.

Bleicher, Joseph. *Contemporary Hermeneutics*. Boston: Routledge & Kegan Paul, 1980: 16-17, 87.
*Review:*
Kurzweil, Edith. *New Vico Studies* 1 (1983): 113-15.

Bloom, Harold. "Emerson: Glory and Sorrows of American Romanticism." In *Romanticism: Vistas, Instances, Continuities*, ed. D. Thorburn and G. Hartmann. Ithaca, NY: Cornell University Press, 1973: 164-65.
_____. *Poetry and Repression*. New Haven, CT: Yale University Press, 1976: ch. 1 *passim*; 158-61, 211, 240, 244.
_____. "The Use of Poetry." *The New York Times* (12 Nov. 1975): 43.
_____. *The Ringers in the Tower. Studies in Romantic Tradition*. Chicago: University of Chicago Press, 1975: 4, 6.
_____. "Poetry, Revisionism, Repression." *Critical Inquiry* 2 (1975): 234-40, 246, 248, 250.
_____. *A Map of Misreading*. Oxford: Oxford University Press, 1975: 9, 55, 67-70, 73, 94.
_____. *Kabbala and Criticism*. New York: Seabury Press, 1975: 107.
*Review:*
Wieseltier, Leon. "Summoning up the Kabbalah." *New York Review of Books* (19 Feb. 1976): 27.

Bloom, Harold. *Wallace Stevens: The Poems of Our Climate*. Ithaca, NY: Cornell University Press, 1976: 28, 205.
_____. *Agon: Toward a Theory of Revisionism*. New York: Oxford University Press, 1982: 98, 115, 142, 151, 157 *et passim*.

Bloomer, Jennifer. *Architecture and the Text: The (S)crypts of Joyce and Piranesi*. New Haven, CT: Yale University Press, 1993: *passim*.

Blumenberg, Hans. *The Origin of the Copernican World*, trans. R. M. Wallace. Cambridge, MA: MIT Press, 1987: 363.
_____. *Work on Myth*, trans. R. M. Wallace. Cambridge, MA: MIT Press, 1985: 60-62, 85, 377-80, 655 n.1.
_____. *The Legitimacy of the Modern Age*, trans. R. M. Wallace. Cambridge, MA: MIT Press, 1983: 285.

Boas, George. *The Cult of Childhood*. London: Warburg Institute, 1966: 62-64.
———. "In Search of the Age of Reason." In *Aspects of the Eighteenth Century*, ed. E. R. Wasserman. Baltimore: Johns Hopkins University Press, 1965: 13-15, 18.

Bobbio, Norberto. *Which Socialism?* Minneapolis: University of Minnesota Press, 1987: 115-84.

Bolt, Sydney. *A Preface to James Joyce*. London: Longman, 1981: 156-57, 158, 163.

Bonaparte, Felicia. Review of *George Eliot and Community: A Study in Social Theory and Fictional Form* (S. Graver). *New Vico Studies* 3 (1985): 226-31.
———. "*Middlemarch*: Genesis of Myth in the English Novel." *Notre Dame English Journal* 13 (1981): 111.
———. *The Triptych and the Cross: Central Myths of Eliot's Imagination*. New York: New York University Press, 1979: 15, 18, 65, 241 [Abstract: *New Vico Studies* 2 (1984): 150].

Boorstin, Daniel J. *The Discoverers*. New York: Vintage Books, 1985: 613-14.

Bore, Paul A. *Mastering Discourse: Politics of Intellectual Culture*. Durham, NC: Duke University Press, 1992: 7, 176.

Borges, Jorje Luis. "'Weak Thought' and Postmodernism: The Italian Departure from Deconstruction." *Social Text* (Winter 1987-88): 41.
———. "The Immortal." In *Labyrinths, Selected Stories, and Other Writings*, ed. D. A. Yates and J. E. Irby. New York: New Directions, 1964: 116, 118n.

Borgman, Albert. *The Philosophy of Language: Historical Foundations and Contemporary Issues*. The Hague: Nijhoff, 1974: 46n., 73-84, 87, 159.

Borradori, Giovanna, ed. *Recoding Metaphysics: The New Italian Philosophy*. Evanston, IL: Northwestern University Press, 1988: 5-8, 16, 19, 25, 148-53.
**Review:**
Struever, Nancy S. *New Vico Studies* 8 (1990): 56-61.

Bosanquet, Bernard. *The Philosophical Theory of the State* (1899). London: Macmillan, 1965: 12, 37-38.

Bosinelli, Rosa Maria, Paola Pugliatti, and Romana Zacchi, eds. *Myriad Minded Man: Jottings on Joyce*. Bologna: Cooperativa Libraria Universitaria Editrice Bologna, 1986: 243, 264.

Boucher, David. *The Social and Political Thought of R. G. Collingwood*. Cambridge: Cambridge University Press, 1989: 11, 13-15, 197.
**Review:**
Levine, Joseph. *New Vico Studies* 10 (1992): 126-28.

Bowen, Zack, and James F. Carens, ed. *A Companion to Joyce Studies.* Westport, CT: Greenwood Press, 1984: 580-85 *et passim.*

Boylan, Francis X. "The Poise of the Ending of *Finnegans Wake*: A Study of Artistic Cunning in Book IV." Unpublished Ph.D. diss. State University of New York (Albany), 1983.

Bradbury, Malcolm, and James McFarlane, ed. *Modernism, 1890-1930.* New York: Penguin, 1976: 32.

Braudel, Fernand. *On History.* Chicago: University of Chicago Press, 1980: 201.

Bray, Paul. "The Influence of Theories of History on the Style of James Joyce's *Finnegans Wake*." Unpublished Ph.D. diss. State University of New York, 1986 [Abstract: *New Vico Studies* 5 (1987): 205-7].

Breisach, Ernst. *Historiography: Ancient, Medieval, Modern.* Chicago: University of Chicago Press, 1983: 201, 203-5, 210-13, 222, 241, 341.

Bridenthal, Renate. "Was There a Roman Homer? Niebuhr's Thesis and Its Critics." *History and Theory* 11 (1972: 205-7).

Bridges, J. H. *Illustrations of Positivism,* ed. H. G. Jones. London: Watts, 1915: 56, 325n., 353f.

Brivic, Sheldon. *Joyce between Freud and Jung.* Port Washington NY: Kennikat Press, 1980: 201.

Brockway, Robert W. *Myth from the Ice Age to Mickey Mouse.* Albany: State University of New York Press, 1993: 79-83, 148-49.

Brombert, Beth A. *Christina: Portrait of a Princess.* New York: Knopf, 1977; University of Chicago Press, 1983: 6, 52-53, 101, 105-7, 163, 257n.

Bronowski, J., and Bruce Mazlish, eds. *The Western Intellectual Tradition from Leonardo to Hegel.* New York: Harper and Bros., 1960: 276, 485.

Brown, Elizabeth A. R. Review of *Medieval French Literature and Law* (R. H. Bloch). *History and Theory* 19 (1980): 319-38 *passim.*

Brown, J. L. *The "Methodus ad Facilem Historiarum Cognitionem" of Jean Bodin: A Critical Study.* Washington, DC: Catholic University Press of America, 1939: 192-93.
*Review:*
Costa, Gustavo. *New Vico Studies* 4 (1986): 150.

Brown, Merle E. *Neo-Idealistic Aesthetics: Croce-Gentile-Collingwood.* Detroit, MI: Wayne State University Press, 1986: 118, 183.

Brown, Norman O. "Rieff's 'Fellow Teachers'." *Salmagundi* 24 (1973): 34-45.

Brown, Richard H. *Social Science as Civic Discourse*. Chicago: University of Chicago Press, 1990: 10, 33, 40, 82-83, 114, 164.
———. "Reason as Rhetorical: On Relations among Epistemology, Discourse, and Practice." In *The Rhetoric of the Human Sciences: Language and Argument in Scholarship and Public Affairs*, ed. J. S. Nelson, A. Megill, and D. McCloskey. Madison: University of Wisconsin Press, 1988: 184-97.
———. "Personal Identity and Political Economy: Western Grammars of the Self in Historical Perspective." *Current Perspectives in Social Theory* 8 (1987): 23-59.
———. *Society as Text. Essays on Rhetoric, Reason and Reality*. Chicago: University of Chicago Press, 1987: 62-67.
**Review:**
Kellner, Hans. *New Vico Studies* 8 (1990): 131-35.

Brown, Richard H. "Social Reality as Narrative Text: Interaction, Institutions, and Politics as Language." *Current Perspectives in Social Theory* 6 (1985): 17-38.
———. "Social Theory as Metaphor: On the Logic of Discovery for the Sciences of Conduct." *Theory and Society* 3 (1976): 171.

Brown, Robert. *The Nature of Social Laws: Machiavelli to Mill*. London: Cambridge University Press, 1984: 158-86 *passim* [Abstract: *New Vico Studies* 2 (1984): 127-28].
**Review:**
Haddock, Bruce A. *New Vico Studies* 4 (1986): 183-85.

Brown, Roger L. *Von Humboldt's Conception of Linguistic Relativity*. The Hague: Mouton, 1967: 30-32, 34.

Brownson, Orestes A. *The Works of Orestes A. Brownson*, ed. H. F. Brownson. New York: AMS Press, 1966: 392-401.

Broyard, Anatole. "Let's Go to the Videotape, Tolstoy." *New York Times Book Review* (6 March 1988).

Bruno, Giordano. *On the Composition of Images, Signs and Ideas*, ed. D. Higgins, trans. C. Doria [Abstract: *New Vico Studies* 10 (1992): 138-39].

Bryan, Ferald Joseph. "Thomas E. Watson vs Henry W. Grady: The Rhetorical Struggle for the Mind of the South, 1880-1980." Unpublished Ph.D. diss. University of Missouri, 1985.

Buber, Martin. *Eclipse of God*. New York: Harper and Bros., 1952: 108.

Buckle, H. T. *Introduction to the History of Civilisation in England*, ed. J. M. Robinson. London, 1904: 91 n.8, 466 n.131, 500.

Buford, Thomas O. "Person, Identity, and Imagination." *Personalist Forum* 5 (1989): 7-25.

Burgess, Anthony. "Mr. Gibbon and the Huns." *New York Times Book Review* (28 Feb. 1988): 37.

Bultmann, Rudolph. *History and Eschatology*. Edinburgh: Edinburgh University Press, 1958: 79-80.
_____. *The Presence of Eternity*. New York: Harper & Row, 1957: 64, 69, 79-81, 85-86.

Bunsen, Christian J. *God in History*. London: Longmans, Green, 1870: 273-75.

Burbank, Rex. *Thornton Wilder*. New York: Twayne, 1961: 103.

Burckhardt, Jacob. *On History and Historians*. New York: Harper & Row, 1965): 172.

Burger, Ronna. *Plato's "Phaedrus": A Defense of a Philosophic Art of Writing*. University: University of Alabama Press, 1980: 113.

Burgess, Anthony. *Joysprick*. New York: Harcourt Brace Jovanovich, 1973: 131, 139, 148, 159.
_____. *Here Comes Everybody*. London: Faber and Faber, 1965 [published simultaneously as *Re Joyce*. New York: Norton: 191].
_____, ed. *A Shorter Finnegans Wake*. New York: Viking, 1965: xii-xiii, xix-xx, xxiv.

Burke, Mary L. "The Verb in Foscolo's Poetic Gestalt." *Forum Italicum* 12 (1978): 528, 541, 548.

Bury, John B. *The Idea of Progress: An Inquiry into Its Origin and Growth*. New York: Macmillan, 1932: 267-71, 277, 308.

Byatt, Anne S. *Possession: A Romance*. New York: Random House, 1990: 3-6 (Vico quoted on 6), 10, 23, 510, 512, 548.
**Review:**
Lehmann-Haupt, Christopher. *New York Times* 119 (21 Oct. 1990): 9.

Cairns, Grace E. *Philosophies of History: Meeting of East and West in Cycle Pattern Theories of History*. New York: Philosophical Library; Toronto: McLeod, 1962: 337-52 *et passim*.

Calendrillo, Linda Therèse. "The Art of Memory and Rhetoric." Ph.D. diss. Purdue University, 1988 [Ann Arbor, MI: University Microfilms, 1988].

Cambon, Glauco. "A Note on Critical Humanism." *Italian Quarterly* 25 (1984): 7-15.
_____. *Ugo Foscolo—Poet of Exile*. Princeton, NJ: Princeton University Press, 1980: 16, 129, 157, 163, 211, 217, 302, 304-5, 312, 316.

Cameron, J. M. "Problems of Literary History." *New Literary History* 1 (1969): 10, 14.

Cammett, John M. *Antonio Gramsci and the Origins of Italian Communism.* Stanford, CA: Stanford University Press, 1967: 42, 60, 203.

Campbell, John Angus. "A Rhetorical Interpretation of History." *Rhetorica* 2 (1984): 228, 229.

Campbell, Joseph. *Way of Animal Powers.* New York: Harper & Row, 1983: 57-58.
_____. *Historical Atlas of World Mythology.* San Francisco: van der Marck Eds., Harper & Row, 1983, 1:57.
_____, and Henry Morton Robinson. *A Skeleton Key to Finnegans Wake.* Harmondsworth: Penguin, 1980: 5-6 [originally published 1944].

Campbell, Richard J. *Truth and Historicity.* Oxford: Clarendon Press, 1992: *passim.*

Campion, Nicholas. "Astrological Historiography in the Renaissance: The Work of Jean Bodin and Louis LeRoy." In *History and Astrology: Clio and Urania Confer,* ed. A. Kitson. Boston: Unwin Paperbacks, 1989: 89-136.

Caponigri, A. Robert. "The Nature of History." *Giornale di metafisica* 17 (1962): 338-39, 363, 376.
_____. *History and Liberty: The Historical Writings of Benedetto Croce.* London: Routledge & Kegan Paul, 1955: 3, 14, 117, 122, 163, 180, 182, 231.

Carlin, John. "Metaphors of Vision: The Mediation of Self and Nature through Language in the Work of Emerson, Thomas Cole, Dickinson, Whitman, and Thomas Eakins." Unpublished Ph.D. diss. Yale University, 1986.

Carmine, James Daniel. "Metaphor of Shame and the Myth of the Primal Scene." Unpublished Ph.D. diss. State University of New York (Stony Brook), 1988.

Carr, David. *Time, Narrative and History.* Bloomington: Indiana University Press, 1986: 1, 4, 146.

Carr, Thomas M. *Descartes and the Resilience of Rhetoric: Varieties of Cartesian Rhetorical Theory.* Carbondale: Southern Illinois University Press, 1990: 1, 2, 170.

Carravetta, Peter. "The Problem of Method and the Quest for Hermeneutics: A Study in the Foundations of Interpretive Thought in Twentieth-Century Italian Literary Criticism." Unpublished Ph.D. diss. New York University, 1983: ch. 3.
_____. "The Postmodernity of D'Annunzio." *Italian Journal* 4 (1987): 45-48.
_____. "Principles of Literary Hermeneutics." In *Italian Literature in North America: Pedagogical Strategies,* ed. J. Picchione and L. Pietropaolo. Ottawa: Biblioteca dei Quaderni d' Italianistica 9 (1990): 156, 162.
_____. *Prefaces to the Diaphora: Rhetoric, Allegory, and the Interpretation of Postmodernity.* West Lafayette, IN: Purdue University Press, 1991: 15, 25, 30, 94, 105, 164, 239-252.

*Review:*
Jacobitti, Edmund E. *New Vico Studies* 10 (1992): 124-26.

Carruccio, Ettore. *Mathematics and Logic in History and in Contemporary Thought*. Chicago: Aldine, 1964: 190-91, 352.

Cascardi, Anthony J. "The Place of Language in Philosophy: or, The Uses of Rhetoric." *Philosophy and Rhetoric* 16 (1983): 223, n. 4.
_____. Review of *After Philosophy: End or Transformation?* (ed. K. Baynes, J. Bohman, and T. McCarthy). *New Vico Studies* 5 (1987): 200-3.

Caserta, Ernesto G. "Croce and Marxism." *Journal of the History of Ideas* 44 (1983): 141-49.
_____. "Croce and Marxism: The Years During and After World War I (1915-1924)." *Italian Quarterly* 27 (1986): 23, 26, 27.

Cassirer, Ernst. *An Essay on Man*. New Haven, CT: Yale University Press, 1944: 114, 153, 172.
_____. *Problem of Knowledge*, trans. W. H. Woglom and C. W. Hendel. New Haven, CT: Yale University Press, 1950: 217, 296.
_____. *Philosophy of the Enlightenment*, trans. F. C. A. Koelin and J. P. Pettegrove. Princeton, NJ: Princeton University Press, 1951: 209.
_____. *Philosophy of Symbolic Forms*, trans. R. Manheim. New Haven, CT: Yale University Press, 1953-57: 1:147-55; 2:3.
_____. *Logic of the Humanities*, trans. C. S. Howe. New Haven, CT: Yale University Press, 1961: 52-55.

Castoriadis, Cornelius. *Philosophy, Politics, Autonomy: Essays in Political Philosophy*. Oxford: Oxford University Press, 1991: 56.

Cellerino, Massimo. Review of *The New Constellation. The Ethical-Political Horizons of Modernity/Postmodernity* (R. J. Bernstein). *New Vico Studies* 11 (1993): 123-29.

Chambliss, J. J. *Social Thought*. New York: Dryden Press, 1954: 366-91.

Chase, Robert. *Quest for Myth*. Baton Rouge: Louisiana State University Press, 1949: 22-27 *et passim*.

Cheng, Vincent John. *Shakespeare and Joyce: A Study of Finnegans Wake*. University Park: Pennsylvania State University Press, 1984: 5, 9, 18-19 *et passim*.

Chill, Emanuel. "Barnave as Philosophical Historian." In *Power, Property, and History: Barnave's Introduction to the French Revolution and Other Writings*. New York: Harper and Row, 1971: 48-49.

Chisholm, Roderick *et al. Philosophy.* Englewood Cliffs, NJ: Prentice Hall, 1964: 94, 99.

Chomsky, Noam. *Rules and Representations.* New York: Columbia University Press, 1980: 9.

Church, Margaret. "Time as an Organizing Principle in the Fiction of Joyce." In *Joyce Centenary Essays*, ed. R. F. Peterson, A. M. Cohn, and E. L. Epstein. Carbondale and Edwardsville: Southern Illinois University Press, 1983: 70-77, 79, 82.

Cicovacki, Oredrag. "Locke on Mathematical Knowledge." *Journal of the History of Philosophy* 28 (1990): 518n.

Cixous, Helene. *The Exile of James Joyce*, trans. S. A. J. Purcell. New York: David Lewis, 1972: 237, 417n., 739.

Clark, G. N. *The Seventeenth Century.* Oxford: Clarendon Press, 1947: 286.

Clark, John S. *Life and Letters of John Fiske.* New York: Houghton, Mifflin, 1917: 1:285.

Clark, Priscilla P. "The Sociology of Literature: A Historical Introduction." In *Research in Sociology of Knowledge, Sciences, and Art*, ed. R. A. Jones. Greenwich, CT: JAI Press, 1978: 1:240-41.

Clark, Robert T. Jr. *Herder—His Life and Thought.* Berkeley: University of California Press, 1955: 24, 31, 179-80, 188, 191, 314, 381.

Clive, John. *Not By Fact Alone. Essays on the Writing and Reading of History.* New York: Knopf, 1989: 52.

Cobb, Edith. *The Ecology of Imagination in Children.* New York: Columbia University Press, 1977: 31, 114.

Cochrane, Eric W. *Tradition and Enlightenment in the Tuscan Academies 1690-1800.* Rome: Edizioni di Storia e Letteratura, 1961: 6, 10, 94, 101, 180, 201.
———. *Florence in the Forgotten Centuries 1527-1800.* Chicago: University of Chicago Press, 1973: 326, 334, 388, 552.

Cohen, G. A. *Marx's Theory of History: A Defense.* Princeton, NJ: Princeton University Press, 1978: 330.

Cohen, J. Bernard. *Revolution in Science.* Cambridge: Harvard University Press, 1985: 259.

Cohen, Morris R. *The Meaning of Human History.* La Salle, IL: Open Court, 1947: 39, 119, 263.

Cohen, Sande. *Historical Culture. On the Recoding of an Academic Discipline.* Berkeley: University of California Press, 1986: 48-61, 218.

*Review:*
Struever, Nancy S. *New Vico Studies* 5 (1987): 193-95.

Cole, William E. "Sociology." In *The Social Sciences*, ed. J. U. Michaelis and A. M. Johnston. Boston: Allyn and Bacon, 1965: 193.

Coleridge, Samuel Taylor. *Hints towards the formation of a more comprehensive theory of life*, ed. Seth B. Watson. London: John Churchill, 1848: 36.
_____. *Unpublished Letters of Samuel Taylor Coleridge*, ed. E. Griggs. New Haven, CT: Yale University Press, 1933: 2:352, 374, 453.
_____. *The Collected Works of Samuel Taylor Coleridge*, ed. by Carl Woodring. Vol. 14 (in 2 parts), *Table Talk*. London: Routledge (Bollingen Series LXXV), Princeton University Press, 1990: 1:129n, 202n, 286-87 (letter of 23 April, 1832), 300n, 301n, 359n, 383n, 450n, 565-66; 2: 87n, 165, 214n.

Coleridge, Sara. *Memoir and Letters of Sara Coleridge*, ed. E. Coleridge. New York: Harper & Bros., 1874: 214.

Collingwood, Robin G. *Speculum Mentis or the Map of Knowledge*. Oxford: Clarendon Press, 1924: 53, 74, 216.
_____. *Principles of Art*. Oxford: Clarendon Press, 1938: 80, 138.
_____. *Essays in the Philosophy of History*, ed. W. Debbins. Austin: University of Texas Press, 1965: 57, 60, 65, 72, 127-30.

Collins, James. *Descartes' Philosophy of Nature*. Oxford: Basil Blackwell, 1971: 19.

Comte, Auguste. *System of Positive Polity*, trans. R. Congreve. New York: Burt Franklin, 1877: 1:512; 3:504.

Cook, Albert. *History/Writing*. Cambridge and New York: Cambridge University Press, 1988: 193-94, 196-97 *et passim*.

Cook, Patricia. Review of *The Ancients and the Moderns: Rethinking Modernity* (S. Rosen). *New Vico Studies* 8 (1990): 115-19.

Cope, Jackson I. *Joyce's Cities: Archaeologies of the Soul*. Baltimore and London: Johns Hopkins University Press, 1981: 112.

Costa, Gustavo. Review of *Theophrastus redivivus: erudizione e ateismo nel Seicento* (T. Gregory). *New Vico Studies 1 (1983): 126-28.*
_____. "Clashing Traditions in the Eighteenth Century: Angelo Calogerà, Scipione Maffei, and Giuseppe Maria Bianchini." *Forum Italicum* 18 (1984): 280, 282, 293, 295.
_____. Review of *Pietro Giannone e il suo tempo: Atti del convegno di studi nel tricentenario della nascita* (ed. R. Ajello). *New Vico Studies* 2 (1984): 128-31.
_____. Review of *Manoscritti napoletani di Paolo Mattia Doria* (ed. G. Belgioioso *et al*). *New Vico Studies* 2 (1984): 143-46.

---------. Review of *Natura umana, società e linguaggio* (Lord Monboddo; ed. A. Verri). *New Vico Studies* 3 (1985): 190-93.

---------. Review of *Verso la "vita civile": Antropologia e politica nelle lezioni accademiche di Gregorio Caloprese e Paolo Mattia Doria* (E. Nuzzo). *New Vico Studies* 3 (1985): 187-90.

---------. Review of *Francis Bacon: Terminologia e fortuna nel XVII secolo. Seminario internazionale, Roma, 1984* (ed. M. Fattori). *New Vico Studies* 4 (1986): 157-60.

---------. Review of *Lexicon philosophicum: Quaderni di terminologia filosofica e storia delle idee* (ed. A. Lamarra and L. P. Xella). *New Vico Studies* 4 (1986): 167-70.

---------. Review of *Paolo Mattia Doria fra rinnovamento e tradizione: Atti del convegno di studi, Lecce, 1982* (ed. G. Papuli). *New Vico Studies* 4 (1986): 170-74.

---------. Review of *Spiritus: IV Colloquio Internazionale* (Rome, 1983) (ed. M. Fattori and M. Bianchi). *New Vico Studies* 4 (1986): 160-64.

---------. Review of *Theophrastus redivivus* (ed. G. Canziani and G. Paganini). *New Vico Studies* 4 (1986): 154-57.

---------. "Arnaldo Momigliano (1908-1987)." *New Vico Studies* 5 (1987): 221-25 [Obituary].

---------. Review of *Galileo e Napoli* (ed. F. Lomonaco and M. Torrini). *New Vico Studies* 6 (1988): 163-67.

---------. Review of *Politics and Culture in Renaissance Naples* (ed. J. H. Bentley). *New Vico Studies* 6 (1988): 160-63.

---------. Review of *Saggio sulla natura e necessità della scienza delle cose e delle storie umane* (C. Jannelli; ed. A. Verri). *New Vico Studies* 7 (1989): 135-37.

---------. Review of *Baltasar Gracian: La logica dell ingegno* (E. Hidalgo-Serna). *New Vico Studies* 10 (1992): 108-13.

---------. Review of *Lex Regia: Diritto, filologia e fides historica nella cultura politico-filosofica dell'Olanda di fine Seicento* (ed. F. Lomonaco). *New Vico Studies* 11 (1993): 120-22.

---------. Review of *Epistolario. Vol. II 1690-1705* (Jean Le Clerc; ed. M. Grazia and M. Sina). *New Vico Studies* 11 (1993): 138-41.

---------. Review of *Lettres à Claude Saumaise et à son entourage (1620-1637)* (N.-C. F. de Peiresc; ed. A. Bresson). *New Vico Studies* 11 (1993): 138-41.

Costa-Lima, Luiz. "Eric Auerbach: History and Metahistory." *New Literary History* 19 (1988): 467-99.

Covino, William A. *The Art of Wondering: A Revisionist Return to the History of Rhetoric.* Portsmouth, MA: Boynton/Cook, 1988: 141.

Cowan, Bernard. Review of *Perspectives on Romanticism: A Transformational Analysis* (D. Morse). London: MacMillan; Totowa NJ: Barnes and Noble, 1981. *The 18th Century: A Current Bibliography*, n.s. 7 (1981): 359.

Cowell, F. R. *Values in Human Society: The Contribution of Pitirim A. Sorokin to Sociology.* Boston: Peter Sargent, 1979: 139.

Cragh, Helge. *An Introduction to the Historiography of Science.* Cambridge: Cambridge University Press, 1987: 5.

Croce, Benedetto. *Benedetto Croce: Essays on Literature and Literary Criticism*, trans. M. E. Moss. Albany: State University of New York Press, 1990: 1, 2, 49, 52, 53, 123, 149, 152, 154.
_____. *Benedetto Croce's "Poetry and Literature: An Introduction to Its Criticism and History,"* ed. G. Gullace. Carbondale: Southern Illinois University Press, 1981: xiii n., *et passim.*
_____. "In Commemoration of an English Friend, A Companion in Thought and Faith, R. G. Collingwood." In *Thought, Action, and Intuition: A Symposium on the Philosophy of Benedetto Croce*, ed. L. M. Palmer and H. S. Harris. Hildesheim and New York: Georg Olms, 1975,: 51, 66.
_____. "A Working Hypothesis: The Crisis of Italy in the *Cinquecento* and the Bond between the Renaissance and the *Risorgimento.*" In *the Late Italian Renaissance 1525-1630*, ed. E. Cochrane. London: Macmillan, 1970: 38-39.
_____. *History of the Kingdom of Naples*, trans. F. Frenaye; ed. H. S. Hughes. Chicago: University of Chicago Press, 1970: *passim.*
_____. *Guide to Aesthetics*, trans. P. Romanell. New York: Bobbs-Merrill, 1965: ix, xiii-xviii, 19, 56, 84.
_____. *My Philosophy: Essays on the Moral and Political Problems of Our Time.* New York: Collier Books, 1962: 13, 91, 205.
_____. *History as the Story of Liberty*, trans. S. Sprigge. New York: Norton, 1941: *passim.*
_____. *European Literature in the Nineteenth Century*, trans. D. Ainslie. New York: Knopf, 1924: 83, 85, 155, 268.
_____. *Shaftesbury in Italy.* Cambridge: Bowes & Bowes, 1924: 8, 21.
_____. *History: Its Theory and Practice*, trans. D. Ainslie. New York: Harcourt, Brace, & Co., 1921; reprinted New York: Russell & Russell, 1960: *passim.*

Croff, Barbara L. *"Stylistic Arrangements": A Study of William Butler Yeats's 'A Vision'.* Lewisburg, PA: Bucknell University Press, 1982: 73, 77, 149.

Cross, Richard K. *Flaubert and Joyce: The Rite of Fiction.* Princeton, NJ: Princeton University Press, 1971: 188.

Crossley, Ceri. *Edgar Quinet (1803-1875). A Study in Romantic Thought.* Lexington, KY: French Forum, 1983: 18-25, 35-39.

Cua, Anthony S. "The Idea of Confucian Tradition." *Review of Metaphysics* 45 (1992): 812.

Culler, Jonathan. *The Pursuit of Signs: Semiotics, Literature, Deconstruction.* Ithaca, NY: Cornell University Press, 1981: 203.

Curran, C. P. *James Joyce Remembered.* London: Oxford University Press, 1968: 86-87, 120-21.

Dalle Vacche, Angela. *The Body in the Mirror—Shapes of History in Italian Cinema.* Princeton, NJ: Princeton University Press, 1992: 10-13, *et passim.*

Dallmayr, Fred R. Review of *Social Science as Civic Discourse: Essays on the Invention, Legitimation, and Uses of Social Theory* (R. H. Brown). *New Vico Studies* 10 (1992): 113-16.

———. *Between Freiburg and Frankfurt: Toward a Critical Ontology.* Amherst: University of Massachusetts Press, 1991: 14, 194; also published as *Life-World—Modernity and Critique: Paths between Heidegger and the Frankfurt School.* Cambridge: Polity Press, 1991 [Abstract in *New Vico Studies* 10 (1992): 137-38].

———. *Critical Encounters: Between Philosophy and Politics.* Notre Dame, IN: University of Notre Dame Press, 1989: 130 [Abstract in *New Vico Studies* 7 (1989): 129].

———. "Between Kant and Aristotle: Ronald Beiner's *Political Judgment.*" *New Vico Studies* 6 (1988): 147-54 [Review].

———. *Language and Politics: Why Does Language Matter to Political Philosophy?* Notre Dame, IN: University of Notre Dame Press, 1984: 148-73 [Abstract in *New Vico Studies* 3 (1985): 219-20].

———. Review of *Beyond Objectivism and Relativism: Science, Hermeneutics, and Praxis* (R. J. Bernstein). *New Vico Studies* 3 (1985): 215-19.

———. *Beyond Dogma and Despair: Toward a Critical Phenomenology of Politics.* Notre Dame, IN: University of Notre Dame Press, 1981: 139-55.

———. *Twilight of Subjectivity: Contributions to a Post-Individualist Theory of Politics.* Amherst: University of Massachusetts Press, 1981: 211-19, 257-63.

———. "Phenomenology and Marxism: A Salute to Enzo Paci." In *Phenomenological Sociology*, ed. G. Psathas. New York: Wiley, 1973: 344 *et passim.*

———. "Political Science and the 'Two Cultures'." *Journal of General Education* 19 (1968): 274.

D'Amico, Robert. *Historicism and Knowledge.* New York and London: Routledge, 1989: 154.

———. *Marx and Philosophy of Culture.* Gainesville: University Presses of Florida, 1981: 5.

Dane, Ernest. *The Critical Mythology of Irony.* Athens: University of Georgia Press, 1991: *passim.*

Danesi, Marcel. "Robert J. di Pietro (1932-1991)." *New Vico Studies* 10 (1992): 142-44 [Obituary].

———. "Rational Thought and Postmodernism: A Commentary on Hwa Yol Jung's Analysis of the Postmodern Mind." *Rivista di Studi Italiani* 9 (1991): 86, 89, 90, 92.

———. "Language and the Senses: New Directions in Linguistics." *Semiotic Review of Books* (1990): 4-6.

———. Review of *The Question of Rationality and the Basic Grammar of Intercultural Texts* (H. Y. Jung). *New Vico Studies* 8 (1990): 119-21.

———. Review of *The Wake of the Imagination* (R. Kearney). *New Vico Studies* 8 (1990): 121-22.

———. Review of *Meaning and Mental Representation* (ed. Umberto Eco, M. Santambrogio, and P. Violi). *New Vico Studies* 7 (1989): 108-10.
———. "The Role of Metaphor in Cognition." *Semiotica* 77 (1989): 526-31.
———. Review of *The Origin of Writing* (R. Harris). *New Vico Studies* 5 (1987): 203-5.
———. "Humanism in Linguistics: The Works of R. J. di Pietro." In *Issues in Language: Studies in Honor of Robert J. di Pietro, Presented to Him by His Students*, ed. M. Danesi. Lake Bluff, IL: Jupiter, 1981: 3-13.

Daniel, Stephen H. "Myth and the Grammar of Discovery in Francis Bacon." *Philosophy and Rhetoric* 15 (1982): 235, 237.
———. "Descartes on Myth and Ingenuity/Ingenium." *Southern Journal of Philosophy* 23 (1985): 158.
———. "Myth and Rationality in Mandeville." *Journal of the History of Ideas* 47 (1986): 597, 603, 608.
———. Review of *William James: His Life and Thought* (G. Meyers). *New Vico Studies* 6 (1988): 181-82.
———. Review of *Transforming the Hermeneutic Context: From Nietzsche to Nancy* (ed. G. L. Ormiston and A. D. Schrift). *New Vico Studies* 8 (1990): 127-29.
———. *Myth and Modern Philosophy*. Philadelphia: Temple University Press, 1990: *passim*.

**Review:**
Jackson, Ronald. *New Vico Studies* 8 (1990): 109-12.

Danto, Arthur. *Analytical Philosophy of History*. Cambridge: Cambridge University Press, 1965: 92.
———. *Narration and Knowledge*—including the integral text of *Analytical Philosophy of History*. New York: Columbia University Press, 1985: 93, 357, 359, 360.
———. *The Philosophical Disenfranchisement of Art*. New York: Columbia University Press, 1987: 59.

Davidson, Alastair. *Antonio Gramsci: Toward an Intellectual Biography*. Atlantic Highlands, NJ: Humanities Press, 1977: 75.

Davies, Stan Gebler. *James Joyce: A Portrait of the Artist*. New York: Stein and Day, 1975: 254.

Davis, Philip J., and Reuben Hersh. *Descartes' Dream: The World According to Mathematics*. San Diego: Harcourt Brace Jovanovich, 1986; reprinted Boston: Houghton Mifflin, 1986: x, 189, 197, 303 [Vico's portrait appears on x].

Davis, Sheila. *The Song-Writers' Idea Book*. Cincinnati: Writer's Digest Books, 1992: *passim*.

Day, Stewart James. "The Place of Difference: A Philosophy of Imagination." Ph.D. diss. Pennsylvania State University, 1988 [Ann Arbor, MI: University Microfilms].

Deane, Seamus. "Joyce and Nationalism." In *James Joyce: New Perspectives*, ed. C. MacCabe. Sussex: Harvester Press; Bloomington: Indiana University Press, 1982: 180.

de Bolla, Peter. *Harold Bloom. Toward Historical Rhetoric.* London and New York: Routledge, 1988: 62-64, 66, 75-76.

De Gennaro, Angelo. *The Philosophy of Benedetto Croce.* New York: Citadel, 1961: 35, 44, 65, 71, 75.

Della Volpe, Galvano. *A Critique of Taste*, trans. M. Caesar. London: NLB, 1978: 1, 22, 23, 84, 87.

de Man, Paul. *Blindness and Insight: Essays in the Rhetoric of Contemporary Criticism.* Minneapolis: University of Minnesota Press, 1983: 168.

De Mauro, Tullio. *Ludwig Wittgenstein: His Place in the Development of Semantics.* Dordrecht, Holland: Dreidel, 1967: 1, 9-14, 16, 18, 19, 22, 23, 53.

Denham, Robert R. *Northrop Frye and Critical Method.* University Park and London: The Pennsylvania State University Press, 1978: 25, 182, 235n.

D'Entrèves, Alessandro Passerin. *Natural Law: Introduction to Legal Philosophy.* London: Hutchinson's University Library, 1951; reprinted as *Natural Law: A Historical Survey.* New York: Harper & Row, 1965: 28, 54, 118.

Derrida, Jacques. *Of Grammatology*, trans. G. Spivak. Baltimore: Johns Hopkins University Press, 1974: 272, 278, 292, 335, 349-52.

de Ruggiero, Guido. *Modern Philosophy*, trans. A. H. Hannay and R. G. Collingwood. New York: Macmillan, 1921: 303-5.

de Sanctis, Francesco. *History of Italian Literature*, trans. J. Redfern. New York: Harcourt, Brace and Co., 1931: 2:*passim*.

Descombes, Vincent. *Modern French Philosophy.* Cambridge: Cambridge University Press, 1980: 32.

de Vries, Jan. *The Study of Religion: A Historical Approach*, trans. K. W. Boole. New York: Harcourt, Brace, and World, 1967: 34-35.

de Waal Malefijt, Annemarie. *Images of Man: A History of Anthropological Thought.* New York: Knopf, 1974: 75-79, 81, 121.
_____. *Religion and Culture.* New York: Macmillan, 1960: 29-32, 34.

Diamond, Stanley. *In Search of the Primitive.* New Brunswick, NJ: Transaction Books, 1974: 301.

Dillworth, David A. *Philosophy in World Perspective: A Comparative Hermeneutic of the Major Theories.* New Haven, CT: Yale University Press, 1989: *passim*.

Dilthey, William. *Descriptive Psychology and Historical Understanding*, trans. R. M. Zaner and K. L. Heiges. The Hague: Martinus Nijhoff, 1977: 7, 7 n.4.
_____. *Selected Works*. Vol. 1. *Introduction to the Human Sciences*, ed. R. A. Makkreel and F. Rodi. Princeton, NJ: Princeton University Press, 1989: 139, 148, 161.
**Review:**
Verene, Donald Phillip. *New Vico Studies* 8 (1990): 140-42.

Dilthey, William. *Selected Works*. Vol. 5. *Poetry and Experience*, ed. R. A. Makkreel and F. Rodi, trans. L. Agosta *et al*. Princeton, NJ: Princeton University Press, 1985.
**Review:**
Daniel, Stephen H. *New Vico Studies* 4 (1986): 175-78.

Di Pietro, Robert J. "The Discovery of Universals in Multilinguism." In *21st Annual Roundtable*, ed. J. E. Alatis. Washington, DC: Georgetown University School of Languages and Linguistics, *Monograph Series on Languages and Linguistics* 23 (1970): 20.
_____. Review of *Language and Interpretation in Psychoanalysis* (M. Edelson). *Centrum* 3 (1975): 100.
_____. *Language as Human Creation*. Washington, DC: Georgetown University Press, 1976: 14.
_____. "Semiotics and the Psychotherapist," *Semiotica* 19 (1977): 149-56.
_____. "The Role of Metaphor in Linguistics." In *Linguistic and Literary Studies in Honor of Archibald A. Hill*, ed. M. A. Jazayery *et al*. The Hague: Mouton, 1978: 1:99-108.
_____. "Language and the Imagination." In *The Fifth LACUS Forum*, ed. W. Wölck *et al*. Columbia, SC: Hornbeam Press, 1979: 443-50.

Di Salvo, Jackie. *War of the Titans: Blake's Critique of Milton and the Politics of Religion*. Pittsburgh: University of Pittsburgh Press, 1983: 87.

Dockhorn, Klaus. "Hans-Georg Gadamer's *Truth and Method*." *Philosophy and Rhetoric* 13 (1980): 167.

Dogana, Fernando. *Suono e senso-Fondamenti teorici e Empirici del simbolismo fonetico*. Milan: F. Angeli, 1983 [Abstract in *New Vico Studies* 2 (1984): 150].

Donadoni, Eugenio. *A History of Italian Literature*, trans. R. Monges. New York: New York University Press, 1969: 305, 310.

Donagan, Alan. *The Later Philosophy of R. G. Collingwood*. Clarendon: Oxford University Press, 1962: 180-81.

Donato, Eugenio. "The Mnemonics of History: Notes for a Contextual Reading of Foscolo's *Dei Sepolcri*." *Yale Italian Studies* 1 (1977): 11-12.

Donoghue, Denis. "Yeats and European Criticism." In *Yeats the European*, ed. A. N. Jeffares. Savage, MD: Barnes and Noble, 1989: 38-48.

Dorfles, Gillo. *Kitsch: The World of Bad Taste*. New York: Universe Books, 1969: 48.

Dray, William H. *Philosophy of History*. Englewood Cliffs, NJ: Prentice-Hall, 1964: 60-62.
―――. *Perspectives on History*. Boston: Routledge & Kegan Paul, 1980: 58, 103.
―――. *On History and Philosophers of History*. Leiden: Brill, 1989: 77, 80, 193, 201.
*Review:*
Kelley, Donald R. *New Vico Studies* 8 (1990): 139-40.

Duro, Aldo. "Humanities Computing Activities in Italy." *Computers and the Humanities* 3 (1968):51.

Dutu, Alexandru. *Romanian Humanists and European Culture: A Contribution to Comparative Cultural History*. Bucharest: Bibliotheca Historical Romaninae (Ed. Acad. Rep. Soc. Romania), 1977: 143-57.

Dyson-Hudson, Neville. "Structure and Infrastructure in Primitive Society: Lévi-Strauss and Radcliffe-Brown." In *The Structuralist Controversy: Languages of Criticism and Sciences of Man*, ed. R. Macksey and E. Donato. Baltimore: Johns Hopkins University Press, 1970: 222.

Eco, Umberto. *A Theory of Semiotics*. Bloomington: Indiana University Press, 1976: 254.
―――. "Metaphor, Dictionary, and Encyclopedia." *New Literary History* 15 (1984): 270.
―――. *Semiotics and the Philosophy of Language*. Bloomington: Indiana University Press, 1984: 87, 107-8, 129.
―――. *The Open Book*. Cambridge: Harvard University Press, 1989: 41.

Edel, Abraham. "A Philosophic Perspective." In *Small Comforts for Hard Times*, ed. M. Mooney and F. Stuber. New York: Columbia University Press, 1977: 353.

Eder, Richard. "Edward Said: Bright Star of English Lit. and P.L.O." *New York Times* (22 Feb. 1980): 2.

Edie, James M. "Expressions and Metaphor." *Philosophy and Phenomenological Research* 23 (1963): 548-49, 552-53.

Ellmann, Richard. *James Joyce*. New York: Oxford University Press, 1959: 351, 565, 575, 706.
―――, and Ellsworth Mason, eds. *The Critical Writings of James Joyce*. New York: Viking, 1959: 134n.

Ellmann, Richard, ed. *Letters of James Joyce*. New York: Viking Press; London: Faber & Faber, 1966: 3:117-18, 463, 480.
Ellmann, Richard. *Ulysses on the Liffey*. New York: Oxford University Press; London: Faber and Faber, 1972: 52-53, 58-59, 84, 118-23, 136, 141-42, 179-83, 190, 192.
―――. *Selected Joyce Letters*. New York: Viking, 1976: 261, 314, 317, 321, 403, 407.

———. *The Consciousness of Joyce*. London: Faber and Faber, 1977: 3, 25, 28-29, 39.
———. "Joyce and Homer." *Critical Inquiry* 3 (1977): 567-82.
———. *James Joyce*. New York: Oxford University Press, 1982: 153, 340, 554, 564, 661n., 664, 693.

Engell, James. *The Creative Imagination*. Cambridge, MA: Harvard University Press, 1981: 112.
**Review:**
Hausman, B. *Journal of Aesthetics and Art Criticism* 40 (1982): 438.

Entwistle, Harold. *Antonio Gramsci*. Boston: Routledge & Kegan Paul, 1979: 66.

Essick, Robert N. *William Blake and the Language of Adam*. Oxford: Clarendon, 1989: 30, 67n, 70n, 122n.

Evans, Simon Domino. "Some Aspects of Sound and Sense in James Joyce's *Finnegans Wake*." Unpublished D. Phil. diss. University of Essex, 1987.

Everett, Alexander H. "Progress and Limits of Social Improvement." *North American Review* 38 (1834): 513.

Farrar, C. C. S. "The Science of History." *De Bow's Review* 5 (1848): 58, 133, 211-14.

Farrington, Benjamin. *Francis Bacon: Philosopher of Industrial Science*. New York: Henry Schuman, 1949: 63.

Faur, José. "Sephardim in the Nineteenth Century: New Directions and Old Values." *Proceedings of the American Academy for Jewish Research* 44 (1977): 29-52.
———. *Golden Doves with Silver Dots: Semiotics and Textuality in Rabbinic Tradition*. Bloomington: Indiana University Press, 1986: xxiii, xxvii, 24-26, 153n.
**Review:**
Luft, Sandra Rudnick. *New Vico Studies* 10 (1992): 129-31.

Faur, José. "De-authorization of the Law: Paul and the Oedipal Model." In *Psychoanalysis and Religion*, ed. J. H. Smith. Baltimore: Johns Hopkins University Press, 1989: 233, 240, 241.
———. Review of *That Nothing Is Known (Quod nihil scitur)* (Francisco Sánches; trans. D. F. S. Thomson). *New Vico Studies* 8 (1990): 104-6.
———. *In the Shadow of History: Jews and 'Conversos' at the Dawn of Modernity*. Albany: State University of New York Press, 1992: 105-214 *passim*.

Feibleman, James K. *An Introduction to Peirce's Philosophy*. New York and London: Harper & Brothers, 1946: 69-70.
———. *In Praise of Comedy: The Classic Works on the Meanings of Comedy from Homer to the New Yorker*. New York: Horizon, 1970: 91-94, 135.
———. *Understanding Civilizations: The Shape of History*. New York: Horizon, 1975: 87 *et passim*.

Fellows, Otis. Review of *Tiphaigne de la Roche: Modèles de l'imaginaire* (J. Marx). *The 18th Century: A Current Bibliography*, n.s. 7 (1981): 353-54.

Femia, Joseph V. "A Historicist Critique of 'Revisionist' Methods for Studying the History of Ideas." *History and Theory* 20 (1981): 115, 120, 123.
_____. *Gramsci's Political Thought*. Oxford: Clarendon Press, 1987: 16, 126, 245.

Ferretti, Silvia. *Cassirer, Panofsky, and Warburg: Symbol, Art, and History*, trans. R. Pierce. New Haven, CT: Yale University Press, 1989: 10, 234. Orig. Italian: *Il demone della memoria. Simbolo e tempo storico in Warburg, Cassirer, Panofsky*. Casale Monferrato: Marietti, 1984 [Abstract: *New Vico Studies* 4 (1986): 178].

Ferry, Luc. *Rights—The New Quarrel between the Ancients and the Moderns*, trans. F. Philip. Chicago and London: University of Chicago Press, 1990: 23.

Fiamingo, G. "Sociology in Italy: The Sociological Tendency of Today." *Quaderni di Sociologia* 29 (1980-81): 267, 270-71.

Fido, Franco. "At the Origins of Autobiography in the 18th and 19th Centuries: The *Topoi* of the Self." *Annali d'Italianistica* 4 (1976): 170-73.

Fisch, Max Harold. "The Academy of the Investigators." In *Science, Medicine, and History: Essays on the Evolution of Scientific Thought and Medical Practice Written in Honour of Charles Singer*, ed. E. A. Underwood. London and Toronto: Oxford University Press, 1953: 1:521-63.
_____. "The Critic of Institutions." *Proceedings and Addresses of the American Philosophical Association* 29 (1956): 42-56. Reprinted in *Studies in Philosophy and in the History of Science: Essays in Honor of Max Fisch*, ed. R. Tursman. Lawrence, KS: Coronado Press, 1970: 182-92.
_____. "The Philosophy of History: A Dialogue." *Philosophy* [*Tetsegaku*. Tokyo: Mita Philosophy Society, Keio University] 36 (1959): 149-70. Reprinted in *Studies in Philosophy and in the History of Science: Essays in Honor of Max Fisch*, ed. R. Tursman. Lawrence, KS: Coronado, 1970: 193-206.
_____. "Justice Holmes, the Prediction Theory of Law, and Pragmatism (1942)." In *Pierce, Semiotic, and Pragmatism: Essays by Max H. Fisch*, ed. K. L. Ketner and C. J. W. Kloesel. Bloomington: Indiana University Press, 1985: 16n, 22.
**Review:**
Barnouw, Jeffrey. *New Vico Studies* 5 (1987): 187-91.

Fisch, Max Harold. Review of *Philosophy in History: Essays on the Historiography of Philosophy* (ed. R. Rorty, J. B. Schneewind, and Q. Skinner). *New Vico Studies* 3 (1985): 208-9.
_____. Review of *Tractatus de signis: The Semiotic of John Poinsot* (trans. J. N. Deely). *New Vico Studies* 4 (1986): 179-82.
_____. "Thomas Goddard Bergin (1904-1987)" *New Vico Studies* 6 (1988): 189-90 [Obituary].

Fischer, Klaus P. *History and Prophecy: Oswald Spengler and the Decline of the West*. Bern: Peter Lang, 1989: 56, 88.

## PART III - WORKS CITING VICO / 109

*Review:*
Hutton, Patrick H. "Should Spengler be Reconsidered?" *New Vico Studies* 10 (1992): 78-82.

Fisher, Peter F. *The Valley of Vision: Blake as Prophet and Revolutionary*. ed. N. Frye. Toronto: University of Toronto Press, 1961: 179-80.

Fletcher, Angus. "Utopian History and the Anatomy of Criticism." In *Northrop Frye in Modern Criticism*, ed. M. Krieger. New York: Columbia University Press, 1966: 38, 45, 53, 71.
_____, ed. *The Literature of Fact*. New York: Columbia University Press, 1976: ix, xv.
_____. Review of *Prophets of Extremity: Nietzsche, Heidegger, Foucault, Derrida* (A. Megill). *New Vico Studies* 3 (1985): 209-11.
_____. "In Memoriam. Northrop Frye (1912-1991)." *New Vico Studies* 9 (1991): 152-54 [Obituary].
_____. *Colors of the Mind. Conjectures on Thinking and Literature*. Cambridge:, MA Harvard University Press, 1991: 12, 132, 147-165, 262.
_____. Review of *Words with Power: Being a Second Study of the Bible and Literature* (N. Frye). *New Vico Studies* 10 (1992): 116-20.
_____. Review of *Zeitgeist in Babel: The Postmodernist Controversy* (ed. I. Hoesterey). *New Vico Studies* 10 (1992): 132-34.

Flint, Robert. *The Philosophy of History in Europe*. Edinburgh: Blackwood, 1874: 1:26, 77, 96 n.1, 206, 286-87, 289, 290, 320-21, 324, 351 n.1.
_____. *Historical Philosophy in France and French Belgium and Switzerland*. London: Blackwood, 1893: 77, 124, 126, 158, 211, 227, 255-56, 264-66, 321, 382-83, 389-90, 480, 526, 530-32, 536, 568, 677, 684.
_____. *Philosophy as Scientia Scientiarum and a History of Classifications of the Sciences*. Edinburgh and London: Blackwood, 1904: 127-29.
*Review:*
Peirce, Charles Sanders. *Nation* 80 (1905): 360.

Forbes, Duncan. "'Scientific' Whiggism: Adam Smith and John Millar." *The Cambridge Journal* 8 (1954): 658.
_____. *The Liberal Anglican Idea of History*. Cambridge: Cambridge University Press, 1952: *passim*.

Formigari, Lia. "Language and Passions—or, I'm lost for words." *Topoi—An International Review of Philosophy* 6 (1987): 99-104.

Foss, Sonia K., Karen A. Foss, and Robert Trapp. *Contemporary Perspectives on Rhetoric*. Prospect Heights, IL: Waveland Press, 1985 (2d ed. 1991): 8, 149-51 *et passim*.

Foucault, Michel. *The Archaeology of Knowledge*, trans. A. M. S. Smith. New York: Harper, 1972: 158, 180.

Frank, Jerome. *Fate and Freedom*. New York: Simon and Schuster, 1945: 81, 237, 338.

Frascari, Marco. "The Professional Use of Signs in Architecture." *Journal of Architectural Education* 36 (1982): 17.
———. "A 'Measure' in Architecture. A Medical-Architectual Theory by Simone Stratico, Architetto Veneto." *res* 9 (1985): 81-83, 86.
———. "A New Angel/Angle in Architectural Research: The Ideas of Demonstration." *Journal of Architectural Education* 43 (1989): 11-19.
———. "The Particolareggiamento in the Narration of Architecture (Architectural Detailing as a Proper Way for Enhancing Architectural Imagination)." *Journal of Architectural Education* 43 (1989): 3-12.

Fraser, G. S. *The Modern Writer and His World*. New York: Penguin, 1964: 14, 277.

French, Marilyn. *The Book as World: James Joyce's "Ulysses."* Cambridge, MA: Harvard University Press, 1976: 279 n. 23.

Fromm, Eric. *Marx's Concept of Man*. New York: Ungar, 1961: 15.
———. *Myth and Metaphor: Selected Essays 1974-1988*, ed. R. D. Denham. Charlottesville: University Press of Virginia, 1990: 9, 22 *et passim*.
———. *Words with Power*. New York: Harcourt Brace Jovanovich, 1990: xii-xiii, 82, 112, 135, 221.

Frye, Northrop. "Quest and Cycle in *Finnegans Wake*." *James Joyce Review* 1 (1957): 41-44. Reprinted in *Fables of Identity—Studies in Poetic Mythology*. New York: Harcourt Brace Jovanovich, 1963: 258.
———. *Anatomy of Criticism: Four Essays*. Princeton, NJ: Princeton University Press, 1957: 62.
———. *The Critical Path*. Bloomington: Indiana University Press, 1971: 34, 38.
———. "The Responsibilities of the Critic." *Modern Language Notes* 91 (1976): 797-813.
———. *Spiritus Mundi—Essays in Literature, Myth, and Society*. Bloomington: Indiana University Press, 1976: 196.
———. *On Culture and Literature. A Collection of Review Essays*, ed. R. Denham. Chicago: University of Chicago Press, 1978: 33, 141, 145.
———. "The Rhythm of Growth and Decay." *Canadian Forum* 29 (1949). Reprinted in *Culture and Literature: A Collection of Review Essays*, ed. R. Denham. Chicago: University of Chicago Press, 1978: 141, 145.
———. *Creation and Recreation*. Toronto: University of Toronto Press, 1980: 6.
———. "Literary History." *New Literary History: A Journal of Theory and Interpretation* 12 (1981): 219, 220, 222. Reprinted as "Literature, History, and Language," in *The Horizon of Literature*, ed. P. Hernadi. Lincoln: University of Nebraska Press, 1982: 43-51.
———. *The Great Code: The Bible and Literature*. New York: Harcourt Brace Jovanovich, 1982: xix, 5, 13, 22, 56, 154.
**Review:**
Schwab, Gweneth B. *Christianity and Literature* 33 (1983): 87.

Frye, Northrop. "Blake's Biblical Illustrations." In *The Essays of Northrop Frye, 1979-1990. Eternal Act of Creation*, ed. R. D. Denham. Bloomington: Indiana University Press, 1993: 66, 69.

Fuentes, Carlos. *Terra Nostra*. New York: Farrar, Strauss, Giroux, 1975: *passim*.
———. "When Don Quixote Left His Village the Modern World Began." *New York Times Book Review* (23 March 1986): 15.
———. *Christopher Unborn*, trans. A. MacAdam and C. Fuentes. New York: Vintage, 1989: 132, 255, 278, 461, 463, 519 [Abstract: *New Vico Studies* 10 (1992): 128-29].

Fugate, Joseph K. *The Psychological Basis of Herder's Aesthetics*. The Hague: Mouton, 1966: 113, 115.

Fuller, Steve. "Does it pay to go post-modern if your neighbors do not?" In *After the Future: Postmodern Times and Places*, ed. G. Shapiro. Albany: State University of New York Press, 1990: 277-78.

Funkenstein, Amos. *Theology and the Scientific Imagination: From the Middle Ages to the Seventeenth Century*. Princeton, NJ: Princeton University Press, 1986: 202-13, 279-90, 328, 345.

Gabin, Rosalind J. Review of *Heracles' Bow: The Rhetoric and Poetics of the Law* (J. B. White). *New Vico Studies* 7 (1989): 146-48.

Gadamer, Hans-Georg. *Truth and Method*. New York: Seabury Press, 1975: 19-26, 30-31, 196, 200, 203, 245, 336.
———. "The Hermeneutics of Suspicion." In *Hermeneutics: Questions and Prospects*, ed. G. Shapiro and A. Sica. Amherst: University of Massachusetts Press, 1984: 55.
———. *The Idea of the Good in Platonic-Aristotelian Philosophy*. New Haven, CT: Yale University Press, 1988: 169.

Gallie, W. B. *Philosophy and the Historical Understanding*. New York: Schocken Books; London: Chatto & Windus, 1964: 11, 55, 127, 174.

Gaonkar, Dilip Parameshwar. "Rhetoric and Its Double: Reflections on the Rhetorical Turn in the Human Sciences." In *Invention and Persuasion in the Conduct of Inquiry*, ed. H. W. Simon. Chicago: University of Chicago Press, 1990: 356.

Gardner, Howard. *The Quest for Mind*. New York: Knopf, 1962: 238.
———. Review of *Language and Learning: The Debate between Piaget and Chomsky* (ed. M. Piattelli-Palmarini). *New Vico Studies* 1 (1983): 112-13.
———. *The Mind's New Science: A History of the Cognitive Revolution*. New York: Basic Books, 1985: 4.

Garrison, J. W. "Newton and the Relation of Mathematics to Natural Philosophy." *Journal of the History of Ideas* 48 (1987): 609-27.

Garver, Eugene. Review of *Rhetoric, Prudence and Skepticism in the Renaissance* (V. Kahn). *New Vico Studies* 5 (1987): 198-99.

Garvin, John. *James Joyce's Disunited Kingdom and the Irish Dimension.* Dublin: Gill; New York: Barnes and Noble, 1976: 126, 128.

Geertz, Clifford. *The Interpretation of Culture.* New York: Basic Books, 1973: 250.

Gehlen, Arnold. *Man: His Nature and Place in the World*, trans. C. McMillan and K. Pillemer. New York: Columbia University Press, 1988: 287, 295.
*Review:*
Schneck, Stephen. *New Vico Studies* 7 (1989): 145-46.

Gellner, Ernest. "Our Current Sense of History." In *The Historian between the Ethnologist and the Futurologist*, ed. J. Dumoulin and D. Moisi. Paris and The Hague: Mouton, 1973: 4-6.
_____. *Spectacles and Predicaments: Essays in Social Theory.* London: Cambridge University Press, 1979: 59.

Gentile, Giovanni. *The Theory of Mind as Pure Act*, trans. H. W. Carr. London: Macmillan, 1922: 15-16, 161, 166n, 196, 209, 215n, 244, 250.
_____. "The Transcending of Time in History." In *Philosophy of History*, ed. R. Klibansky and H. J. Paton. Oxford: Clarendon Press, 1936. Reprinted: New York: Harper & Row, 1963: 91.

Giddens, Anthony. *Studies in Social and Political Theory.* New York: Basic Books, 1977: 25.

Gifford, D., and Robert J. Seidman. *Notes for Joyce.* New York: E. P. Dutton, 1974: 20-21.

Gilbert, Katherine Everett, and Helmuth Kuhn. *A History of Esthetics.* New York: Macmillan, 1939: 268-74.

Gilbert, Katherine Everett. "Cassirer's Placement of Art." In *The Philosophy of Ernst Cassirer*, ed. P. A. Schilpp. Evanston, IL: Library of Living Philosophers, 1949. Reprinted New York: Tudor, 1958: 616; La Salle, IL: Open Court, 1973.

Gilbert, Stuart. "Prolegomena to *Work in Progress.*" In *Our Exagmination Round His Factification for Incamination of Work in Progress*, ed. S. Beckett *et al.* Paris: Shakespeare & Co; Norfolk, CT: New Directions, 1929: 51-54, 56.
_____. *James Joyce's "Ulysses."* New York: Vintage Press, 1955: 39 *et passim.*
_____, ed. *Letters of James Joyce.* New York: Viking, 1957: 241.

Giles, Henry. "The Leading Theories on the Philosophy of History." *North American Review* 95 (1862): 167-70.

Gillespie, Michael Patrick. *Inverted Volumes Improperly Arranged: James Joyce and His Trieste Library.* Ann Arbor: University of Michigan Research Press, 1980: 20.

Ginsberg, Robert, ed. *The Philosopher as Writer: The Eighteenth Century.* Cranbury, NJ: Susquehanna University Press, 1987: 9.

Giorgi, Amedeo. Review of *Actual Minds, Possible Worlds* (J. Bruner). *New Vico Studies* 6 (1988): 171-73.

Giovene, Andrea. *The Book of Sansevero*, trans. M. Waldman. Boston: Houghton Mifflin, 1970: 11.

Goethe, Johann Wolfgang von. *Italian Journey*, trans. W. H. Auden and E. Mayer. New York: Random, 1962: 183 (entry for 5 March 1787).

Goldberg, S. L. *The Classical Temper: A Study of Joyce's "Ulysses"*. London: Chatto and Windus, 1961: 67, 321.

Golden, James L., Goodwin F. Berquist, and William E. Coleman. *The Rhetoric of Western Thought* (3d ed). Dubuque, IA: Kendall-Hunt, 1983: 133-37.

Goldstein, Leon J. "Human Nature and Historical Knowledge." *History and Theory* 31 (1992): 56-65.

Goodfield, June. "Humanity in Science: A Perspective and a Plea." *Science* 198 (1977): 580-85.

Gordon, John. *James Joyce's Metamorphoses*. London: Gill; New York: Barnes and Noble, 1981: 2-3, 5, 10.

Gorman, David. "The Worldly Text: Writing as Social Action, Reading as Historical Reconstruction." In *Literary Theory Future(s)*, ed. J. Natoli. Urbana: University of Illinois Press, 1989: 185-86.

Gorman, Herbert. *James Joyce*. New York and Toronto: Farrar & Rinehart, 1929: 332-35.

Gorman, J. L. *The Expression of Historical Knowledge*. Edinburgh: Edinburgh University Press, 1982: 110-13 [Abstract: *New Vico Studies* 2 (1984): 140-41].
**Review:**
Palmer, Humphrey. *Philosophical Books* 24 (1983): 112.

Gose, Elliot B. *The Transformation Process in Joyce's "Ulysses."* Toronto: University of Toronto Press, 1980: xii, 60, 96.

Gottfried, Roy K. *The Art of Joyce's Syntax in "Ulysses."* Athens: University of Georgia Press, 1980: 43.

Gottschalk, Louis. *Understanding History*. New York: Knopf, 1950: 215.

Gould, Warwick. "A Crowded Theater: Yeats and de Balzac." In *Yeats the European*, ed. A. N. Jeffares. Savage, MD: Barnes and Noble, 1989: 69-90.

Gracia, Jorge J. E. *Philosophy and its History: Issues in Philosophical Historiography*. Albany: State University of New York Press, 1991: 68, 123.

Grafton, Anthony. "The Availability of Ancient Works." In The *Cambridge History of Renaissance Philosophy*, ed. C. B. Schmidt and Q. Skinner. Cambridge: Cambridge University Press, 1988: 781.

_____. *Defenders of the Text: The Traditions of Scholarship in an Age of Science, 1450-1800*. Cambridge, MA: Harvard University Press, 1991: 224.

Gramsci, A. *The Modern Prince and Other Writings*, trans. L. Marks. New York: International Publishers, 1957: 25.

_____. *Selections from the Prison Notebooks*, ed. Q. Hoare and G. N. Smith. New York: International Publishers, 1971: *passim*.

_____. *Letters from Prison*, trans. L. Lawner. New York: Harper & Row, 1973: 243.

_____. *Selections from Political Writings (1910-1920)*, ed. Q. Hoare. London: Lawrence and Wishart, 1977: 10.

Grassi, Ernesto. "Can Rhetoric Provide a New Basis for Philosophizing?" *Philosophy and Rhetoric* 11 (1978): 7, 79.

_____. "Italian Humanism and Heidegger's Thesis of the End of Philosophy." *Philosophy and Rhetoric* 13 (1980): 79, 92-94, 96.

_____. "The Philosophical and Rhetorical Significance of Ovid's Metamorphoses." *Philosophy and Rhetoric* 15 (1982): 261.

_____. *Heidegger and the Question of Renaissance Humanism*. Binghamton, NY: Center for Medieval and Early Renaissance Studies, 1983: 26-28, 38-39, 47, 61, 74, 78, 98, 99, 102 [Abstract: *New Vico Studies* 2 (1984): 139-40].

_____. "Remarks on German Idealism, Humanism, and the Philosophical Function of Rhetoric." *Philosophy and Rhetoric* 19 (1986): 127, 129, 131.

_____. *Folly and Insanity in Renaissance Literature*. Binghamton, NY: Center for Medieval and Early Renaissance Studies, 1986: *passim*.

_____. "The Originary Quality of the Poetic and Rhetorical Word: Heidegger, Ungaretti, and Neruda." *Philosophy and Rhetoric* 20 (1987): 248-60.

_____. *Renaissance Humanism. Studies in Philosophy and Poetics*. Binghamton, NY: Center for Medieval and Early Renaissance Studies, 1988: 35, 36, 71, 122, 125.

**Review:**
Blackwell, Jerome. *Journal of the History of Philosophy* 29 (1991): 486.

Grasso, Anthony Robert. "The Epistemology and Structure of Tennyson's 'In Memoriam': A Study of Poetic Development." Unpublished Ph.D. diss. University of Toronto, 1985.

Gratton, C. "Summaries of Selected Works on the Value of the Human." *Humanitas* 15 (1979): 241-46.

Gravelle, Sarah Stever. "Lorenzo Valla's Comparison of Latin and Greek, and the Humanist Background." *Bibliothèque d'Humanisme et Renaissance—Travaux et Documents*, vol. 44. Geneva: Libraire Droz, 1982: 271.

Gray, John. "The Unavoidable Conflict: Isaiah Berlin's Agonistic Liberalism." Review of *Isaiah Berlin: A Celebration* (ed. E. Ullmann-Margalit and A. Ullmann-Margalit). *London Times Literary Supplement* (5 July 1991): 3.

Greenblatt, Stephen J. *Learning to Curse: Essays in Early Modern Culture*. New York: Routledge, 1990: 31-32.

Greenleaf, W. H. *Order, Empiricism and Politics: Two Traditions of English Political Thought 1500-1700*. London: Oxford University Press, 1964: 264.

Grilli, Marcel. "The Nationality of Philosophy and Bertrando Spaventa." *Journal of the History of Ideas* 2 (1941): *passim*.

Grimsley, Ronald. *The Age of Enlightenment*. Harmondsworth: Penguin, 1979: 108-10, 116-27, 139, 140, 390.

Groden, M. *"Ulysses" in Progress*. Princeton, NJ: Princeton University Press, 1977: 36.

Grose, Kenneth. *James Joyce*. London: Evans Brothers Ltd., 1975: 129, 132, 138, 140.

Gross, John. *James Joyce*. New York: Viking Press, 1970: 25, 79.

Grosso, Michael. *The Final Choice—Playing the Survival Game*. Walpole, NH: Stillpoint, 1985: 300-27.

Grote, George. *A History of Greece*. 2d ed. London: John Murray, 1869-70: 1:341-43.

Grottanelli, Vinigi. "Ethnology and/or Cultural Anthropology in Italy: Traditions and Developments." *Current Anthropology* 18 (1977): 594.

Grun, Bernard. *The Timetables of History*. New York: Simon and Schuster, 1979: 304, 330, 342.

Gruner, Rolf. "Progressivism and Historicism." *Clio* 10 (1981): 279-90.

Guardiani, Francesco. "Interview with Northrop Frye." *Quaderni d'Italianistica* 9 (1986): 318-19.

Guardini, Romano. *The End of the Modern World*, ed. D. Wilhelmsen. New York: Sheed and Ward, 1956: 4.

Gueroult, Martial. *Descartes; Philosophy Interpreted According to the Order of Reasons*, trans. R. Ariew. Minneapolis: University of Minnesota Press, 1984: 1:258.

Gullace, Vincenzo. "Benedetto Croce and the Problem of Translation." *Italian Quarterly* 25 (1984): 15-27.

Gunn, Peter. *Naples: A Palimpsest.* London: Chapman and Hall, 1961: 130, 131, 135, 136, 160, 196, 253.

Gunnell, John G. *Political Philosophy and Time: Plato and the Origins of Political Vision.* Chicago: University of Chicago Press, 1987: 228, 249.

Gutmann, James. "Cassirer's Humanism." In *The Philosophy of Ernst Cassirer*, ed. P. A. Schilpp. New York: Tudor, 1958: 448.

Haac, Oscar A. *Jules Michelet.* Boston: Twayne Publishers, 1982: *passim*.
*Review:*
Piccolomini, Manfredi. *New Vico Studies* 2 (1984): 125-27.

Habermas, Jürgen. *Knowledge and Human Interests*, trans. J. Shapiro. Boston: Beacon Press, 1971: 148-49.
_____. *Theory and Practice*, trans. J. Viertel. Boston: Beacon Press, 1973: *passim*.

Haddock, B. A. *An Introduction to Historical Thought.* London: Edward Arnold, 1980: *passim* [Abstract: *New Vico Studies* 1 (1983): 117-18].
_____. Review of *Homer's Original Genius: Eighteenth-Century Notions of the Early Greek Epic (1688-1798)* (K. Simonsuuri). *New Vico Studies* 1 (1983): 109-11.
_____. Review of *The Iliad: A Commentary*, vol. 1 (Bks. 1-4) (G. S. Kirk). *New Vico Studies* 4 (1986): 185-86.
_____. "Sir Edmund Leach (1910-1989)." *New Vico Studies* 7 (1989): 156-57 [Obituary].

Hall, Vernon. "Joyce Eye to Eye with History." *Clio* 5 (1976): 303-306, 311, 312.

Halper, Nathan. *Studies in Joyce.* Ann Arbor: University of Michigan Research Press, 1983: 15, 16, 55.

Hamilton, Kenneth Gordon. *The Two Harmonies: Poetry and Prose in the Seventeenth Century.* Westport, CT: Greenwood Press, 1978: 178-80.

Hamilton, Peter. *Knowledge and Social Structure: An Introduction to the Classical Argument in the Sociology of Knowledge.* London: Routledge & Kegan Paul, 1974: 1-14.

Hamlyn, D. W. *The Penguin History of Western Philosophy.* London: Penguin Books, 1988: 206, 214-16.

Hampshire, Stuart. "Freedom and Explanation." In *The Idea of Freedom*, ed. A. Ryan. Oxford: Oxford University Press, 1979: 72, 75.
_____. *Morality and Conflict.* Cambridge, MA: Harvard University Press, 1983: 166-67.
*Review:*
Simon, Lawrence H. *New Vico Studies* 2 (1984): 131-34.

Hampshire, Stuart. *Innocence and Experience*. Cambridge, MA: Harvard University Press, 1989: 45-46.
_____. "Morality and Conflict." In *Anti-Theory in Ethics and Moral Conservatism*, ed. S. G. Clarke and E. Simpson. Albany: State University of New York Press, 1989: 152-53.

Hampson, Norman. *A Cultural History of the Enlightenment*. New York: Pantheon Books, 1968: 108, 234-38 [reprinted as *The Enlightenment*. Harmondsworth: Penguin, 1979].

Hardy, Henry. "A Bibliography of Isaiah Berlin." In *The Idea of Freedom*, ed. A Ryan. Oxford: Oxford University Press, 1979: 272, 280-81, 283-88.

Harris, H. S. "Another Unknown Page from the Last Months of Hegel's Life." In Harris and L. M. Palmer, eds., *Thought, Action, and Intuition: A Symposium on the Philosophy of Benedetto Croce*. Hildesheim and New York: Georg Olms Verlag, 1975: 136-40, 143.

Harris, Marvin. *The Rise of Anthropological Theory: A History of Theories of Culture*. New York: Crowell Press, 1968: 19-20, 27-28, 65, 269.

Harrison, Andrew. *Making and Thinking*. London: Harvester Press, 1978: 152.

Harrison, Barbara Grizzuti. *Italian Days*. New York: Weidenfeld & Nicholson, 1989: 167 *et passim*.

Hart, Clive. *Structure and Motif in "Finnegans Wake."* London: Faber and Faber, 1962: *passim*.

Hartmann, Geoffrey. "Romanticism in France." In *Romanticism: Vistas, Instances, Continuities*, ed. E. Thornburn and G. Hartman. Ithaca, NY: Cornell University Press, 1973: 55.
_____. *Criticism in the Wilderness. The Study of Literature Today*. New Haven, CT: Yale University Press, 1980: 33, 90, 111, 187, 215, 249n., 268.
_____. *Saving the Text: Literature, Derrida, Philosophy*. Baltimore: Johns Hopkins University Press, 1981: xv, 63.

Haskell, Francis. *Patrons and Painters: Art and Society in Baroque Italy*. New Haven, CT: Yale University Press, 1980: 320.

Haskell, Robert E., ed. *Cognition and Synthetic Structures: The Psychology of Metaphoric Transformation*. Norwood, NJ: Ablex, 1987: 67-82 *et passim*.

Hassan, Ihab. *The Postmodern Turn. Essays in Postmodern Theory and Culture*. Columbus: Ohio State University Press, 1987: 100, 113.

Hatton, Ragnhild. *Europe in the Age of Louis XIV*. New York: Harcourt, Brace & World, 1969: 180.

Hawkes, Terence. *Structuralism and Semiotics*. Berkeley: University of California Press, 1977: 11-15, 17-18, 32-33, 142, 160, 168, 185.

Hawkins, Richmond L. *August Comte and the United States*. Cambridge, MA: Harvard University Press, 1936: 42, 46, 119, 126.

Hayek, F. A. von. *Law, Legislation, and Liberty*, vol. 1. Chicago: University of Chicago Press, 1982.

Hazard, Paul. *European Thought in the Eighteenth Century*, trans. J. L. May. New Haven, CT: Yale University Press, 1954: 33, 35-37, 152, 246, 406.
―――. *The European Mind, 1680-1715*, trans. J. L. May. New York: World Publishing/ Meridian Books, 1963: 76, 130, 311, 412-14.

Headlam, Cecil. *The Story of Naples*. London: J. M. Dent and Sons, 1927: 174, 349.

Heath, Stephen. "Joyce in Language." In *James Joyce: New Perspectives*, ed. C. MacCabe. Sussex: Harvester Press; Bloomington: Indiana University Press, 1982: 129-31, 146 n.12.

Henke, Suzette A. *James Joyce and the Politics of Desire*. New York: Routledge, 1990: 166, 169, 190, 196, 208-9, 210.

Herberg, Will. *Faith Enacted As History: Essays in Biblical Theology*, ed. B. W. Anderson. Philadelphia: Westminster, 1976: 104-5, 108, 113.

Herkless, John L. Review of *Vorlesungen zur Geschichtheorie II* (K. Kluxen). *History and Theory* 22 (1983): 322.

Hermans, Hubert J. M. *et al.* "The Dialogical Self: Beyond Individualism and Rationalism." *American Psychologist* (Jan. 1992): 23-33.

Herr, Cheryl. *Joyce's Anatomy of Culture*. Chicago: University of Illinois Press, 1986: 13.

Hersey, George L. "Delacroix's Imagery in the Palais Bourbon Library." *Journal of the Warburg and Courtauld Institutes* 31 (1968): 389-403.
―――. *Architecture, Poetry, and Number in the Royal Palace at Caserta*. Cambridge: MIT Press, 1983: *passim* [Abstract in *The 18th Century: A Current Bibliography* n.s. 11 (1985): 293].
**Reviews:**
Braham, Allan. *London Times Literary Supplement* (14 Oct. 1983): 1122.
Pelzel, Thomas. *The 18th Century: A Current Bibliography*, n.s. 9 (1983): 342-43.
Coffin, David R. *Renaissance Quarterly* 37 (1984): 264-67.
Costa, Gustavo. *New Vico Studies* 2 (1984): 146-49.
Armstrong, Alison. *Progressive Architecture* 11 (1985): 135-36.
Saisselin, R. G. *The Eighteenth Century. Theory and Interpretation* 26 (1985): 178-86.

Herzen, Aleksander. *From the Other Shore*; and *The Russian People and Socialism: An Open Letter to Jules Michelet*, ed. I. Berlin. London and New York: G. Braziller, 1956: 34, 147.

Herzfeld, Michael. *Anthropology through the Looking Glass: Critical Ethnography in the Margins of Europe.* Cambridge: Cambridge University Press, 1987: vi, 3, 17, 22, 23-25, 32, 78-81.
*Reviews:*
Stewart, Charles. *Times Literary Supplement* (London) (6-12 Jan. 1989): 18.
White, Hayden. *New Vico Studies* 7 (1989): 126-29.

Herzfeld, Michael. "Of Definitions and Boundaries: The Status of Culture in the Culture of the State." In *Discourse and the Social Life of Meaning*, ed. P. P. Choch and J. R. Wyman. Washington: Smithsonian Institution, 1986: 75-76.

Hidalgo-Serna, Emilio. "The Philosophy of *Ingenium*: Concept and Ingenious Method in Baltasar Graciàn." *Philosophy and Rhetoric* 13 (1980): 245, 263n.
———. "*Ingenium* and Rhetoric in the Work of Vives." *Philosophy and Rhetoric* 16 (1983): 238n., 240n.

Highwater, Jamake. *The Primal Mind.* New York: New American Library, 1981: 21, 22.

Hill, Melvin A. "The Fictions of Mankind and the Stories of Man." In Hill, ed., *Hannah Arendt: The Recovery of the Public World.* New York: St. Martin Press, 1979: 298.

Hillman, James. *Re-Visioning Psychology*. New York: Harper & Row, 1975: *xi*, 16, 43, 156, 233-49 *passim.*

Hintikka, Jaakko. "Practical versus Theoretical Reason—An Ambiguous Legacy." In *Practical Reason*, ed. S. Körner. Oxford: Blackwell, 1974: 87-88.

Hirsch, E. D. Jr. *Validity in Interpretation*. New Haven and London: Yale University Press, 1967: 273.
———. *The Aims of Interpretation*. Chicago: University of Chicago Press, 1976: 41-42.

Hirschman, Albert O. *The Passions and the Interests. Political Arguments for Capitalism before Its Triumph*. Princeton, NJ: Princeton University Press, 1977: 14, 17, 19, 130.

Hobsbawm, Eric J., ed. *Marxism in Marx's Day. The History of Marxism*. Bloomington: Indiana University Press, 1982: 1:110, 198, 219n.

Hodgart, Matthew. *James Joyce: A Student's Guide.* London: Routledge & Kegan Paul, 1978: 133-34, 136-38, 149, 168, 170, 182.

Hodgen, Margaret Trabue. *Early Anthropology in the 16th and 17th Centuries.* Philadelphia: University of Pennsylvania Press, 1964: 492-97, 513.

Hodges, Herbert Arthur. *The Philosophy of Wilhelm Dilthey*. London: Routledge & Kegan Paul, 1952: xii, xvi, 186, 190, 236.

Holborn, Hajo. *History and the Humanities*. Garden City, NY: Doubleday, 1972: 16, 113.

Holbrook, Paul Evans, Jr. "The Metaphoric Function: Myth, Metaphor, and the Achievement of Meaning." Ph.D. diss. University of Kentucky, 1988 [Ann Arbor, MI: University Microfilms].

Hollinger, D. A. "Survival by Critical Selection in the Natural History of Art and Literature." *New Literary History* 6 (1975): 651-52.

Holmes, George F. "Schlegel's Philosophy of History." *Southern Quarterly Review* 3 (1843): 274-79.

Holub, Renate. "Critical Illiteracy: Humanism, Heidegger, Anti-Humanism." *Differentia* 3-4 (1989): 79-89.
_____. *Antonio Gramsci: Beyond Marxism and Postmodernism*. London and New York: Routledge, 1992: 170 n.37, 227-28.

Hone, Joseph. *W. B. Yeats*. New York: Macmillan, 1943: 95, 393f., 444.

Hopper, S. R., and D. L. Miller, eds. *Interpretation: The Poetry of Meaning*. New York: Harcourt, Brace and World, 1967: 105.

Howard, Roy J. *Three Faces of Hermeneutics*. Berkeley and Los Angeles: University of California Press, 1982: 82, 106.

Hoyningen-Huene, Paul. *Reconstructing Scientific Revolutions: Thomas S. Kuhn's Philosophy of Science*, trans. A. T. Levine. Chicago: University of Chicago Press, 1993: 128 (Vico quoted), 301.

Hughes, H. Stuart. *Oswald Spengler: A Critical Estimate*. New York: Scribner's Sons, 1952: 38-40, 53, 81, 94, 141.
_____. *Consciousness and Society: The Reorientation of European Social Thought, 1890-1930*. New York: Random House, 1958: 171-72, 198, 202, 205-6, 212, 270, 428.
_____. *History as Art and as Science*. New York: Harper & Row, 1964: 26-30, 36.

Hughes, Peter. *Spots of Time*. Toronto: CBC Publications, 1969: 23-26.
_____. "Language, History, and Vision: An Approach to Eighteenth-Century Literature." In Hughes and D. Williams, eds., *The Varied Pattern: Studies in the Eighteenth Century*. Toronto: A. M. Hakkert, 1971: 83, 88, 90, 92.
_____. "Restructuring Literary History: Implications for the Eighteenth Century." *New Literary History* 8 (1977): 258-60, 262-64, 270-74.

Humphries, J. "Shards from the Wreckage of History: Antimaxims in Modern Poetry." *South Atlantic Quarterly* 86 (1987): 22-23.

Hundert, E. T. "A Cognitive Ideal and Its Myth: Knowledge and Power in the Lexicon of the Enlightenment." *Social Research* 53 (1986): 149.

Huppert, George. *The Idea of Perfect History*. Urbana: University of Illinois Press, 1970: 166-67.

Hutchins, Patricia. *James Joyce's World*. London: Methuen and Co., 1957: 5.

Huth, Alfred H. *The Life and Writings of H. T. Buckle*. New York: Scribner & Welford, 1880: 234-49 *passim*.

Hutton, Patrick H. Review of *Cultural Analysis: The Work of Peter L. Berger, Mary Douglas, Michel Foucault, and Jürgen Habermas* (R. Wuthnow et al.). *New Vico Studies* 3 (1985): 211-13.
_____. Review of *The Structure of the Mind in History* (P. Romper). *History and Theory* 25 (1986): 191.
_____. Review of *Philosophical Profiles: Essays in the Pragmatic Mode* (R. J. Bernstein). *New Vico Studies* 4 (1986): 186-88.
_____. "The Art of Memory Reconceived: From Rhetoric to Psychoanalysis." *Journal of the History of Ideas* 48 (1987): 373, 376-92. Reprinted in *The History of Ideas: Canon and Variations*, ed. D. R. Kelley. Rochester: University of Rochester Press, 1990: 295-308 [Abstract in *New Vico Studies* 5 (1987): 209-10].
_____. Review of *Mythistory and Other Essays* (W. H. McNeill). *New Vico Studies* 6 (1988): 179-81.
_____. Review of *The Rise and Fall of the Great Powers: Economic Change and Military Conflict from 1500 to 2000* (P. Kennedy). *New Vico Studies* 7 (1989): 110-13.
_____. Review of "Fin-de-Siècle America" (P. Kennedy). *New York Review of Books* (28 June 1990). *New Vico Studies* 9 (1991): 136-37.
_____. "The Role of Memory in the Historiography of the French Revolution." *History and Theory* 30 (1991): 60, 61, 63, 65, 67, 68.

Iggers, Georg G. *The Doctrine of Saint-Simon*. New York: Schocken Books, 1958: 32.
_____. *The German Conception of History. The National Tradition of Historical Thought from Herder to the Present*. Middletown, CT: Wesleyan University Press, 1968: 30, 33, 219, 289.
_____. *New Directions in European Historiography*. Middletown, CT.: Wesleyan University Press, 1975: 15, 126.

Ijsseling, Samuel. *Rhetoric and Philosophy in Conflict: A Historical Survey*, trans. P. Dunphy. The Hague: Martinus Nijhoff, 1976: 57f.
**Review:**
Frankel, Margherita. *New Vico Studies* 1 (1983): 102-4.

Inman, Billie Andrew. *Walter Pater's Reading: A Bibliography of His Library Borrowings and Literary References, 1858-1873.* New York and London: Garland, 1981: 80, 148-57, 159, 166, 202, 206.

"Italian Literature of the Eighteenth Century." *Foreign Quarterly Review* 2 (1828): 628.

Jacobitti, Edmund. "Hegemony before Gramsci: The Case of Benedetto Croce." *Journal of Modern History* 52 (1980): 66-84 *et passim.*
_____. *Revolutionary Humanism and Historicism in Modern Italy.* New Haven, CT: Yale University Press, 1981 [Abstract: *New Vico Studies* 1 (1983): 115-17].
_____. "Taking Humanism Seriously: Science and Rhetoric in the Postmodern World." *Differentia* 3-4 (1989): 91-115.

Jacoby, Russell. "Isaiah Berlin: With the Current." *Salmagundi* 55 (1982): 235-36, 239.

James, Patrick. "Is *The Theory of History* (1914) Collingwood's First Essay on the Philosophy of History?" *History and Theory* 29: *Reassessing Collingwood* (1990): 1-13 *et passim.*

Jameson, Fredric. *Marxism and Form.* Princeton, NJ: Princeton University Press, 1971: 181.
_____. *The Prison House of Language: A Critical Account of Structuralism.* Princeton, NJ: Princeton University Press, 1971: 79, 80, 181-82.
_____. *The Political Unconsciousness.* Ithaca, NY: Cornell University Press, 1981: 28, 90, 130.

Jauss, Hans Robert. *Aesthetic Experience and Literary Hermeneutics.* Minneapolis: University of Minnesota Press, 1982: 52-54.

Jay, Martin. *The Dialectical Imagination: A History of the Frankfurt School and the Institute of Social Research, 1923-1950.* Boston: Little, Brown, 1973: 25, 49, 81, 257-58, 269.
_____. "Should Intellectual History Take a Linguistic Turn? Reflections on the Habermas-Gadamer Debate." In *Modern European Intellectual History*, ed. D. La Capra and S. Kaplan. Ithaca, NY: Cornell University Press, 1982: 87, 90.
_____. *Marxism and Totality.* Berkeley and Los Angeles: University of California Press, 1984: 32-39 *et passim.*

Jennings, J. R. *Georges Sorel—The Character and Development of His Thought.* New York: St. Martin's, 1985: 62-66, *et passim.*
**Review:**
Haddock, Bruce A. *New Vico Studies* 5 (1987): 191-92.

John-Steiner, Vera, and Marta Field. "Integrative Views of the Life of the Mind." Review of *Vygotsky and the Social Formation of the Mind* (J. V. Wertsch). *New Vico Studies* 6 (1988): 143-45.

Johnston, William H. *The Formative Years of R. G. Collingwood.* The Hague: Martinus Nijhoff, 1967: 67-68, 74-76, 87, 89 *et passim.*

Joll, James. *Antonio Gramsci*. Middlesex, UK: Penguin, 1977: 32, 142f., 148.

Joyce, James. *Finnegans Wake*. New York: Viking, 1939: 26, 32, 134, 215, 255, 260, 262, 452, 551, 614 *et passim*.
———. *Notes, Criticism, Translations, & Miscellaneous Writings*, ed. H. Gabler. New York: Garland, 1979: 2:391-93.

Jung, Hwa Yol. "Phenomenology as a Critique of Politics." *Human Studies* 5 (1982): 173, 175, 178-79.
———. *Rethinking Political Theory: Essays in Phenomenology and the Study of Politics*. Athens: Ohio University Press, 1993: 38-41 *et passim*.

Kadir, Djelal. *Questing Fictions. Latin America's Family Romance*. Minneapolis: University of Minnesota Press, 1986: ch. 2.

Kaempffert, W. "Story of a Materialist." *Saturday Review of Literature* (17 June 1944): 40.

Kahler, Erich. *The Meaning of History*. New York: G. Braziller, 1964: 41, 147, 157f., 214.
———. *Man the Measure*. Meridian Books, 1967 (originally published 1943): 582.

Kahn, Beverly H. "Hegemony and Italian History: The Philosophy of Antonio Gramsci." *Italian Quarterly* 24 (1983): 75, 93.

Kanai, Yoshihiko. "Stylistic Movement as Historical Pattern in James Joyce's *Ulysses*." *Shiron* 24 (1985): 59-78.

Kann, Robert A. *The Problem of Restoration: A Study in Comparative Political History*. Berkeley and Los Angeles: University of California Press, 1968: 28, 55.

Kaufmann, Edgar, Jr. "Memmo's Lodoli." *Art Bulletin* 46 (1964): 167-68, 170, 172.
———. "Lodoli, Carlo (Fra)" *Encyclopaedia of the Architects*. New York: Macmillan, 1982: 3:17-20.

Kearns, Sheila M. "Writing the Self: A Study in Romantic Autobiography." Unpublished Ph.D. diss. University of California (Irvine), 1984.

Kelley, Donald R. "Historical Thought and Legal Scholarship in Sixteenth Century France." Unpublished Ph.D. diss. Columbia University, 1962: *passim*.
———. *Foundations of Modern Historical Scholarship*. New York: Columbia University Press, 1970: 1, 6, 7, 44, 301, 303-5.
———. "History as a Calling: The Case of La Popelinière." In *Renaissance Studies in Honor of Hans Baron*, ed. A. Molho and J. A. Tedeschi. DeKalb: Northern Illinois University Press, 1971: 773.
———. "*Vera Philosophia*: The Philosophical Significance of Renaissance Jurisprudence." *Journal of the History of Philosophy* 14 (1976): 267-68, 271, 275, 279.

———. "Louis Le Caron Philosophe." In *Philosophy and Humanism: Renaissance Essays in Honor of Paul Oskar Kristeller*, ed. E. P. Mahoney. Leiden: E. J. Brill, 1976: 30-49 *passim*.

———. "The Metaphysics of Law: An Essay on the Very Young Marx." *American Historical Review* 83 (1978): 353.

———. "*Gaius Noster*: Substructures of Western Social Thought." *American Historical Review* 84 (1979): 637, 641-43, 647 [Abstract: *New Vico Studies* 1 (1983): 104.

———. Review of books by Seifert, Hassinger, Dubois, and Schlobach. *Journal of Modern History* 54 (1982): 321-22.

———. *Historians and the Law in Post-Revolutionary France*. Princeton, NJ: Princeton University Press, 1984: *passim*.

**Review:**
Stone, Harold. *New Vico Studies* 3 (1985): 197-98.

Kelley, Donald R. *History, Law and the Human Sciences*. London: Variorum Reprints, 1984: 27, 30 *et passim*.

———. Review of *A Study in the History of Classical Scholarship*, vol. 1, *Textual Criticism and Exegesis* (J. Scaliger). *History and Theory* 24 (1985): 84.

———. "Horizons of Intellectual History: Retrospect, Circumspect, Prospect." *Journal of the History of Ideas* 48 (1987): 148, 152, 153, 154, 156, 159, 163, 164, 167 [reprinted in D. R. Kelley, ed., *The History of Ideas: Canon and Variations*. Rochester, NY: University of Rochester Press, 1990: 322, 323, 333, 336].

———. "Ancient Verses on New Ideas: Legal Tradition and the French Historical School." *History and Theory* 26 (1987): 324-27, 335.

———. "The Theory of History." In *The Cambridge History of Renaissance Philosophy*, ed. C. B. Schmidt and Q. Skinner. Cambridge: Cambridge University Press, 1988: 757, 761.

———. "'History of Ideas': Canon and Variations." *Intellectual History Newsletter* 11 (1989): 29, 33, 34, 35, 36.

———. *The Human Measure: Social Thought in the Western Legal Tradition*. Cambridge and London: Havard University Press, 1990: 2, 44, 62, 191, 234-39 *et passim*.

**Reviews:**
Frier, Bruce W. *American Historical Review* 96 (1991): 1503-4.
Pocock, J. G. A. *New Vico Studies* 10 (1992): 101-6.

Kelley, Donald R. "What Is Happening to the History of Ideas?" *Journal of the History of Ideas* 51 (1990): 3, 8, 9, 10, 23.

———. *Renaissance Humanism*. Twayne's Studies in Intellectual and Cultural History, vol. 2. Boston: G. K. Hall, 1991: *passim*.

———, and Richard Popkin, eds. *The Shapes of Knowledge from the Renaissance to the Enlightenment*. International Archives of the History of Ideas, vol. 124. Dordrecht: Kluwer Academic Publishers, 1991: 2, 14, 15, 16, 18, 35.

Kelley, Donald R., ed. *Versions of History from Antiquity to the Enlightenment*. New Haven, CT: Yale University Press, 1991: 3, 5, 7, 16-17, 440, 474-77, 499, 503.

*Review:*
Hutton, Patrick. *New Vico Studies* 11 (1993): 111-14.

Kelley, Donald R. "*Tacitus Noster:* The *Germania* in the Renaissance and Reformation." In *Tacitus and the Tacitean Tradition*, ed. T. J. Luce and A. J. Woodman. Princeton, NJ: Princeton University Press, 1993: 165-67.

Kellner, Hans. "A Bedrock of Order: Hayden White's Linguistic Humanism." *History and Theory* 19 (1980): 3, 5, 6, 14, 24, 28.
_____. *Language and Historical Representation: Getting the Story Crooked*. Madison: University of Wisconsin Press, 1989: 198-200 *et passim*.

Kelly, A., and Henry Hardy, eds. *Russian Thinkers*. New York: Penguin, 1979: xvi, 140.

Kiernan, S. "Biography and Historiography in Early 18th-Century Italy: Their Ideological Function." *Eighteenth-Century Life* 11 (1987): 50-65.

Kim, Seong-Kon. "Journey into the Past: The Historical and Mythical Imagination of Barth and Pynchon." Unpublished Ph.D. diss. State University of New York (Buffalo): 1984: *passim*.

Kinsley, James. "The Music of the Heart." In *Critical Essays on Robert Burns*, ed. D. A. Low. London: Routledge and Kegan Paul, 1975: 124-36.

Kippur, Stephen A. *Jules Michelet: A Study of Mind and Sensibility*. Albany: State University of New York Press, 1981: xi, 25-27, 30-35, 37, 41, 45, 73, 77.
*Review:*
Piccolomini, Manfredi. *New Vico Studies* 2 (1984): 125-27.

Kitch, S. L. "Feminist Literary Criticism as Irony." *Rocky Mountain Review of Language and Literature* 41 (1987): 7-19.

Klein, A. M. "A Shout in the Street: An Analysis of the Second Chapter of Joyce's *Ulysses*." *New Directions in Prose and Poetry* 13 (1951): 327-45 *passim*.

Klein, Jacob. "History and the Liberal Arts." In *Lectures and Essays*, ed. R. B. Williamson and E. Zuckerman. Annapolis: St. John's University Press, 1985: 133-35.

Klemm, D. E. "Toward a Rhetoric of Postmodern Theology: Through Barth and Heidegger." *Journal of the American Academy of Religion* 55 (1987): 443-69.

Klibansky, Raymond, and H. J. Paton, eds. *Philosophy of History*. Oxford: Clarendon Press, 1936: 34-35, 324 (reprinted New York: Harper & Row, 1963).

Knapp, W. F. "Jules Michelet." *History Today* 2 (1952): 91.

Knight, William. *Philosophy of the Beautiful*. London: J. Murray, 1891: 146.

Knox, T. M. Preface to *The Idea of History* (R. G. Collingwood). London: Oxford University Press, 1946: viii.

Kolakowski, Leszek. *Main Currents of Marxism*, trans. P. Falla. Oxford: Clarendon Press, 1978: 2:144, 152, 155, 162, 178, 211; 3:524.
_____. "The Fantasy of Marxism." *Encounter* 50 (1978): 84.

Komesu, Okifumi. *The Double Perspective of Yeats's Aesthetic*. Totowa, NJ: Barnes and Noble, 1984: 36.

Kosik, Karel. *Dialectics of the Concrete*, trans. K. Kovanda (with J. Schmidt). Dordrecht, Holland: Reidel, 1976: 91.

Kovacs, Betty J. "The Return to the Goddess Creatrix in German Romanticism: A Challenge to the Masculine Trinity of Western Consciousness." Ph.D. diss. University of California (Irvine), 1987 [Ann Arbor, MI: University Microfilms].

Krader, Lawrence. *Introduction to the Ethnological Notebooks of Karl Marx*. Assen: Van Gorcum, 1972: 16, 52, 70, 391.

Kreiswirth, Martin. "Trusting the Tale: The Narrative Turn in the Human Sciences." *New Literary History* 23 (1992): 635.

Krieger, Leonard. *Time's Reasons. Philosophies of History, Old and New*. Chicago: University of Chicago Press, 1989: 36, 37-39, 43.

Kristeller, Paul Oskar. *Renaissance Thought: The Classic, Scholastic, and Humanistic Strains*. New York: Harper & Row, 1961: 18.
_____. *Renaissance Thought II: Papers on Humanism and the Arts*. New York: Harper & Row, 1965: 188.
_____. *Renaissance Thought and Its Sources*, ed. M. Mooney. New York: Columbia University Press, 1979: 13, 28, 250.
_____. "Philosophy and Its Historiography." *Journal of Philosophy* 82 (1985): 619.

Krois, John Michael. "Peirce's Speculative Rhetoric and the Problem of Natural Law." *Philosophy and Rhetoric* 14 (1981): 30n.
_____. Review of *Das Gesprach als Ereignis: Ein Semiotisches Problem*, ed. E. Grassi and H. Schmale. *Philosophy and Rhetoric* 17 (1984): 243, 244.
_____. *Cassirer: Symbolic Forms and History*. New Haven, CT: Yale University Press, 1987: xi, 123, 160.
**Review:**
Bergstrom, Timothy. *New Vico Studies* 6 (1988): 176-79.

Kukathas, Chandran. *Hayek and Modern Liberalism*. Oxford: Clarendon Press, 1989: 91, 206, 208.

Kunze, Donald E. Jr. "Commentary on 'Metaphorical Vision'." *Annals of the Association of American Geographers* 73 (1983): 153-56.

Kuypers, K. "The Relation between Knowing and Making as an Epistemological Principle." *Philosophy and Phenomenological Research* 35 (1974): 60-78, *passim*.

Kuzminski, Adrian. "Defending Historical Realism." *History and Theory* 18 (1979): 326, 335.

Labriola, Antonio. *Essays on the Materialist Conception of History*, trans. C. H. Kerr. New York and London: *Monthly Review* Press, 1966: 120-21, 163, 215-18, 232-33.

Lacan, Jacques. *Speech and Language in Psychoanalysis*, trans. A. Wilden. Baltimore: Johns Hopkins University Press, 1968: 132-33.

La Capra, Dominick. "A Poetics of Historiography: Hayden White's *Tropics of Discourse*." *Modern Language Notes* 93 (1978): 1037-43, *passim*. Reprinted in La Capra, *Rethinking Intellectual History: Texts, Contexts, Language*. Ithaca, NY: Cornell University Press, 1983: 73, 76-78.

Lachterman, David R. *The Ethics of Geometry: A Genealogy of Modernity*. New York: Routledge, 1989: xii, 7-9, 18, 71, 132, 209.
**Review:**
Page, Carl. "Mathematics and Modernity." *New Vico Studies* 8 (1990): 62-70.

Lachterman, David R. "Mathematics, Method, and Metaphysics: Essays toward a Genealogy of Modern Thought." Unpublished Ph.D. diss. The Pennsylvania State University, 1984.

Ladner, G. B. *The Idea of Reform: Its Impact on Christian Thought and Action in the Age of the Fathers*. New York: Harper Torchbooks, 1959: 23-24.

Lafargue, Paul. *Reminiscences of Marx and Engels*. Moscow: Foreign Languages Publishing House [n.d.]: 78.
_____. *Karl Marx: His Life and Work*. New York: International Publishers, 1943: 15.

Lana, Robert. *The Foundations of Psychology*. Hillsdale, NJ: Lawrence Erlbuam Associates, 1976: 41-47.

Land, Stephen K. "Universalism and Relativism: A Philosophical Problem of Translation in the Eighteenth Century." *Journal of the History of Ideas* 35 (1974): 606-8.
_____. *From Signs to Propositions: The Concept of Form in Eighteenth-Century Semantic Theory*. New York: Longman, 1974: 50-74.

Lang, Berel. *Philosophy and the Art of Writing*. Lewisburg: Bucknell University Press, 1983: 30.

Lasch, Christopher. *The World of Nations*. New York: Knopf, 1973: 312.

Leach, Edmund. *Claude Lévi-Strauss*. New York: Viking Press, 1970: 35, 129n.
_____. *Culture and Communication, The Logic by Which Symbols Are Created*. London: Cambridge University Press, 1976: 4.
_____. Review of *The Parable of the Tribes: The Problem of Power in Social Evolution* (A. B. Schmookler). *New Vico Studies* 4 (1986): 189-91.
_____. "Arian Warlords in Their Chariots." Review of *Black Athena: The Afro-Asiatic Roots of Classical Civilization*, vol. 1, *The Fabrication of Ancient Greece 1785-1985* (M. Bernal). *London Review of Books* (2 April 1987): 11.
_____. Review of *Anthropology and Myth: Lectures 1951-1982* (C. Lévi-Strauss). *New Vico Studies* 6 (1988): 173-76.
_____. "Word of Mouth." Review of *The Interface between the Written and the Oral* (J. Goody). *London Review of Books* (3 March 1988): 22.

Lecky, Elisabeth. *A Memoir of the Right Hon. William Edward Hartpole Lecky*. New York: Longmans, Green, 1909: 68f.

Lee, Vernon. *Studies of the 18th Century in Italy*. London: J. Fisher Unwin, 1907: 15, 28, 55, 226, 232, 367.

LeGoff, Jacques. *History and Memory*, trans. S. Rendall and E. Claman. New York: Columbia University Press, 1992: 163, 186.

Lentricchia, Frank. *After the New Criticism*. Chicago: University of Chicago Press, 1980: 107.

Levi, Albert William. *Philosophy and the Modern World*. Bloomington: Indiana University Press, 1959: 108, 520.
_____. *Literature, Philosophy, and the Imagination*. Bloomington: Indiana University Press, 1962: 60, 221-25.

Levin, Harry. *James Joyce: A Critical Introduction*. Norfolk, CT: New Directions, 1941: 133, 142-48, 156-57, 166, 168, 172, 177, 181-83, 190, 199.
_____. "Some Meanings of Myth." *Daedalus* 88 (1959): 226, 228.

Levin, Samuel R. *Metaphoric Worlds: Conceptions of a Romantic Nature*. New Haven, CT: Yale University Press, 1988.

Lévi-Strauss, Claude. *Structural Anthropology*, trans. M. Layton. New York: Basic Books, 1976: 2:332 [reprinted University of Chicago Press, 1983: 332].
_____. *The View from Afar*, trans. J. Neugroschel and P. Hoss. New York: Basic Books, 1984: 34-35.

***Reviews:***
Merquior, José Guilherme. *New Vico Studies* 3 (1985): 205-7.
Leach, Edmund. *New Vico Studies* 4 (1986): 191-96.

Lichtheim, George. *George Lukács.* New York: Viking Press, 1970: 16, 21-22, 33, 121, 132.
_____. *From Marx to Hegel.* New York: Herder and Herder, 1971: 16, 101, 111, 119.
_____. *Europe in the Twentieth Century.* London: Weidenfield and Nicholson, 1972: 221, 357, 358-62, 371.

Lieberson, Jonathan, and Sidney Morgenbesser. "The Questions of Isaiah Berlin." *New York Review of Books* (6 March 1980): 38, 40-42 *passim*; and *New York Review of Books* (20 March 1980): 31, 36. Reprinted in *Isaiah Berlin: A Celebration*, ed. E. and A. Ullmann-Margalit. London: Hogarth, 1991: see 2, 8, 10-15, 17, 24, 29- 30, 124, 140, 163-64..

Lieberson, Jonathan. "Karl Popper." *Social Research* 49 (1982): 98.

Lilla, Mark. "On Goodman, Putnam, and Rorty: The Return to the 'Given'." *Partisan Review* 2 (1984): 234.

Littleford, Michael. Review of *The Closing of the American Mind: How Higher Education Has Failed Democracy and Impoverished the Souls of Today's Students* (A. Bloom). *New Vico Studies* 6 (1988): 169-71.
_____. "Toward a Pragmatic Metaphysics: Comments on a Speculative Approach." Review of *Speculative Pragmatism* (S. B. Rosenthal). *Man and World* 26 (1993): 346n, 347n, 348n.

Litz, A. Walton. *The Art of James Joyce.* London: Oxford University Press, 1961: 60-62, 76, 96-97.
_____. *James Joyce.* New York: Twayne Publishers, 1966: 102-5.

Livingston, Donald W., and James T. King, eds. Introduction to *Hume: A Re-Evaluation.* New York: Fordam University Press, 1976: 15; see also D. W. Livingston, "Hume's Historical Theory of Meaning," 236.

Livingston, Donald W. *Hume's Philosophy of Common Life.* Chicago and London: University of Chicago Press, 1984: ix, 2, 129, 251, 287-88.

Lobner, Corinna del Greco. *James Joyce's Italian Connection: The Poetics of the Word.* Iowa City: University of Iowa, 1989: ix, 8, 82, 108.
***Review:***
Reynolds, Mary T. *New Vico Studies* 9 (1991): 134-35.

Lovejoy, Arthur O. "Herder and the Enlightenment Philosophy of History." In Lovejoy, *Essays in the History of Ideas*. Baltimore: Johns Hopkins University Press, 1948 [reprinted G. P. Putnam's Sons, 1960: 75].

Lovekin, David. "Technique and the Commonplace of the Commonplace." In *Commonplaces: Essays on the Nature of Place*, ed. D. W. Black, D. Kunze, and J. Pickles. Lenham, MD: University Press of America, 1989: 44-47.

Lucente, Gregory L. *The Narrative of Realism and Myth. Verga, Lawrence, Faulkner, Pavese*. Baltimore and London: Johns Hopkins University Press, 1981: 16, 26, 28-31, 32, 36, 51, 93, 140, 159 n.3, 164 n.1.
**Reviews:**
Cecchetti, Giovanni. *Italica* 62 (1985): 268.

Lucente, Gregory L. Review of *The Content of the Form: Narrative Discourse and Historical Representation* (H. White). *New Vico Studies* 6 (1988): 156-59.

Luft, Sandra Rudnick. "The Legitimacy of Hans Blumenberg's Conception of Originary Activity." *Annals of Scholarship* 5 (1987): 28-30, 35-36 [Abstract in *New Vico Studies* 7 (1989): 150-52].

Lukàcs, John. *Historical Consciousness or the Remembered Past*. New York: Harper and Roy, 1968: 17, 259-60.
———. "The Future of Historical Thinking." Review of *Clio and the Doctors* (J. Barzun). *Salmagundi* 30 (1975): 93.

MacCabe, Colin. *James Joyce and the Revolution of the World*. London: Macmillan, 1979: 157.
———, ed. *James Joyce: New Perspectives*. Sussex: Harvester Press; Bloomington: Indiana University Press, 1982: 33-35, 39.

McCabe, Joseph. *A Biographical Dictionary of Modern Rationalists*. London: Watts: 1920: 842f.

Mac Cannell, Juliet Flower. *Figuring Lacan. Criticism and the Cultural Unconscious*. Lincoln: University of Nebraska Press, 1986: 91.

McCarthy, Patrick A. *The Riddles of "Finnegans Wake."* Rutherford, NJ: Fairleigh Dickinson University Press; London and Toronto: Associated University Presses, 1980: 31 *et passim*.

McCarthy, Thomas. *The Critical Theory of Jürgen Habermas*. Cambridge: MIT Press, 1978: 1.

McCormack, W. J., and Alistair Stead, eds. *James Joyce and Modern Literature*. London and Boston: Routledge & Kegan Paul, 1982: 169, 173-74, 181, 186, 203, 211.

McCormick, Peter. *Modernity, Aesthetics, and the Bounds of Art*. Ithaca, NY: Cornell University Press, 1990: 71, 72, 80, 167 *et passim*.

McGee, Patrick. *Paperspace: Style as Idealogy in Joyce's Ulysses.* Lincoln: University of Nebraska Press, 1988: 12, 202, 213.

Machievich, W. "The Philosophy of Stanislaw Brzozowski: Its Origin and Influence." *Dialectics and Humanism* 2 (1980): 103-13.

McHugh, Roland. *The Sigla of "Finnegans Wake."* Austin: University of Texas Press, 1976: 5, 18, 60, 62, 67, 92, 101, 118-19.

_____. *The "Finnegans Wake" Experience.* Berkeley: University of California Press; Dublin: Irish Academic Press, 1981: 4-5, 18, 22, 29-30, 48, 100, 105.

McInnes, Neil. "Georges Sorel." In *The Encyclopedia of Philosophy*, vol. 7. New York: Collier-Macmillan, 1967: 498.

MacIntyre, Alasdair. *A Short History of Ethics.* New York: Macmillan, 1966: 179.

_____. *After Virtue: A Study in Moral Theory.* Notre Dame, IN: University of Notre Dame Press, 1981: 5, 201 [Vico mention on 201 reprinted in A. J. Ayer and J. O'Grady, eds., *A Dictionary of Philosophical Quotations.* Oxford: Basil Blackwell, 1992: 275].

_____. "The Relationship of Philosophy to Its Past." In *Philosophy in History*, eds. R. Rorty, J. B. Schneewind, and Q. Skinner. Cambridge: Cambridge University Press, 1984: 47.

_____. "Relativism, Power, and Philosophy." *Proceedings and Addresses of the American Philosophical Association* 59 (1985): 6, 9, 21 [reprinted in *After Philosophy: End or Transformation?*, ed. K. Baynes *et al.*, Cambridge: MIT Press, 1987: 387, 392, 410].

_____. "The Relationship of Philosophy to History: Postscript to the Second Edition of *After Virtue.*" In *After Philosophy: End or Transformation?* (K. Baynes *et al.*). Cambridge, MA: MIT Press, 1987: 413.

_____. *Whose Justice? Which Rationality?* Notre Dame, IN: University of Notre Dame Press, 1988: 57, 222.

_____. "Epistemological Crises, Dramatic Narrative and the Philosophy of Science." In *Anti-Theory in Ethics and Moral Conservatism*, ed. S. G. Clarke and E. Simpson. Albany: State University of New York, 1989: 246.

_____. *Three Rival Versions of Moral Enquiry: Encyclopaedia, Genealogy, and Tradition: Being Gifford Lectures Delivered in the University of Edinburgh in 1988.* Notre Dame, IN: University of Notre Dame Press, 1990: 22.

McKeon, Richard. "The Philosophic Bases of Art and Criticism." In *Critics and Criticism*, ed. R. S. Crane. Chicago: University of Chicago Press, 1952: 503-4.

McLain, Evelyn N. "'Alle Schiffe Brücken': Joyce's 'Ulysses' Resolved." *South Central Bulletin* 30 (1970): 209-11.

McLuhan, Marshall. *The Gutenberg Galaxy: The Making of Typographic Man.* Toronto: University of Toronto Press, 1962: 249-50.

_____. *The Interior Landscape*, ed. E. McNamara. New York: McGraw-Hil, 1969: 161.

_____. *Letters of Marshall McLuhan*, ed. M. Molmaro, L. McLuhan, and W. Toye. Toronto: Oxford University Press, 1987: 221, 339n, 369, 375n, 385, 525.

_____, and Eric McLuhan. *Laws of Media: The New Science*. Toronto: University of Toronto Press, 1988: *x-xi*, 219-23, 250.
**Review:**
Weir, Lorraine. *New Vico Studies* 8 (1990): 142-45.

McMullen, Roy. *Art, Affluence, and Alienation*. New York: F. A. Praeger, 1968: 259.

MacNeice, Louis. *The Poetry of W. B. Yeats*. New York: Oxford University Press, 1941: 126.

McNeil, Lynda D. *Recreating the World/Word. The Mythic Mode as Symbolic Discourse*. Albany: State University of New York Press, 1992: 30, 40, 63.

Maddox, James H., Jr. *Joyce's "Ulysses" and the Assault upon Character*. New Brunswick, NJ: Rutgers University Press, 1978: 180.

Madison, G. B. *The Hermeneutics of Postmodernity: Figures and Themes*. Bloomington: Indiana University Press, 1988: 164.
**Review:**
Palmer, Lucia M. *New Vico Studies* 11 (1993): 116-19.

Maestro, Marcello. *Cesare Beccaria and the Origins of Penal Reform*. Philadelphia: Temple University Press, 1973: 4.

_____. "Gaetano Filangieri and His 'Science of Legislation.'" *Transactions of the American Philosophical Society* 66 (n.s.) (1976): 6, 9, 55.

Magalaner, Marvin. *Time of Apprenticeship: The Fiction of Young James Joyce*. London: Abelard-Schuman, 1959: 34.

_____. and Richard M. Kain. *Joyce: The Man, the Work, the Reputation*. New York: New York University Press, 1956: 205 *et passim*.

Mahootian, Farzad. "The Relevance of Myth to Science." Unpublished Ph.D. diss. Fordham University, 1990.

Mailer, Norman. *Harlot's Ghost*. New York: Random House: 1991: *passim*.
**Review:**
Leonard, John. "The Trouble with Harry." *The Nation* (18 Nov. 1991): 622, 628.

Major-Poetzl, Pamela. *Michel Foucault's Archaeology of Western Culture*. Chapel Hill: University of North Carolina Press, 1983: 199, 242 n.12.

Makkai, Adam. "Idiomaticity and Phraseology in Post-Chomskian Linguistics: The Coming-of-Age of Semantics beyond the Sentence." *Semiotica* 64 (1987): 171-87.

Makkreel, Rudolf A. Review of *Wilhelm Dilthey: The Critique of Historical Reason* (M. Ermarth). *History and Theory* 19 (1980): 362.
_____. *Imagination and Interpretation in Kant*. Chicago: University of Chicago Press, 1990: 157, 165, 167.

Mandelbaum, Maurice. *History, Man, and Reason: A Study of Nineteenth-Century Thought*. Baltimore: Johns Hopkins University Press, 1971: 182, 481n.
_____. *The Anatomy of Historical Knowledge*. Baltimore: Johns Hopkins University Press, 1977: 157.

Manganiello, Dominic. *Joyce's Politics*. London: Routledge & Kegan Paul, 1980: 58, 224-28.

Manion, Christopher. "The Philosophy of History of Juan Donoso Cortes." Unpublished Ph.D. diss. University of Notre Dame, 1980.

Manuel, Frank E. "In Defense of Philosophical History." *Antioch Review* 20 (1960): 331-43.
_____. *The Prophets of Paris*. Cambridge, MA: Harvard University Press, 1962; reprinted New York: Harper & Row, 1965: 14 *et passim*.
_____. *Isaac Newton Historian*. Cambridge: Cambridge University Press, 1963: 43.
_____. *Shapes of Philosophical History*. Stanford, CA: Stanford University Press, 1965: 40 *et passim*.
_____. "The Use and Abuse of Psychology in History." *Daedalus* 100 (1971): 188-90; reprinted in *Varieties of Psychohistory*, ed. G. M. Kren and L. H. Rappoport. New York: Springer Publishing Co., 1976: 40-41.
_____. *Freedom from History and Other Untimely Essays*. New York: New York University Press, 1971: 7, 18-19, 25-27, 54-58, 61-64, 244.
_____. "Michelet and the Philosophy of History." *Clio* 6 (1977): 149-65 *passim*.
_____. *The Changing of the Gods*. Hanover, NH: University Press of New England, 1983: 54 *et passim*.
_____, and Fritzie P. Manuel. *Utopian Thought in the Western World*. Cambridge, MA: Belknap Press, 1979: 317 *et passim*.

Manzoni, Alessandro. *On the Historical Novel*, trans. S. Bermann. Lincoln: University of Nebraska Press, 1984: *passim*.
**Review:**
Burke, John J. Jr. *The 18th Century: A Current Bibliography*, n.s. 10 (1984): 475-77.

Marassi, Massimo. "Rhetoric and Historicity. An Introduction." *Philosophy and Rhetoric* 21 (1988): 245, 248, 251, 258.

Marcel, Gabriel. "I and Thou." In *The Philosophy of Martin Buber*, ed. P. A. Schilpp and M. Friedman. London: Cambridge University Press, 1967: 47.

Márcus, György. "The Paradigm of Language: Wittgenstein, Lévi-Strauss, Gadamer." In *The Structural Allegory: Reconstructive Encounters with the New French Thought*, ed. J. Fekete. Minneapolis: University of Minnesota Press, 1984: 109.

Marcus, John T. *Sub Specie Historiae: Essays in the Manifestation of Historical and Moral Consciousness*. Rutherford, NJ: Fairleigh Dickinson Press, 1980: 52, 146-47.

Marcus, Phillip L. *Yeats and the Beginning of the Irish Renaissance* (2d ed.). Syracuse, NY: Syracuse University Press: 1987: 244, 272.

Margalit, Edna Ullmann, and Avishai Margalit, eds. *Isaiah Berlin: A Celebration*. Chicago: Hogarth, 1991: 2, 8, 10-15, 17, 24, 29, 30, 128, 140, 163, 164.

Marino, John A. "The State and the Shepherds in Pre-Enlightenment Naples." *Journal of Modern History* 58 (1986): 126, 138-39.

Martin, Kingsley. *French Liberal Thought in the Eighteenth Century*. New York: Harper Torchbooks, 1962: 148, 152.

Martindale, Colin. "Theories of the Evolution of Consciousness." *Journal of Altered States of Consciousness* 3 (1977-78): 261-78 *passim*.

Marvin, F. S. *The Century of Hope: A Sketch of Western Progress from 1815 to the Great War*. Oxford: Clarendon Press, 1921: 68.

Marwick, Arthur. *The Nature of History*. New York: Alfred A. Knopf, 1971: 37, 45.

Marx, Karl. *Capital*, ed. F. Engels, trans. S. Moore and E. Aveling. Moscow: Progress Publishers, 1965: 372 n.3. Reprinted New York: International Publishers, 1967: 367 n.1.

Masur, Gerhard. *Prophets of Yesterday: Studies in European Culture, 1890-1914*. New York: Harper, 1961: 265.

Mayr, Ernst. *The Growth of Biological Thought*. Cambridge, MA and London: Belknap Press of Harvard University, 1982: 40, 311.

Mazlish, Bruce. *A New Science: The Breakdown of Connections, and the Birth of Sociology*. New York: Oxford University Press, 1990: 175, 176, 192, 210.

Mazzeo, Joseph A. *Renaissance and Seventeenth Century Studies*. New York: Columbia University Press, 1964: 51-52.
———. "Some Interpretations of the History of Ideas." *Journal of the History of Ideas* 33 (1972): 381.
———. *Varieties of Interpretation*. Notre Dame, IN: University of Notre Dame Press, 1978: 27-28, 32-33, 39.

Mazzotta, Giuseppe. *Dante's Vision and the Circle of Knowledge*. Princeton, NJ: Princeton University Press, 1992: x, xi, 15, 152.

Megill, Allan. "Aesthetic Theory and Historical Consciousness in the Eighteenth Century." *History and Theory* 17 (1978): 29-62 *passim.*
_____. Review of *The Anti-Aesthetic: Essays on Postmodern Culture* (ed. H. Foster). *New Vico Studies* 3 (1985): 212-15.
_____. Review of *The Rhetoric of Economics* (D. N. McCloskey). *New Vico Studies* 4 (1986): 195-96.
_____. "On Postmodernism." *New Vico Studies* 11 (1993): 67-76.

Meisel, James H. *The Myth of the Ruling Class: Gaetano Mosca and the 'Elite'.* Ann Arbor: University of Michigan Press, 1958. Reprinted Ann Arbor, MI: Ann Arbor Paperbacks, 1962: 30, 39, 139, 200, 242, 258, 267.

Melko, Matthew. *The Nature of Civilizations.* Boston: Porter-Sargent Books, 1969: 5, 189, 194, 197.
***Review:***
Toynbee, A. *History and Theory* 10 (1971): 24-48 *passim.*

Mellor, Ronald. *Tacitus.* New York and London: Routledge, 1993: 154-55.

Melotti, Umberto. *Marx and the Third World*, trans. P. Ransford. Atlantic Highlands, NJ: Humanities Press, 1977: 92.

Merquior, José Guilherme. *The Veil and the Mask.* Boston: Routledge & Kegan Paul, 1979: 116.

Meszaros, Istvan. *Marx's Theory of Alienation.* London: Merlin Press, 1970: 41, 70, 316.

Meyerhoff, Hans. *The Philosophy of History in Our Time.* Garden City, NY: Doubleday, 1959: 5, 7.

Michelet, Jules. *The People*, trans. J. P. McKay. Urbana: University of Illinois, 1973: xv, xviii, 121.

Middleton, Robin. "Giovan Battista Piranesi (1730-1778): Review of Recent Literature." *Journal of the Society of Architectural Historians* 41 (1982): 339.

Milbank, John. "Theology without Substance: Christianity, Signs, Origins." *Literature and Theology* 2 (1988): 1-17, 131-52 *passim.*

Mill, John Stuart. *System of Logic, Ratiocinative and Inductive* (London, 1843), vol. 2, ch. 3. Reprinted in *Collected Works.* London: Routledge & Kegan Paul; Toronto: University of Toronto Press, 1974: 8:914.

Milman, Henry Hart. "Origin of the Homeric Poems." *Quarterly Review* 44 (1831): 128f.

Mink, Louis O. *Mind, History, and Dialectics: The Philosophy of R. G. Collingwood.* Bloomington: Indiana University Press, 1969: 6, 174, 196, 208.

Mitzman, Arthur. *Michelet, Historian: Rebirth of Romanticism in 19th-Century France.* New Haven, CT and London: Yale University Press, 1990: 14f., 47, 180.
*Review:*
Rearick, Charles. *American Historical Review* 96 (1991): 1555-56.

Mohan, Robert Paul. *Philosophy of History.* New York: Bruce, 1970: 51-65 *passim.*

Momigliano, Arnaldo. "Ancient History and the Antiquarian." *Studies in Historiography.* New York: Harper & Row; London: Wiedenfeld and Nicholson, 1966: 19, 106.
_____. "Gibbon from an Italian Point of View." *Daedalus* 107 (1976): 128-30, 132-34.
_____. "Polybius between the English and the Turks." In *Sesto Contributo alla storia degli studi classici e del mondo antico.* Rome: Edizioni di Storia e Letterature, 1980: 1:125-41.
_____. *On Pagans, Jews, and Christians.* Middletown, CT: Wesleyan University Press, 1987: 6, 26.
_____. *The Classical Foundations of Modern Historiography.* Berkeley: University of California Press, 1990: 75, 127.
*Review:*
Page, Carl. *New Vico Studies* 9 (1991): 114, 115.

Monas, Sidney. Review of *After Bakhtin: Essays on Fiction and Criticism* (D. Lodge). *New Vico Studies* 10 (1992): 134-36.

Montagu, M. F. Ashley. "Cassirer on Mythological Thinking." In *The Philosophy of Ernst Cassirer*, ed. P. A. Schilpp. New York: Tudor, 1958: 368.

"Monti and the Italian Writers of the Eighteenth Century." *Athenaeum* (22 Oct. 1828): 825 *et passim.*

Mooney, Michael. "In Memoriam. A. Robert Caponigri." *New Vico Studies* 2 (1984): 174-76 [Obituary].
_____. Review of "Retoriche e poetiche dominanti" (A. Battistini and E. Raimondi). *New Vico Studies* 4 (1986): 196-99.

Moravia, Sergio. *Filosofia e scienze umane nell'età dei lumi.* Florence: Sansoni, 1982 [Abstract in *New Vico Studies* 2 (1984): 155].

Morison, G. B. *The Hermeneutics of Postmodernity. Figures and Themes.* Bloomington: Indiana University Press, 1988: 164.

Morrall, John B. *The Medieval Imprint: The Founding of the Western European Tradition.* New York: Penguin, 1967: 21-22.

Morris, Wesley. *Toward a New Historicism*. Princeton, NJ: Princeton University Press, 1972: 72, 95, 97, 139n.

Morse, J. Mitchell. "Where Terms Begin." In M. H. Begnal and F. Senn, eds., *A Conceptual Guide to "Finnegans Wake."* University Park and London: The Pennsylvania State University Press, 1974.

Moseley, Virginia. *Joyce and the Bible*. DeKalb: Northern Illinois University Press, 1967: 134, 147-48.

Moss, Myra E. *Benedetto Croce Reconsidered: Truth and Error in Theories of Art, Literature, and History*. Hanover, NH: University Press of New England, 1987: 10, 13, 22, 35, 36, 41, 43, 44, 61, 98, 110.
_____. "The Crocean Concept of the Pure Concept." *Idealistic Studies* 17 (1987): 39-52.
_____, ed. and trans. *Benedetto Croce: Essays on Literature and Literary Criticism*. Albany: State University of New York Press, 1990: 1-2, 49, 52-53, 123, 149, 152, 154.

Mueller, Lauren E. "Semiotics in Italy: Cesare Segre, Gianfranco Bettini, Pier Paolo Pasolini, Emilio Garroni." Unpublished Ph.D. diss. Purdue University, 1982.

Mueller-Vollmer, Kurt, ed. *The Hermeneutic Reader: Texts of the German Tradition from the Enlightenment to the Present*. New York: Continuum, 1985: 19, 260.

Mumford, Lewis. *The Condition of Man*. New York: Harcourt, Brace and World, 1944: 263, 271, 274, 365-66.
_____. *Interpretations and Forecasts: 1922-1972*. New York: Harcourt Brace Jovanovich, 1972: 185, 189, 191, 202.
_____. *My Works and Days: A Personal Chronicle*. New York: Harcourt Brace Jovanovich, 1979: 16, 192, 479.

Munz, Peter. Introduction to *Italian Humanism* (E. Garin), trans. P. Munz. New York: Harper & Row, 1965: xxii *et passim*.
_____. *When the Golden Bough Breaks: Structuralism or Typology?* London: Routledge & Kegan Paul, 1973: 107, 120-21 [Abstract: *New Vico Studies* 1 (1983): 105-7].
_____. "Early European History and African Anthropology." *New Zealand Journal of History* 10 (1976): 44.
_____. *The Shapes of Time*. Middletown, CT: Wesleyan University Press, 1977: 2, 11, 43, 190n., 210, 250, 338f., 348 [Abstract: *New Vico Studies* 1 (1983): 107-9].
*Review:*
Kelley, Donald R. *Humanities in Society* 2 (1979): 170.

Munz, Peter. "Gesta Dei per Australianos." *Australia 1888* 3 (1979): 23-24.
_____. Review of *On Pursuit of Truth: Essays on the Philosophy of Karl Popper on the Occasion of His 80th Birthday* (ed. P. Levinson) and of *Popper Selections* (ed. D. Miller). *New Vico Studies* 3 (1985): 207-8.

_____. *Our Knowledge of the Growth of Knowledge. Popper or Wittgenstein?* London: Routledge & Kegan Paul, 1985: 78.
**Review:**
Perkinson, Henry. *New Vico Studies* 4 (1986): 204-7.

Munz, Peter. "The Rhetoric of Rhetoric." *Journal of the History of Ideas* 51 (1990): 136, 139, 141.
_____. "What's Postmodern, Anyway?" *Philosophy and Literature* 16 (1992): 348.
_____. *Philosophical Darwinism. On the Origin of Knowledge by Means of Natural Selection.* London and New York: Routledge, 1993: 112.

Murillo, L. A. *The Critical Night: Irony in James Joyce and Jorge Luis Borges.* Cambridge, MA: Harvard University Press, 1968: 99.

Murray, Michael. *Modern Philosophy of History: Its Origin and Destination.* The Hague: Martinus Nijhoff, 1970: 89-91.

Natoli, Joseph, ed. *Literary Theory's Future.* Urbana: University of Illinois Press, 1989: 10, 27 n.12.

Neff, Emery. *The Poetry of History.* New York: Columbia University Press, 1947: 83-88, 96, 98, 131-33, 136-37, 140, 157.

Nelson, John S. "Ironic Politics: Critical Commitment in the Fourth Age." Unpublished Ph.D. diss. University of North Carolina (Chapel Hill), 1977.
_____, and Allan Megill. "Rhetoric of Inquiry: Projects and Prospects." *Quarterly Journal of Speech* 72 (1986): 20-37.

Neumann, Franz. Introduction to *The Spirit of the Laws of Baron de Montesquieu,* trans. T. Nugent. New York: Hafner, 1966: xxxviii.

Nichols, Stephen G., Jr. "The Spirit of Truth: Epic Modes in Medieval Literature." *New Literary History* 1 (1970): 372.

Nisbet, Robert. *History of the Idea of Progress.* New York: Basic Books, 1980: 136, 160-67 *passim*, 182.

Noakes, Susan. *Timely Reading—Between Exegesis and Interpretation.* Ithaca, NY: Cornell University Press, 1988 [Abstract in *New Vico Studies* 7 (1989): 141].
_____. Review of *The Hermeneutic Tradition: From Ast to Ricoeur* (ed. G. L. Ormiston and A. D. Schrift). *New Vico Studies* 8 (1990): 126-27.
_____. Review of *Ascoltare il silenzio: la retorica come teoria.* Collezione di testi e di studi. Linguistica e critica letteraria (P. Valesio). *New Vico Studies* 8 (1990): 130-31.

Noland, Aaron. "History and Humanity: The Proudhonian Vision." In *The Uses of History,* ed. H. White. Detroit, MI: Wayne State University Press, 1968: 69-70.

Nordau, Max. *The Interpretation of History*, trans. M. A. Hamilton. New York: Willey Book Company, 1910: 68, 71, 297, 319, 357.

Norris, Margot. *The Decentered Universe of "Finnegans Wake."* Baltimore, MD: Johns Hopkins University Press, 1974: 54-61 *passim*.

Novak, Erwin Emilian. "Providence and the West: The Hungarian Catalyst." Unpublished Ph.D. diss. University of Dallas (Texas), 1974: pt. 3.

Nun, J. "Elements for a Theory of Democracy: Gramsci and Common-sense." *Boundary Two—A Journal of Postmodern Literature and Culture* 14 (1988): 197ff.

Oakeshott, Michael. "The Voice of Poetry in the Conversation of Mankind." In *Rationalism and Politics*. New York: Basic Books, 1962: 240 n.2. Reprinted Liberty Press, 1991: 533 n.34.

O'Banion, John D. *Reorienting Rhetoric: The Dialectic of History and Story*. University Park: Pennsylvania State University Press, 1991: 3, 89, 150, 183, 194, 196, 245, 273.

Ollman, Bertell. *Alienation: Marx's Concept of Man in Capitalist Society*. Cambridge: The University Press, 1971: 259 n.24.

Olsson, Gunnar. "Of Ambiguity or Far Cries from a Memorializing Mamafesta." In *Humanistic Orientations in Geography*, ed. D. Ley and M. Samuels. Chicago: Maroufa Press, 1978: 109-20 *passim*.
_____. "The New Social Science: Toward a Mandala of Thought and Action." In *Analysis and Decision in Regional Policy*, ed. I. G. Cullen. London: Pion, 1979: 7-19 *passim*.
_____. "On Yearnings for Home: An Epistemological View of Ontological Transformations." In *Humanistic Geography and Literature*, ed. D. C. D. Pocock. London: Croom Helm, 1981: 121-29 *passim*.
_____. "Thunderbolts on Herons Shore." In *Space and Time in Geography. Essays Dedicated to Torsten Hagerstrand*, ed. A. R. Pred. Lund Studies in Geography 48, ser. B (Lund [Sweden]: CWK Cleerup), 1981: 122-26 *passim*.

O'Neill, John. *Making Sense Together*. New York: Harper, 1974: 14, 27-28, 31-38.
_____. "Breaking the Signs: Roland Barthes and the Literary Body." In *The Structural Allegory: Reconstructive Encounters with the New French Thought*, ed. J. Fekete. Minneapolis: University of Minnesota Press, 1984: 184-94.
_____. *The Communicative Body. Studies in Communication, Philosophy, Politics, and Society*. Evanston, IL: Northwestern University Press, 1989: 3-4, 192, 201.
_____. *Critical Conventions: Interpretation in the Literary Arts and Sciences*. Norman: Oklahoma University Press, 1992: 166, 169, 175, 177-79, 250, 281-96.

Ong, Walter J. *In the Human Grain: Further Explorations in Contemporary Culture*. New York: Macmillan; London: Collier-Macmillan, 1964: 65.
_____. *Orality and Literacy: The Technologizing of the Word*. London: Methuen, 1982: 44.

Orsini, Gian N. *Benedetto Croce: Philosopher of Art and Literature*. Carbondale: Southern Illinois University Press, 1961: 14 *et passim*.

———. *Coleridge and German Idealism*. Carbondale: Southern Illinois University Press, 1969: 41, 164-65, 245, 262.

O'Shea, Michael Joseph. *James Joyce and Heraldry*. Albany: State University of New York, 1986: 3, 7, 92-93, 95, 125, 127.

Pachter, Henry. "Defining an Event: Prolegomenon to Any Philosophy of History." *Social Research* 41 (1974): 439.

Paci, Enzo. *The Function of the Sciences and the Meaning of Man*, trans. P. Piccone and J. Hansen. Evanston, IL: Northwestern University Press, 1972: 55.

Pacifici, Sergio. *A Guide to Contemporary Italian Literature*. New York: Meridian Books, 1962: 120, 259.

Padover, Saul K., ed. *On History and People*. The Karl Marx Library. New York, 1977: 7:311-12.

Page, Carl. "David Rapport Lachterman (1944-1991)." *New Vico Studies* 9 (1991): 155-56 [Obituary].

Paglia, Camille. *Sex, Art, and American Culture*. New York: Vintage, 1992: 102-3, 223.

Palmer, Lucia M. Review of "The Construal of Reality: Criticism in Modern and Postmodern Science" (S. Toulmin); *Consequences of Pragmatism* (R. Rorty); and *The Later Works, 1925-1953*, vol. 4 (John Dewey). *New Vico Studies* 3 (1985): 175-79.

———. Review of "The Recovery of Practical Philosophy" (S. Toulmin). *New Vico Studies* 7 (1989): 129-33.

———. Review of *The Breakdown of Cartesian Metaphysics* (R. A. Watson). *New Vico Studies* 8 (1990): 112-15.

Panofsky, Erwin. *Meaning in the Visual Arts*. Chicago: University of Chicago Press, 1972 [1st ed. Doubleday, 1955]: 219.

Pap, Arthur. *Elements of Analytic Philosophy*. New York: Macmillan, 1969: 21.

Parker, Theodore. *American Scholar*, ed. G. W. Cooke. London: Fischer Unwin, 1907: 364.

Parry, Adam, ed. *The Making of Homeric Verse: The Collected Papers of Milman Parry*. Oxford: Clarendon Press, 1971. Reprinted Oxford: Clarendon Press, 1987: xiii, xvi, li.

Patel, Cyrus R. K. *Joyce's Use of History in Finnegans Wake*. Cambridge: Harvard University Press, 1983: 3-4, 9, 11-22, 29, 33, 47.

Peake, C. H. *James Joyce: The Citizen and the Artist*. Stanford, CA: Stanford University Press, 1977: 355-56, 364.

Peer, Larry A. "Mimesis in Manzoni's Literary Theory." In S. Matteo and L. A. Peer, eds., *The Reasonable Romantic—Essays on Alessandro Manzoni*. New York: Peter Lang, 1987: 86.

Perelman, Chaim H. *The Realm of Rhetoric*, trans. W. Kluback. Notre Dame, IN: University of Notre Dame Press, 1982: 38.

———, and Lucie Olbrechts-Tyteca. *The New Rhetoric: A Treatise on Argumentation*, trans. J. Wilkinson and P. Weaver. Notre Dame, IN: University of Notre Dame Press, 1969: 23, 84, 144, 175-76, 178, 217-18, 236, 392-93, 408, 429, 444, 448, 488.

Perkinson, Henry. Review of *The Unschooled Mind: How Children Think and How Schools Should Teach* (H. Gardner). *New Vico Studies* 11 (1993): 131-35.

Perlove, Shelley. "Piranesi's Tomb of the Scipios of *le Antichità Romane* and Marc-Antoine Laugier's Primitive Hut." *Gazette des Beaux Arts* 113 (1989): 115-20.

Perniola, Mario. "The Difference of the Italian Philosophical Culture." *Graduate Faculty Philosophy Journal* 10 (1984): 105.

Pesciarelli, Enzo. "The Italian Contribution to the Four-Stages Theory." *History of Political Economy* 10 (1978): 604-7.

Peterson, Richard F. "Stephen and the Narrative of *A Portrait of the Artist as a Young Man*." In *Joyce Centenary Essays*, ed. Peterson, A. M. Cohn, and E. L. Epstein. Carbondale: Southern Illinois University Press, 1983: 24-25.

Phinney, A. W. "Wordsworth's Winander Boy and Romantic Theories of Language." *Wordsworth Circle* 18 (1987): 66-72.

Piccolomini, Manfredi. Review of *A Defense of Life: Lorenzo Valla's Theory of Pleasure* (M. de P. Lorch). *New Vico Studies* 4 (1986): 208-9.

———. "Croce." In *European Writers*, ed. G. Stade. New York: Charles Scribner's Sons, 1989: 8:322-56 *passim*.

Piccone, Paul. *Italian Marxism*. Berkeley: University of California Press, 1983: 15, 17, 96n.

Pietropaolo, Domenico. "On the Dignity of *Voluptas*: Valla's Philosophy of Pleasure" [a note on *A Defense of Life: Lorenzo Valla's Theory of Pleasure* (M. de P. Lorch)]. *Quaderni d'Italianistica* 9 (1988): 67, 74.

Pipa, Arshi. "Albanian Literature: Social Perspectives." *Albanische Forschungen* 19. Munich: Trofenik, 1978: 7, 20, 28, 31, 196.

———. "Gramsci as a (non)Literary Critic." *Telos* 57 (1983): 84.

Pocock, J. G. A. *The Ancient Constitution and the Feudal Law: A Study of English Historical Thought in the Seventeenth Century*. Cambridge: Cambridge University Press, 1957: 246, 248.

Polkinghorne, Donald E. *Narrative Knowing and the Human Sciences*. Albany: State University of New York Press, 1988: 194 n. 55.

Pons, Alain. Review of *La création littéraire sur la création littéraire chez Dostoievsky* (J. Catteau) [Vico cited by Dostoevsky]. *New Vico Studies* 2 (1984): 151-52.

Popkin, Richard H. Review of *Nicolas-Antoine Boulanger (1722-1759) ou avant nous le deluge* (P. Sardin). *The 18th Century: A Current Bibliography*, n.s. 12 (1986): 412-13.
_____. *Isaac La Peyrère (1594-1676): His Life, Work and Influence*. Leiden: Brill, 1987: 89, 91, 175, 197.

Popper, Karl R. *The Poverty of Historicism*. London: Routledge & Kegan Paul, 1957: 110.
_____. *The Open Society and Its Enemies*. New York: Harper Torchbooks, 1962: 1:221; 2:306.

Porter, Roy. *Edward Gibbon: Making History*. London: Weidenfeld and Nicolson, 1988: 23, 142.

Potts, Willard, ed. *Portraits of the Artist in Exile: Recollections of James Joyce by Europeans*. Seattle and London: University of Washington Press, 1979: 80, 207, 251.

Prezzolini, Giuseppe. *Machiavelli*, trans. G. Savini. New York: Farrar, Straus and Giroux, 1967: 292-305.

Price, Martin. *Swift's Rhetorical Art*. New Haven, CT: Yale University Press, 1953: 1-35 *passim*.

Procacci, Giuliano. *History of the Italian People*, trans. A. Paul. Harmondsworth: Penguin, 1978: 213-14.

Pruitt, Raymond D. "The Sciences, the Humanities, and the Illusion of Progress: A Comment on Kuhn's *Structure of Scientific Revolutions* and Berlin's 'Divorce between the Sciences and the Humanities'." *Perspectives in Biology and Medicine* 25 (1981).

Psathas, George, ed. *Phenomenological Sociology: Issues and Applications*. New York: John Wiley, 1973: 113, 124n, 344-46.

Puhvel, Jaan. *Comparative Mythology*. Baltimore: Johns Hopkins University Press, 1987: 11, 13.

Punter, David. *Blake, Hegel and Dialectic*. Amsterdam: Rodopi, 1982: 77, 132, 133, 171, 217.

Putnam, Hilary. *Realism and Reason: Philosophical Papers*. New York: Cambridge University Press, 1973: 3:149, 195.
_____. *Reason, Truth and History*. Cambridge: Cambridge University Press, 1981: 117.
_____. "Cognitive Psychology and Interpretation Theory." In *Artificial Intelligence: The Case Against*, ed. R. Born. London: Croom Helm, 1987: 12.

Quartermain, P. "Only-is-Order-Othered-Nought-is-Nulled: *Finnegans Wake* and Middle and Late Zukofsky." *English Literary History* 54 (1987): 957-78.

Quigley, Hugh. *Italy and the Rise of a New School Criticism in the Eighteenth Century*. Glasgow: Munro, Scott and Perth, 1921: 21-24, 44.

Radman, Zdravko. "The Multidimensionality of Metaphor." *Synthesis Philosophica* 6 (facs. 1) (Zagreb, 1991): 3-4.

Ramos, Peter. *Francis Bacon's Idea of Science and the Maker's Knowledge Tradition*. Oxford: Oxford University Press, 1988: 189-95.

Rand, Calvin. "Two Meanings of Historicism in the Writings of Dilthey, Troeltsch, and Meinecke." *Journal of the History of Ideas* 25 (1964): 503-18 *passim*.

Rasula, Jed. "The Poetics of Embodiment: A Theory of Exceptions." Unpublished Ph.D. diss. University of California (Santa Cruz), 1989.

Read, Herbert. *Form in Modern Poetry*. London: Sheed & Ward, 1932: 36-38.
_____. *Anarchy and Order: Essays in Politics*. London: Faber and Faber, 1954: 24, 184.
_____. *The Philosophy of Modern Art*. New York: Meridian, 1955: 293-94.
_____. *The Forms of Things Unknown: Essays Toward an Aesthetic Philosophy*. New York: Horizon Press, 1960: 109-11, 115-16, 118-19.
_____. *In Defence of Shelley and Other Essays*. Freeport, NY: Books for Libraries Press, 1968: 151-56.

Rearick, Charles. "Symbol, Legend, and History: Michelet as Folklorist-Historian." *French Historical Studies* 7 (1971): 75-76, 78-79.

Rée, Jonathan. "Descartes' Comedy." *Philosophy and Literature* 8 (1984): 163.

Reese, W. L. *Dictionary of Philosophy and Religion*. Atlantic Highlands, NJ: Humanities Press, 1991; 1980: 612.

Reynolds, Mary T. *Joyce and Dante: The Shaping Imagination*. Princeton, NJ: Princeton University Press, 1981: *passim*.

Rice, Thomas Jackson. *James Joyce: A Guide to Research*. New York: Garland Publishing, 1982: *passim*.

Ricci, Gabriel Robert. "The Category of the Creative in the Historicism of Ernst Troeltsch and Martin Heidegger." Unpublished Ph.D. diss. Temple University, 1986.

Ricciardelli, Michele. *Writings on Twentieth Century Italian Literature. Forum Italica*: Filibrary Monograph Series, 1992: 105.

Richards, John, and Ernst von Glasersfeld. "The Control of Perception and the Construction of Reality: Epistemological Aspects of the Feedback-Control System." *Dialectica* 33 (1979): 54.

Richardson, R. C. "Methodologies of History." *Literature and History* 5 (1979): 220-24.

Richter, Payton E. *Perspectives in Aesthetics: Plato to Camus*. New York: Odyssey, 1967: 90, 119, 355.

Rickman, H. P. "Rhetoric and Hermeneutics." *Philosophy and Rhetoric* 14 (1981): 111.
———. *The Adventure of Reason: The Uses of Philosophy in Sociology*. Westport, CT: Greenwood, 1983: 35.
———. *Dilthey Today—A Critical Appraisal of the Contemporary Relevance of His Work*. Westport, CT: Greenwood, 1988: 142, 181.

Riddel, Joseph. "Decentering the Image." In *Textual Strategies: Perspectives in Post-Structuralist Criticism*, ed. J. V. Harari. Ithaca, NY: Cornell University Press, 1979: 358.

Riesterer, Berthold. "Karl Löwith's Anti-Historicism." In *The Uses of History*, ed. H. White. Detroit: Wayne State University Press, 1968: 157.

Riquelme, John Paul. *Teller and Tale in Joyce's Fiction*. Baltimore and London: Johns Hopkins University Press, 1983: 33-34 *et passim*.

Riverso, Emmanuele. *Esperienza e riflessione. Le tappe della filosofia e della scienza nella cultura occidentale*. 3 vols. Rome: Borla, 1985 [Abstract: *New Vico Studies* 3 (1985): 202].

Roberts, David D. *Benedetto Croce and the Uses of Historicism*. Berkeley: University of California Press, 1987: 162-63 *et passim*.

Robertson, G. F. *Studies in the Genesis of the Romantic Theory in the Eighteenth Century*. Cambridge: Cambridge University Press, 1923: 288.

Robertson, J. M. *A History of Freethought*. London: Watts, 1906: 1:26n; 2:310f, 379.
———. *A History of Freethought in the Nineteenth Century*. London: Watts, 1930: 355, 359 n.1.

Robinson, Henry Crabb. *Henry Crabb Robinson on Books and Their Writers*, ed. E. Morley. London: J. M. Dent, 1938: 1:320-21.

Rockmore, Tom. *Irrationalism: Lukáks and the Marxist View of Reason.* Philadelphia: Temple University Press, 1992: 17, 60, 107-8, 143, 197.
_____, and Beth J. Singer, eds. *Anti-foundationalism Old and New.* Philadelphia: Temple University Press, 1992: 9.

Romanyshyn, Robert D. *Psychological Life: From Science to Metaphor.* Austin: University of Texas Press, 1982: 91-93.

Rorty, Richard. *Philosophical Papers.* Cambridge University Press, 1991: 1:87.

Rosnow, Ralph. *Paradigms in Translation: The Methodology of Social Inquiry.* Oxford and New York: Oxford University Press, 1981: 106, 108, 116, 153.

Rossi, Paolo. *Francis Bacon: From Magic to Science.* Chicago: University of Chicago Press, 1968: *passim*.

Rotenstreich, Nathan. *Basic Problems of Marx's Philosophy.* New York: Bobbs-Merrill, 1965: 48.
_____. "Convertibility and Alienation." In *Substance and Form in History*, ed. L. Pompa and W. H. Dray. Edinburgh: University of Edinburgh Press, 1981: 77-79, 83-85.

Rubanowich, Robert T. "Ernst Troeltsch's History of the Philosophy of History." *Journal of the History of Philosophy* 14 (1976): 85-86.

Rubel, Mary. "Savage and Barbarian: Historical Attitudes in the Criticism of Homer and Ossian in Britain 1760-1800." *Nieuwe Reeks* 96 (1978): 7.

Russell, Bertrand. *Wisdom of the West*, ed. P. Foulkes. New York: Doubleday, 1959: 206-9, 216-17, 274-75, 277, 290.

Rust, Eric C. *Toward a Theological Understanding of History.* New York: Oxford University Press, 1963: 26-30 *et passim*.

Russo, J. P. "Ovidian Tales of the Modern: Franco Rella's Racconto Method of Criticism." *Italian Quarterly* 27 (1986): 51-68 *passim*.

Ryan, Alan, ed. *The Idea of Freedom.* Oxford: Oxford University Press, 1979: 2.

Rykwert, Joseph. "Lodoli on Function and Representation." *Architectural Review* 160 (1976): 24-25.
_____. *The First Moderns: The Architects of the Eighteenth Century.* Cambridge, MA: MIT Press, 1980: 280-82 *et passim*.
_____. *On Adam's House in Paradise: The Idea of the Primitive Hut in Architectural History.* New York: Museum of Modern Art, 1972: 49, 56, 61-62 [reprinted Cambridge, MA: MIT Press, 1981].

Sahlins, Marshall. "Other Times, Other Customs." *American Anthopologist* 85 (1983): 517-44 *passim*.
_____. *Islands of History*. Chicago: University of Chicago Press, 1985: 32, 35.

Said, Edward. "Labyrinth of Incarnations: The Essays of Maurice Merleau-Ponty." *Kenyon Review* 29 (1967): 53-68 *passim*.
_____. "Molestation and Authority." In *Aspects of Narrative*, ed. J. H. Miller. New York: Columbia University Press, 1971: 58-61.
_____. "The Text as Practice and as Idea." *Modern Language Notes* 88 (1973): 1073, 1078, 1080, 1090, 1100.
_____. "On Repetition." In *The Literature of Fact: Selected Papers from the English Institute*, ed. A. Fletcher. New York: Columbia University Press, 1976: 135-58 *passim*. [Abstract in *The 18th Century: A Current Bibliography*, n.s. 2 (1976): 394.]
_____. "Roads Taken and Not Taken in Contemporary Criticism." *Contemporary Literature* 17 (1976): 337.
_____. *Orientalism*. New York: Pantheon, 1978: 4, 25, 53, 117-20, 132f, 147f.
_____. "The Text, the World, the Critic." In *Textual Strategies: Perspectives in Post-Structuralist Criticism*, ed. J. V. Harari. Ithaca, NY: Cornell University Press, 1979: 188.
_____. *The World, the Text, and the Critic*. Cambridge, MA: Harvard University Press, 1982: 2, 7, 25, 53, 111-18, 120, 208, 227, 290-91.
_____. "Opponents, Audiences, Constituencies, and Community." *Critical Inquiry* 9 (1982): 10-12. Reprinted in *The Anti-Aesthetic: Essays in Postmodern Culture*, ed. H. Foster. Port Townsend, WA: Bay Press, 1983: 143-45.
_____. "Secular Criticism. *Raritan* 2 (1983): 2, 23.
_____. "Orientalism Reconsidered." *Cultural Critique* 1 (1985): 101.
_____. "Expanding Humanism: An Interview." In *Wild Orchids and Trotsky*, ed. M. Edmundson. New York: Penguin Books, 1993: 104.

Sailer, Susan Shaw. "Reading the 'Wake': Language, Contexts, Perspectives." Ph.D. diss. University of Washington, 1988 [Ann Arbor, MI: University Microfilms, 1988].

Saintsbury, George A. *A History of Criticism and Literary Taste in Europe from the Earliest Texts to the Present Day*. 2d ed. New York: Dodd, Mead, 1902-1905: 3:9n, 146, 152-57 *et passim*.

Sanborn, Frank B. "Social Science in the Nineteenth Century." *Journal of Social Science* 9 (1878): 2-3.

Sandulescu, C. George. *The Language of the Devil: Texture and Archetype in Finnegans Wake*. Chester Springs, PA: Dufour Editions, 1987: 10, 97, 111-13.

Scaglione, Aldo. *The Classical Theory of Composition from its Origin to the Present: A Historical Survey*. Chapel Hill: University of North Carolina Press, 1972: 243, 248, 254, 265, 295-96, 304, 315.

Schaeffer, John D. "Ironic Discourse and the Creation of Secularity." *Soundings* 66 (1983): 319-30 *passim*.
_____. Review of *After Virtue: A Study in Moral Theory* (A. MacIntyre). *New Vico Studies* 2 (1984): 134-35.
_____. Review of *Hermeneutics: Questions and Prospects* (ed. G. Shapiro and A. Sica). *New Vico Studies* 3 (1985): 199-201.
_____. Review of *The Great Cat Massacre and Other Episodes in French Cultural History* (R. Darton). *New Vico Studies* 3 (1985): 201.
_____. "Mapping the Edges of the Abyss." *Isis* 77 (1986): 320-23.
_____. Review of *Ethics and the Limits of Philosophy* (B. Williams). *New Vico Studies* 4 (1986): 209-11.
_____. Review of *Shapes of Culture* by Thomas McFarland. *New Vico Studies* 5 (1987): 192-93.
_____. Review of *Words and the Word: Language, Poetics, and Biblical Interpretation* (S. Prickett). *New Vico Studies* 5 (1987): 210-12.
_____. Review of *Seven Theories of Human Nature: Christianity, Freud, Lorenz, Marx, Sartre, Skinner, Plato* (2d ed.) (L. Stevenson); and *Social Action and Human Nature* (A. Honneth and H. Joas). *New Vico Studies* 8 (1990): 137-39.
_____. Review of *The Presence of Myth* (L. Kolakowski). *New Vico Studies* 8 (1990): 106-8.
_____. Review of *Anti-Theory in Ethics and Moral Conservatism* (ed. S. G. Clarke and E. Simpson). *New Vico Studies* 8 (1990): 135-37.
_____. Review of "The Narrative Construction of Reality" (J. Bruner). *New Vico Studies* 11 (1993): 135-37.

Schiffman, Zachary Sayre. "Renaissance Historicism Reconsidered." *History and Theory* 24 (1985): 171, 176.

Schmidt, James. "Jürgen Habermas and the Difficulties of Enlightenment." *Social Research* 49 (1982): 188.

Schmitt, Charles B., Quentin Skinner, and Eckhard Kessler, eds. *The Cambridge History of Renaissance Philosophy*. Cambridge: Cambridge University Press, 1988: 757, 761, 781.

Schras, Francis. "Social Science and Social Practice." *Inquiry* 26 (1983): 107-24.

Schumpeter, J. A. *History of Economic Analysis*. New York: Oxford University Press, 1954: 28, 135-37, 300, 791-92.

Scott, Bonnie Kline. *James Joyce*. Atlantic Highlands, NJ: Humanities Press, 1987: 84-85.

Scott, Nathan A. Jr. *The Broken Center. Studies in the Theological Horizons of Modern Literature*. New Haven, CT: Yale University Press, 1966: 43-44, 48, 56.

Scott, Wilbur. *Five Approaches of Literary Criticism*. London: Collier Macmillan Publishers, 1963: 123.

Scruton, Roger. "Humane Education." *American Scholar* 49 (1980): 491, 498.

Sebba, Helen, Anibal A. Bueno, and Hendrikus Boers, eds. *The Collected Essays of Gregor Sebba: Truth, History and the Imagination*. Baton Rouge and London: Louisiana State University Press, 1991: 168n, 452.

Seebohm, Thomas M. "The Problem of Hermeneutics in Recent Anglo-American Literature: Part II." *Philosophy and Rhetoric* 10 (1972): 272-74.

Seidel, Michael. *Epic Geography: James Joyce's "Ulysses."* Princeton, NJ: Princeton University Press, 1976: *passim*.
_____. *Satiric Inheritance: Rabelais to Sterne*. Princeton, NJ: Princeton University Press, 1979: *passim*.
_____. "Satire and Metaphoric Collapse: The Bottom of the Sublime." In *Satire in the Eighteenth Century*, ed. J. D. Brown. New York: Garland, 1983: 116-23 *passim*.

Senn, Fritz. "Joyce the Verb." In *Coping with Joyce*, ed. M. Beja and S. Benstock. Columbus: Ohio State University Press, 1989: 25-54.

Sennet, Richard. *Authority*. New York: Vintage Books, 1981: 6.

Sewell, Elizabeth. *The Orphic Voice: Poetry and Natural History*. London: Routledge & Kegan Paul, 1961; reprinted New York: Harper Torchbooks, 1971: 181-84.
**Review:**
Steiner, George. *The Nation* (4 Feb. 1961): 102.

Sewell, Elizabeth. *The Human Metaphor*. Notre Dame, IN: University of Notre Dame Press, 1964: 16, 65, 121n, 128, 158n.

Shackleton, Robert. *Montesquieu: A Critical Biography*. London: Oxford University Press, 1961: 114-16.

Shepherd, Michael. "The Psycho-Historians." *Encounter* 52 (1979): 38.

Shibles, Warren A. *Metaphor: An Annotated Bibliography and History*. Whitewater, WI: Language Press, 1971: 88, 92, 185, 297, 366, 383, 402.

Shotter, John. "A Poetics of Relational Forms: The Sociality of Everyday Social Life." *Cultural Dynamics* 4 (1991): 379-96.

Simons, Herbert W., ed. *The Rhetorical Turn. Invention and Persuasion in the Conduct of Inquiry*. Chicago: University of Chicago Press, 1990: 270, 273, 356.
**Review:**
Struever, Nancy S. *New Vico Studies* 11 (1993): 119-20.

Simons, Herbert W., and T. Melia. *The Legacy of Kenneth Burke*. Madison: University of Wisconsin Press, 1988: 7.

***Review:***
Gabin, Rosalind J. *New Vico Studies* 7 (1989): 148-50.

Simpson, Evan. "Introduction: Colloquimur, ergo sumus." In Simpson, ed., *Antifoundationalism and Practical Reasoning; Conversations between Hermeneutics and Analysis*. Edmonton, Alberta: Academic Printing and Publishing, 1987: 1.
***Review:***
Palmer, Lucia M. *New Vico Studies* 9 (1991): 129-30.

Singleton, Charles. *Commedia: Elements of Structure*. Cambridge, MA: Harvard University Press, 1954: 74, 79.

Sitter, John. *Literary Loneliness in Mid-Eighteenth Century England*. Ithaca, NY: Cornell University Press, 1982: 181, 183, 185.

Skagestad, Peter. "The Expression of Historical Knowledge." *History and Theory* 23 (1984): 116-32.

Skinner, B. F. *Beyond Freedom and Dignity*. New York: Knopf, 1971: 180-81.

Slaniceanu, A. "The Calculating Woman in Cervantes' *La Fuerza de la Sangre*." *Bulletin of Hispanic Studies* 64 (1987): 101-10.

Smitten, Jeffrey. "Blackstone's Commentaries as Constitutive Rhetoric." *Studies in Eighteenth-Century Culture* 17 (1987): 173-89 *passim*.

Snukal, Robert. *High Talk: The Philosophical Poetry of W. B. Yeats*. Cambridge: Cambridge University Press, 1973: 238.

Snyder, Howard R. "The Emergence of a Contextualist Theory of Language: A Historical and Comparative Review." Unpublished Ph.D. diss. University of Washington, 1989.

Snyder, Louis L. *The Age of Reason*. Princeton, NJ: Van Nostrand, 1955: 13, 50.

Sorel, Albert. *Europe and the French Revolution: The Political Traditions of the Old Regime*. London: Collins and Fontana, 1969: 417.

Sorokin, Pitirim A. *Society, Culture, and Personality: A System of General Sociology*. New York: Cooper Square, 1962: 15, 20-21, 31, 110, 538, 588, 686-87.
―――. *Sociocultural Causality, Space, Time*. New York: Russell & Russell, 1964: 34, 234.

Spanos, W. V., Paul A. Bove, and Daniel O'Hara, eds. *The Question of Textuality: Strategies of Reading in Contemporary American Criticism*. Bloomington and London: Indiana University Press, 1987: 9.

Sparshott, Francis. *The Theory of the Arts*. Princeton, NJ: Princeton University Press, 1982: 625.

Sprinker, Michael. "Gerard Manley Hopkins on the Origin of Language." *Journal of the History of Ideas* 41 (1980): 113-14.
———. "Fictions of the Self: The End of Autobiography." In *Autobiography: Essays Theoretical and Critical*, ed. J. Olney. Princeton, NJ: Princeton University Press, 1980: 325-29, 342.

Stabb, Martin S. *Jorge Luis Borges.* New York: Twayne Publishers, 1970: 132.

Stafford, Barbara Maria. *Body Criticism. Imaging the Unseen in Enlightenment Art and Medicine.* Cambridge, MA: MIT Press, 1991: 176, 235-36.

Stam, James H. *Inquiries into the Origin of Language: The Fate of a Question.* New York: Harper & Row, 1976: 3-4, 9-19 *et passim.*
**Review:**
Frankel, Margherita. *New Vico Studies* 1 (1983): 111-12.

Stanford, W. B. *The Ulysses Theme: A Study in the Adaptability of a Traditional Hero.* Oxford: Blackwell, 1954: 161, 185-87.

Stanley, John L. *The Sociology of Virtue. The Political and Social Theories of Georges Sorel.* Berkeley: University of California Press, 1982: *passim.*

Stapleton, Laurence. *Justice and World Society.* Chapel Hill: University of North Carolina Press, 1944: 34-35, 37-48 *passim.*

Stark, Werner. *The Sociology of Knowledge.* London: Routledge & Kegan Paul, 1960: ix, 115, 160, 165, 328.
———. *Montesquieu: Pioneer of the Sociology of Knowledge.* London: Routledge & Kegan Paul, 1960: ix, x, 52.
———. *The Fundamental Forms of Social Thought.* New York: Fordham University Press, 1963: 8, 11-12, 219-22.

"State of Historical Science in France." *Eclectic Magazine* 1 (1844): 163f.

Steadman, John M. *The Lamb and the Elephant: Ideal Imitation and the Context of Renaissance Allegory.* San Marino, CA: Huntington Library, 1974: 230n.

Steegmuller, Francis. "The Abbé Galiani—The Laughing Philosopher." *The American Scholar* (Autumn, 1988): 592.

Steinberg, Michael. "The Twelve Tables and Their Origins: An Eighteenth-Century Debate." *Journal of the History of Ideas* 43 (1982): 379-96 [Abstract in *New Vico Studies* 2 (1984): 151; Abstract in *The 18th Century: A Current Bibliography*, n.s. 8 (1982): 223].

Steiner, George. "An Aesthetic Manifesto" [1964]. In *Language and Silence: Essays on Language, Literature, and the Inhuman.* New York: Atheneum, 1967: 340, 344.

_____. "Orpheus with His Myths: Claude Lévi-Strauss" [1965]. *Psychiatry and Social Science Review* (15 Aug. 1970): 15-20; *Psychiatry and Social Science Review* (15 Sept. 1970): 13-15. Reprinted in *Language and Silence: Essays on Language, Literature, and the Inhuman*. New York: Atheneum, 1967: 243, 247.

_____. "Whorf, Chomsky, and the Student of Literature." *New Literary History* 4 (1972): 15-34 *passim*. Reprinted in *On Difficulty and Other Essays*. Oxford: Oxford University Press, 1978: 139, 143.

_____. *After Babel*. New York: Oxford University Press, 1975: 75-80 *passim*, 88, 102, 190.

_____. *Martin Heidegger*. New York: Viking Press, 1979; reprinted: Middlesex: Penguin Books, 1980: 52; reprinted: Chicago: University of Chicago Press, 1989: 52.

_____. "The Historicity of Dreams." *Salmagundi* 61 (1983): 7.

_____. *Antigones*. Oxford: Clarendon Press, 1986: 110.

_____. "The Total Experience: Hegel's Dogged Quest for the Meaning Beyond Representation." Review of *Hegel und di heroischen Jahre der Philosophie: Eine Biographie* (H. Althaus). *Times Literary Supplement* [London] (8 May 1992): 3.

Steinman, Michael. *Yeats's Heroic Figures: Wilde, Parnell, Swift, Casement*. Albany: State University of New York Press, 1983: 120, 122, 132.

Stephens, Walter. *Giants in Those Days: Folklore, Ancient History, Nationalism*. Lincoln: University of Nebraska Press, 1989: 75, 92, 366 n.77.

Stewart, J. I. M. *James Joyce*. London: Longmans, Green & Co., 1957: 33.

Stillman, Edmund. "Before the Fall." *Horizon* 10 (1968): 1011.

Stock, Brian. "The Middle Ages as Subject and Object: Romantic Attitudes and Academic Medievalism." *New Literary History* 5 (1974): 531, 539.

Stockton, Constant Noble. "Economics and the Mechanism of Historical Progress in Hume's History." In *Hume: A Re-Evaluation*, ed. D. W. Livingston and J. T. King. New York: Fordham University Press, 1976: 236.

Stone, Harold. "The Record of the Loser: A Consideration of Pietro Giannone." *The American Scholar* 54 (Winter 1984-1985): 111.

Struever, Nancy. *The Language of History in the Renaissance: Rhetoric and Historical Consciousness in Florentine Humanism*. Princeton, NJ: Princeton University Press, 1970: *passim*.

_____. Review of *Rhetoric and Philosophy in Renaissance Humanism* (J. Siegel). *History and Theory* 11 (1972): 73-74.

_____. "The Study of Language and the Study of History." *Journal of Interdisciplinary History* 4 (1974): 412-13.

_____. "Classical Investigations." *New Literary History* 5 (1974): 523-25.

_____. "Topics in History." *History and Theory*, Beiheft 19 (1980): 70.

_____. "Fables of Power." *Representations* 4 (1983): 114-27 *passim*.
_____. Review of *The Rhetoric of the Human Sciences: Language and and Argument in Scholarship and Public Affairs* (ed. J. S. Nelson et al). *New Vico Studies* 7 (1989): 101-5.
_____. *Theory as Practice. Ethical Theory in the Renaissance*. Chicago: University of Chicago Press, 1992: 93, 151, 210-24, 128, 212-12, 216, 220, 222, 225, 220-24, 231-32.

Sullivan, Edmund V. *Psychology as an Interpretive Activity*. Toronto: Ontario Institute for Studies in Education (Informal Series 18), 1980: *passim*.
_____. *Critical Psychology: Interpretation of the Personal World*. New York and London: Plenum, 1984 [Abstract in *New Vico Studies* 3 (1985): 231-32].

Sullivan, Kevin. *Joyce among the Jesuits*. New York: Columbia University Press, 1958: 82-83.

Sumner, Charles. "The Law of Human Progress." In *The Works of Charles Sumner*. Boston: Lee and Shepard, 1849: 14-15.

Suttle, B. B. "The Passion of Self-Interest: The Development of the Idea and Its Changing Status." *American Journal of Economics and Sociology* 46 (1987): 459-72.

Swearingen, James. "Philosophical Hermeneutics and the Renewal of Tradition." *The Eighteenth Century* 22 (1981): 196.

Szacki, Jerzy. *History of Sociological Thought*. Westport, CT: Greenwood, 1979: 45-47, 185.

Tagliacozzo, Giorgio. "The Tree of Knowledge." *American Behavioral Scientist* 4 (1960): 6.
_____. "General Education: The Mirror of Culture." *American Behavioral Scientist* 6 (1962): 23, 25n.
_____. "Culture and Education: The Origins." *American Behavioral Scientist* 7 (1963): 10.
_____. "In Memoriam. Edgar Kaufmann, Jr. (1910-1989)." *New Vico Studies* 7 (1989): 158-61 [Obituary].
_____. "In Memoriam. Elio Gianturco (1900-1987)." *New Vico Studies* 4 (1986): 215-18 [Obituary].

Tanner, Tony. *Adultery in the Novel*. Baltimore: Johns Hopkins University Press, 1980: 93, 101, 111, 148, 158-66 *passim*.
_____. "'Antony and Cleopatra': Boundaries and Excess." *Hebrew University Studies in Literature and the Arts* 15 (1987): 78-104.

Tarnas, Richard. *The Passion of the Western Mind: Understanding the Ideas That Have Shaped Our World View*. New York: Harmony Press, 1991: 330, 369, 457.

Tatarkiewicz, Wladijslaw. "A Note on the Modern System of the Arts." *Journal of the History of Ideas* 24 (1963): 422.
_____. *History of Aesthetics* (trans. from 1967 Polish original). The Hague: Mouton; Paris: PLW-Polish-Scientific-Publishers-Warsaw, 1974: 3:xix, 435, 441-42, 444-47, 449-57 *passim*.

Teggert, Frederick J. *Theory and Processes of History*. Berkeley and Los Angeles: University of California Press, 1960: 1.

Tejera, Vittorino. "On the Nature of Reflective Discourse in Politics." *Philosophy and Rhetoric* 17 (1984): 66.

Thompson, Edward P. *The Poverty of Theory and Other Essays*. New York: *Monthly Review Press*, 1978: 84-88 *et passim*.

Thompson, John Hinsdale. "*Finnegans Wake*." In *Modern Poetry: American and British*, ed. K. Friar and M. J. Brinnin. New York: Appleton-Century-Crofts, 1951: 88-97 *passim*.

Thompson, James Westfall, and Bernard J. Holm. *A History of Historical Writing*. New York: Macmillan, 1942: 2:65 n.22, 92-94, 135, 233, 239, 608.

Thompson, William Irwin. *Passages about Earth: An Exploration of the New Planetary Culture*. New York: Harper & Row, 1974: 5, 121, 124.
_____. *The Time Falling Bodies Take to Light*. New York: St. Martins Press, 1981: 4-5.

Thornton, Weldon. *Allusions in "Ulysses."* Chapel Hill: University of North Carolina Press, 1961: 29-30, 389.

Throop, W. M., and M. L. Knight. "A Pragmatic Reconstruction of the Naturalism/Anti-Naturalism Debate." *Journal for the Theory of Social Behavior* 17 (1987): 93-112.

Tice, Terrence, and Thomas P. Slavens. *Research Guide to Philosophy. Source of Information in the Humanities*. Chicago: American Library Association, 1983: 98-100, 101, 111, 193, 428, 430.

Timpanaro, Sebastiano. *The Freudian Slip*. London: Verso, 1976. Reprinted 1985: 188, 193.

Tindall, William York. *James Joyce: His Way of Interpreting the Modern World*. New York: Charles Scribner's Sons, 1950: *passim*.
_____. *A Readers' Guide to James Joyce*. New York: Noonday Press, 1959: *passim*.
_____. *A Readers' Guide to "Finnegans Wake."* New York: Farrar, Strauss, Giroux, 1969: *passim*.

Todorov, Tzvetan. *Theories of the Symbol*. Ithaca, NY: Cornell University Press, 1982: 148, 224, 231-32, 234-35, 287.
*Review:*
Megill, Allan. *New Vico Studies* 4 (1986): 193-95.

"Tokyo Congress: Le deuxiéme Renaissance" (April 1984). *New Vico Studies* 3 (1985): 235 [Report].

Tolomeo, Diane. "The Final Octagon of *Ulysses*." *James Joyce Quarterly* 10 (1973): 439-54 *passim*.

Tonelli, G. "Croce as Historian of Eighteenth-Century Aesthetics." In *Thought, Action, and Intuition: A Symposium on the Philosophy of Benedetto Croce*, ed. L. M. Palmer and H. S. Harris. Hildesheim: Georg Olms Verlag, 1975: 252-53.

Topolsky, Jerzy. *Methodology of History*, trans. O. Wojtasiewicz. Dordrecht: D. Reidel Publishing Co., 1976: 91, 95, 108, 266, 595.

Toulmin, Stephen. *Human Understanding*. Princeton, NJ: Princeton University Press, 1972: 23, 426, 491, 501.
———. "From Form to Function: Philosophy and History of Science in the 1950s and Now." *Daedalus* 106 (1977): 145.
———. *The Return to Cosmology*. Berkeley and Los Angeles: University of California Press, 1982: 161, 167, 263.
**Review:**
Palmer, Lucia M. *New Vico Studies* 2 (1984): 135-38.

Toulmin, Stephen. *Cosmopolis: The Hidden Agenda of Modernity*. New York: Free Press, 1990: 145.
**Reviews:**
Cellerino, Massimo. *New Vico Studies* 9 (1991): 92-99.
Hutton, Patrick H. *New Vico Studies* 9 (1991): 85-91.
Jacobitti, Edmund E. *New Vico Studies* 9 (1991): 77-84.

Toynbee, Arnold J. *A Study of History*. Oxford: The University Press, 1961: 12:40n, 131n, 161n, 252, 584-87, 607, 653n.

Trilling, Lionel. *Matthew Arnold*. New York: Columbia University Press, 1949: 51-53, 63.

Trompf, G. W. *The Idea of Historical Recurrence in Western Thought*. Berkeley: University of California Press, 1979: xi, 237, 277, 312.

Trotsky, Leon D. *The History of the Russian Revolution*, trans. M. Eastman. Ann Arbor: University of Michigan Press, 1932: 3.
———. *My Life*. New York: Pathfinder Press, 1970: 119, 122.

Trousdale, Marion. *Shakespeare and the Rhetoricians*. Chapel Hill: University of North Carolina Press, 1982: 32-33, 37-38, 179n, 180n.

Tucker, Lindsey Ann Sale. "Stephen and Bloom at Life's Feast: Alimentary Symbolism and the Creative Process in James Joyce's *Ulysses*." Unpublished Ph.D. diss. University of Delaware, 1981.

Tully, John. *A Discourse on Property: John Locke and His Adversaries*. Cambridge: Cambridge University Press, 1980: 12, 23-24, 27, 32, 58.

Tursman, Richard, ed. *Studies in Philosophy and in the History of Science: Essays in Honor of Max Fisch.* Lawrence, KS: Coronado Press, 1970: 207-10, 211-19.

Tuttle, Howard N. "The Negation of History." *Southwest Philosophical Studies* 7 (1982): 7-9, 13.

Tyrrell, R. Emmett, Jr. "Clintons Shouldn't Cater to Zealots." *Conservative Chronicle* 8, no. 25 (23 June 1993): 13.

Tysdahl, B. J. *Joyce and Ibsen: A Study in Literary Influence.* Oslo: Norwegian Universities Press; Atlantic Highlands, NJ: Humanities Press, 1968: 138, 148, 160-62, 179, 212.

Ullmann, Stephen. "Semantic Universals." In *Universals of Language*, ed. J. H. Greenberg. 2d ed. Cambridge, MA: MIT Press, 1963: 241.

Unamuno, Miguel de. *The Tragic Sense of Life in Men and Nations.* Princeton, NJ: Princeton University Press, 1972: 56-57, 429n., 445n.

Updike, John. *Bech: A Book.* New York: Random House, 1980: 176.

Valdes, Mario J. *Phenomenological Hermeneutics and the Study of Literature.* Toronto: University of Toronto Press, 1987: 3, 5, 8-9, 12, 16-18, 20, 23-26, 67.
**Review:**
Lucente, Gregory L. *New Vico Studies* 10 (1992): 97-100.

Valesio, Paolo. *Gabriele D'Annunzio. The Dark Flame.* New Haven, CT: Yale University Press, 1992: 2, 77, 195.
**Review:**
Lucente, Gregory L. *New Vico Studies* 11 (1993): 129-31.

Van Atta, John R. "Insights to the Art of Studying History." *Indiana Social Studies Quarterly* 29 (1976): 20-22, 28.

van der Dussen, Johannis. *History as a Science: Collingwood's Philosophy of History.* Leiden: Krips Repro, 1980: 1, 3, 52, 88, 361, 330.

Vattimo, Gianni. "Myth and the Destiny of Secularization." *Social Research* 52 (1985): 348, 359.
_____. *The End of Modernity. Nihilism and Hermeneutics in Postmodern Culture.* Baltimore: Johns Hopkins University Press, 1989: 96.
**Review:**
White, Hayden. *New Vico Studies* 9 (1991): 61-67.

Veit, Walter. "The Potency of Imagery—the Impotence of Rational Language: Ernesto Grassi's Contribution to Modern Epistemology." *Philosophy and Rhetoric* 17 (1984): 233-34.

Venturi, Franco. *Italy and the Enlightenment*, trans. S. Corsi. New York: Longman, 1972: *passim*.

Venturi, Lionello. *History of Art Criticism*. New York: Dutton 1964: 137, 161-62, 330.

Verene, Donald Phillip. "The Philosophy of Culture and the Problem of Human Existence." In *Akten des XIV. Internationalen Kongresses für Philosophie*, ed. L. Gabriel. Vienna: Herder, 1969: 4:497.
_____. "Categories and the Imagination." In *Categories: A Colloquium*, ed. H. W. Johnstone, Jr. University Park, PA: Department of Philosophy, The Pennsylvania State University, 1978: 185-207 *passim*.
_____. "Technique and the Directions of the Human Spirit: Laughter and Desire." In D. Lovekin and D. P. Verene, eds., *Essays in Humanity and Technology*. Dixon, IL: Sauk Valley College, 1978: 87, 90-93.
_____. "On Rhetoric and Imagination as Kinds of Knowledge." *Section Papers of the 16th World Congress of Philosophy*. Düsseldorf: World Congress of Philosophy, 1978: 675-78 *passim*.
_____. "Culture, Categories, and the Imagination." In *Presentations on Art Education Research: Aesthetics and Culture* (No. 5), ed. R. Staley and D. Pariser. Montréal: Concordia University, 1979: 37-73 (English and French texts).
_____. "Rhetoric and Imagination: Topic and Metaphor." *Journal of the Faculty of Letters* (University of Tokyo) 5 (1980): 279-82 *passim*.
_____. "Technology and the Ship of Fools." In *Research in Philosophy and Technology*, ed. P. T. Durbin. Greenwich, CT and London: JAI Press, 1982: 5:281-98 *passim*.
_____. "Cassirer's Philosophy of Culture." *International Philosophical Quarterly* 22 (1982): 133-44 *passim*.
_____. "Technological Desire." In *Research in Philosophy and Technology*, ed. P. T. Durbin. Greenwich, CT and London: JAI Press, 1984: 7:99, 110-11.
_____. *Hegel's Recollection: A Study of Images in the Phenomenology of Spirit*. Albany: State University of New York Press, 1985: 66 [Abstract in *New Vico Studies* 4 (1986): 211].
_____. "Response to Grassi." *Philosophy and Rhetoric* 19 (1986): 136.
_____. "The 1922 and 1984 Editions: Some Philosophical Considerations." In *Assessing the 1984 "Ulysses,"* ed. C. G. Sandulescu and C. Hart. Gerrards Cross, Bucks: Colin Smythe; Totowa, NJ: Barnes & Noble, 1986: 214, 216.
_____. "Philosophy, Argument, and Narration." *Philosophy and Rhetoric* 22 (1989): 141-44.
_____. "Lewis Mumford (1896-1990)." *New Vico Studies* 8 (1990): 162 [Obituary].
_____. "Ernesto Grassi (1902-1991)." *New Vico Studies* 10 (1992): 140-41 [Obituary].
_____. "The Limits of Argument: Argument and Autobiography." *Philosophy and Rhetoric* 16 (1993): 1-8.

Verri, Antonio. "On the Porset Edition of Rousseau's *Essai sur l'origine des langues*." *Studies on Voltaire and the Eighteenth Century*. Oxford: The Voltaire Foundation, 1976: 2170-71.
_____. "Jules Michelet e il progetto di ritrovare nelle lingue la storia della civiltà." In *Studi in onore di Dinu Adamesteanu*. Lecce: Galatina, 1983: 275-89.
**Review:**
Piccolomini, Manfredi. *New Vico Studies* 2 (1984): 125-27.

Vickers, Brian. "Territorial Disputes: Philosophy *vs* Rhetoric." In Vickers, ed. *Rhetoric Revalued*, Binghamton, NY: Center for Medieval and Renaissance Studies, 1982: 236, 247, 257.
*Review:*
Shapiro, Gary. *New Vico Studies* 5 (1987): 195-98.

Vickers, Brian. *In Defence of Rhetoric*. Oxford and New York: Clarendon Press and Oxford University Press, 1988: 183, 184, 207, 210, 382, 439-42, 447, 448, 451, 457.
*Reviews:*
Nehamas, Alexander. "The School of Eloquence." *Times Literary Supplement* (15-21 July 1988): 771.
Struever, Nancy S. *New Vico Studies* 7 (1989): 101-5.

Vickers, Brian. "The Dangers of Dichotomy." *Journal of the History of Ideas* 51 (1990): 158.
———. "Francis Bacon and the Progress of Knowledge." *Journal of the History of Ideas* 53 (1992): 495-518.

Vignoli, Tito. *Myth and Science. An Essay*. New York: D. Appleton and Co., 1882: 229, 295.

Vincenzo, Joseph. "Discovery of Italian Humanism: The Case of Ernesto Grassi." *Italian Culture* 8 (1990): 163-85 *passim*.

Voegelin, Eric. *Amamnesis*, trans. and ed. G. Niemeyer. Notre Dame, IN: University of Notre Dame Press, 1978: 25.

von Bertalanffy, Ludwig. *General Systems Theory*. New York: Braziller, 1968: 11, 110, 117, 198-99.

von Glaserfeld, Ernst. *The Construction of Knowledge. Contributions to Conceptual Semantics*. Seaside, CA: Intersystems, 1987: xiii.
———. "Cognition, Construction of Knowledge, and Teaching." *Synthèse* 80 (1989): 121-25.
———. "Constructivism in Education." In *International Encyclopedia of Education*, ed. T. Husen and T. N. Postlewhaite. London: Pergamon, 1989 [supplement]: 1:162-63.

Vucinich, Alexander. *Darwin in Russian Thought*. Berkeley: University of California Press, 1988: 199.

Walsh, William H. *An Introduction to Philosophy of History*. London and New York: Hutchinson's University Library, 1964: 11, 121, 165-66.
———. "Bradley and Critical History." In *The Philosophy of F. H. Bradley*, ed. A. Manser and G. Stock. Oxford: Oxford University Press, 1984: 50.

Warneke, Georgia. *Gadamer: Hermeneutics, Tradition and Reason*. Stanford, CA: Stanford University Press, 1987: 39.

Wartofsky, Marx W. "From Praxis to Logos: Genetic Epistemology and Physics." In *Cognitive Development and Epistemology*, ed. T. Mischell. New York: Academic Press, 1971: 130.

Weber, Eugen. "Michelet Reconsidered." *The American Scholar* (Winter 1991): 55, 56, 60, 64.

Weinberg, Kurt. "Language as Mythopoesis: Mallarmé's Self-Referential Sonnets." In *Yearbook of Comparative Criticism*. University Park: The Pennsylvania State University Press, 1980: 141-42, 145, 173, 176.

Weinsheimer, Joel C. *Gadamer's Hermeneutics—A Reading of "Truth and Method."* New Haven, CT: Yale University Press, 1985: 74, 149, 152.

Weintraub, Karl Joachim. "Autobiography and Historical Consciousness." *Critical Inquiry* 1 (1975): 831.
———. *The Value of the Individual: Self and Circumstance in Autobiography*. Chicago: University of Chicago Press, 1978: ch. 11.

Weir, Lorraine. "From Catechism to Catachresis: Aspects of Joycean Pedagogy in *Ulysses* and *Finnegans Wake*." In *Coping with Joyce*, ed. M. Beja and S. Benstock. Columbus: Ohio State University Press, 1989: 288-98.
———. *Writing Joyce. A Semiotics of the Joyce System*. Bloomington and Indianapolis: Indiana University Press, 1989: 3, 9, 10, 53, 54-81, 83, 84, 86, 99, 115 n. 11.
**Review:**
Lucente, Gregory L. *New Vico Studies* 8 (1990): 147-49.

Weiss, Paul. *History: Written and Lived*. Carbondale: Southern Illinois University Press, 1962: 24, 114.

Wellek, René. *A History of Modern Criticism 1750-1950*. New Haven, CT: Yale University Press, 1955: 1: *passim*.
———. *Concepts of Criticism*. New Haven, CT: Yale University Press, 1963: 12, 38, 82.
———. *The Rise of English Literary History*. New York: McGraw-Hill, 1966: 75, 86.
———, and Austin Warren. *Theory of Literature*. New York: Harcourt, Brace, and World, 1956: 113, 191.

West, Cornell. *The American Evasion of Philosophy: A Genealogy of Pragmatism*. Madison: University of Wisconsin Press, 1989: 11, 69.

Whalley, George. *Poetic Process*. London: Routledge and Kegan Paul, 1953; Westport, CT: Greenwood Press, 1973: xiv, 20, 71-72, 213.

White, David A. *The Grand Continuum: Reflections on James Joyce and Metaphysics*. Pittsburgh, PA: University of Pittsburgh Press, 1983: 4, 7, 9, 10-11, 41, 72.

White, Hayden. "Literary History: The Point of It All." *New Literary History* 2 (1970): 179.

———. "The Irrational and the Problem of Historical Knowledge in the Enlightenment." In *Eighteenth Century Studies*, ed. H. E. Pagliaro. Cleveland, OH: The Press of Case Western Reserve University, 1972: 2:313-19 *passim*.

———. "Foucault Decoded: Notes from Underground." *History and Theory* 12 (1973): 48.

———. *Metahistory: The Historical Imagination in Nineteenth-Century Europe*. Baltimore: Johns Hopkins University Press, 1973: *passim*.

**Reviews:**
Carroll, David. "On Tropology: The Forms of History." *Diacritics* 6 (1976): 58-64.
Jameson, Fredric. "Figural Relativism, or the Poetics of Historiography." *Diacritics* 6 (1976): 2.

White, Hayden. *Tropics of Discourse*. Baltimore: Johns Hopkins University Press, 1978: *passim*.

**Review:**
Johnston, William M. *New Vico Studies* 1 (1983): 86-90.

White, Hayden. "The Problem of Style in Realistic Representation: Marx and Flaubert." In *The Concept of Style*, ed. B. Lang. Philadelphia: University of Pennsylvania Press, 1979: 228.

———. Review of *After Philosophy: End or Transformation?* (ed. K. Baynes, J. Bohman, and T. McCarthy). *New Vico Studies* 6 (1988): 167-68.

White, Morton. *The Age of Enlightenment*. New York: Mentor Books, 1956: 44, 45.

Whitney, Charles. *Francis Bacon and Modernity*. New Haven, CT: Yale University Press, 1986: 154.

Whitton, Brian J. "Herder's Critique of the Enlightenment: Cultural Community vs Cosmopolitan Rationalism." *History and Theory* 22 (1988): 154.

Whyte, Lancelot Law. "A Scientific View of the 'Creative Energy' of Man." In *Aesthetics Today*, ed. M. Philipson. New York: World Publishers/Meridian, 1961: 353.

———, ed. *Robert Joseph Boscovich: Studies of His Life and Work on the 250th Anniversary of His Birth*. London: Allen & Unwin, 1961: 118-19, 125.

Widgery, Alban G. *Interpretations of History: Confucius to Toynbee*. London: Allen & Unwin, 1961: 152-57.

———. *The Unconscious before Freud*. Garden City, NY: Doubleday, 1962: 45, 93-97, 186, 188.

Wiener, Philip P., ed. *Dictionary of the History of Ideas*. New York: Charles Scribner's Sons, 1968-74: 4:*passim*.

Wiggins, David. "Truth, Invention, and the Meaning of Life." *Proceedings of the British Academy* 62 (1976): 331-78.

_____. *Needs, Values, Truth: Essays in the Philosophy of Value*. Cambridge, MA: Basil Blackwell, 1979; 2d ed. 1991: 162 n. 21.

Wilcox, Donald J. *The Measure of Times Past*. Chicago: University of Chicago Press, 1987: 214-20, 261, 269.

Wilder, Thornton. *Theophilus North*. New York: Harper & Row, 1973: 108, 110.

Wilkerson, Kenneth E. "Michael Herzfeld's NEH Seminar, 'The Poetics of Social Life'." *New Vico Studies* 9 (1991): 151 [Report].

Wilkins, Ernst Hatch. *A History of Italian Literature*. Cambridge, MA: Harvard University Press, 1954: 334-41, 383.

Williams, Raymond. *Marxism and Literature*. Oxford: Oxford University Press, 1977: 16-17, 20, 23-24, 29, 31.

Wilson, Edmund. "The Historical Interpretation of Literature." In Wilson, *The Triple Thinkers. Twelve Essays on Literary Subjects* (1938). Reprinted New York: Farrar, Strauss & Giroux, Noonday Books, 1976: 258-60.
_____. *To the Finland Station* (1940). Reprinted New York: Farrar, Strauss & Giroux, 1972: 1-7, 62, 141, 193, 467.

Wilson, F. A. C. *W. B. Yeats and Tradition*. New York: Macmillan, 1958: 63, 149, 150.
_____. *Yeats's Iconography*. London: Victor Gollancz, 1960: 146, 157-58.

Wilson, Robert Anton. "Coincidance." *SEMIOTEXT[E] USA*. Philosophy Hall, Columbia University: Autonomedia, Inc., 1987: 172.
_____. *The Earth Will Shake: The Historical Illuminatus Chronicles*. New York: Penguin, 1982: 1:75, 129.

Wilson, William A. "Herder, Folklore, and Romantic Nationality." *Journal of Popular Culture* 6 (1973): 821, 823, 825-26.

Wimsatt, William K., and Cleanth Brooks. *Literary Criticism: A Short History*. New York: Knopf, 1962: 246, 350, 366, 417, 500, 529, 600, 631, 700.

Winch, Peter. "Nature and Convention." *Proceedings of the Aristotelian Society* 60 (1959-60): 241, 251.
_____. "Understanding a Primitive Society." *American Philosophical Quarterly* 1 (1964): 324. Reprinted in *Rationality*, ed. B. R. Wilson. Evanston, IL: Harper & Row, 1970: 107.

Windelband, W. *A History of Philosophy*, trans. J. H. Tufts. New York: Macmillan, 1901: 526, 528.

Wright, O. W. "Primary Law of Political Development in Civil History." *North American Review* 88 (1859): 387-88.

Wundt, Wilhelm Max. *Elements of Folk Psychology*, trans. E. L. Schaub. New York: Macmillan, 1916: 516.

Yeats, William Butler. *The Words upon the Window-Pane*. Dublin: Cuala Press, 1934: 13-15.
_____. *Wheels and Butterflies*. New York: Macmillan, 1935: 16f.
_____. *A Vision*. London: Macmillan, 1937: 261f.
_____. *On the Boiler*. Dublin: Cuala Press, 1938: 22.

Young, Louise Merwin. *Thomas Carlyle and the Art of History*. Philadelphia: University of Pennsylvania Press, 1939: 39, 21-22, 46, 55, 67.

Zagorin, Perez. "Hobbes on Our Mind." *Journal of the History of Ideas* 51 (1990): 323.

Zhang, Lonxi. "The Critical Legacy of Oscar Wilde." *Texas Studies in Literature and Language* 30 (1988): 87-103.
_____. "The Myth of the Other: China in the Eyes of the West." *Critical Inquiry* 15 (1988): 114, 115, 116.
_____. "Profile: Professor Zhu Guang Qian." *New Vico Studies* 4 (1986): 213-14 [Obituary].

# Appendix

## Bibliographies of Work on Vico
(In chronological order)

Croce, Benedetto. *Bibliografia Vichiana*. Naples: Alfonso Tessitore e Figlio, 1904.

Falzon, Paul L. "Some Additions to Croce's Bibliography of Vico." *Melita Theologica* 1 (1921): 488-95, 526-33.

Croce, Benedetto. *Bibliografia Vichiana*. Revised and enlarged by Fausto Nicolini. 2 vols. Naples: Riccardo Ricciardi Editore, 1947-1948.
*Review:*
Fisch, Max Harold. *Philosophical Review* 58 (1949): 528-29.

Gianturco, Elio. *A Selective Bibliography of Vico Scholarship (1948-1968)*. *Forum Italicum*, supplement. Florence: Grafica Toscana, 1968.
*Review:*
Palmer, Lucia M. *Journal of the History of Philosophy* 8 (1970):220-22.

Tagliacozzo, Giorgio. "Works Published in English during the Past Fifty Years Dealing Wholly or Partly with Vico." In *Giambattista Vico. An International Symposium*, ed. Tagliacozzo; H. V. White, Co-editor. Baltimore: The Johns Hopkins Press, 1969: 615-19.

Molinaro, J. A. "Vico." In "Bibliography of Italian Studies in America." *Italica* 46 (1969): 216-18; see also "Translations," 209-10.

Donzelli, Maria. *Contributo alla bibliografia vichiana (1948-1970)*. Naples: Guida Editori, 1973.

Verene, Molly Black. "Critical Writings on Vico in English." In *Giambattista Vico's Science of Humanity*, ed. G. Tagliacozzo and D. P. Verene. Baltimore and London: Johns Hopkins University Press, 1976: 457-80.
_____. "Critical Writings on Vico in English: A Supplement." *Social Research* 43 (1976): 904-14.

Mooney, Michael. "Vico's Writings." In *Giambattista Vico's Science of Humanity*, ed. G. Tagliacozzo and D. P. Verene. Baltimore, MD: Johns Hopkins University Press, 1976: xix-xxviii.

Crease, Robert. *Vico in English: A Bibliography of Writings by and about Giambattista Vico (1668-1744)*. Atlantic Highlands, NJ: Humanities Press, 1978.
_____. *Supplement to Vico in English*. Atlantic Highlands, NJ: Humanities Press, 1981 [Abstract: *New Vico Studies* 1 (1983): 125].

*Reviews:*
American Reference Books Annual 11 (1980): 488.
Costa, Gustavo. *Forum Italicum* 15 (1981): 89.

Battistini, Andrea. *Nuovo contributo alla bibliografia vichiana (1971-1980)*. Studi vichiani 14. Naples: Guida, 1983. [The *Centro di Studi Vichiani* occasionally publishes bibliographic supplements.]
*Review:*
Costa, Gustavo. *New Vico Studies* 2 (1984): 172-73.

Battistini, Andrea. "Bibliography of some Natural Law Writings about Vico." *Vera Lex* 5, no. 1 (1985): 23-24.

Tagliacozzo, Giorgio, Donald Phillip Verene, and Vanessa Rumble. *A Bibliography of Vico in English 1884-1984*. Bowling Green, OH: Philosophy Documentation Center, 1986.
*Reviews:*
Bedani, G. L. C. *New Vico Studies* 4 (1986): 137-38.
Bynagle, Hans W. *American Reference Books Annual*. Littleton, CO: Libraries Unlimited, Inc., 1987: 523.
*Choice* 24 (1987): 51.
Pietropaolo, Domenico. *Quaderni d'Italianistica* 8 (1987): 130-32.

*New Vico Studies* published 9 bibliographies supplement to the above collection, each inclusive of the earlier lists, as follows:
Nelli, Anna. 3 (1985): 241-47.
Bergstrom, Timothy. 4 (1986): 219-32.
Tagliacozzo, Giorgio. 5 (1987): 227-46.
Bergstrom, Timothy. 6 (1988): 191-214.
Wilson, Jeffrey. 7 (1989): 162-91.
Bertland, Alexander. 8 (1990): 163-95.
_____. 9 (1991): 157-93.
Rust Murray, Jennifer. 10 (1992): 145-86.
Smith, Charlotte. 11 (1993): 142-88.

Croce, Benedetto. *Bibliografia Vichiana*. Ristampa anastatica della prima edizione del 1904, con una presentazione di Raffaello Franchini. Naples: Morano Editore, 1987.
*Review:*
Verene, Donald Phillip. *Idealistic Studies* 20 (1990): 179-80.

Sanna, Manuela. *Catalogo vichiano napoletano*. *Bollettino del Centro di Studi Vichiani*. Supplement to Anno XVI (1986). Naples: Bibliopolis, 1987: 493-659.
*Review:*
Costa, Gustavo. *New Vico Studies* 5 (1987): 182-87.

Mazzola, Roberto, ed. *Terzo contributo alla bibliografia vichiana (1981-1985). Bollettino del Centro di Studi Vichiani.* Supplement to Anni XVII-XVIII (1987-1988). Naples: Bibliopolis, 1987: 387-501.
*Review:*
Costa, Gustavo. *New Vico Studies* 7 (1989): 114-19.

Mazzola, R., and M. Sanna, eds. *Contributo al catalogo vichiano nazionale: Supplemento al "Bollettino del Centro di Studi Vichiani" XIX, 1989.* Naples: Bibliopolis, 1989: 321-434.
*Review:*
Costa, Gustavo. *New Vico Studies* 8 (1990): 95-99.

# Index

Aarsleff, H.   15, 17
Abbagnano, N.   85
Abbott, D. P.   6, 15
Abbs, P.   85
Abel, B.   7
Accomando, J. A.   61
Adair-Toteff, S.   85
Adams, B.   85
Adams, H.   85
Adams, H. P.   1, 15, 77
Adams, R. M.   85
Adamson, W. L.   85
Adorno, T. W.   38, 85
Agrimi, M.   65
Albano, M. E.   1, 61
Alberti, A.   12, 15
Alker, H. R.   15
Alleman, B.   85
Allen, R. van R.   61
Althusser, L.   85
Altieri, C.   85
Amari, V. M.   61
Americo, R.   65
Amsler, M. E.   15
Anderle, O. F.   85
Anderson, P.   89
Angeli, G.   79
Angelil, M.   86
Apel, K.-O.   24, 86
Arendt, H.   86
Arias, J.   86
Arieti, S.   15, 86
Aristotle   3, 21, 61, 62
Armour, L.   12
Armstrong, A.   118
Armstrong, A. M.   3
Arnheim, R.   86
Arnold, M.   25
Aronovitch, H.   15
Atherton, J. S.   86
Auber, J.   86
Auerbach, E.   15, 16, 58, 77, 86

Ausmus, H. J.   48
Ausubel, H.   87
Auxier, R. E.   8
Averill, J. R.   15, 51
Avineri, S.   87
Avis, P.   1

Bacon, F.   16, 51
Badaloni, N.   15, 65
Bagby, P.   87
Bahti, T.   16, 87
Bair, D.   87
Baker, J. J.   6
Bakhtin, M.   36, 42
Ball, T.   16
Ballanche, P.-S.   40
Bank, B. H.   61
Barbi, M.   87
Bardis, P. D.   87
Barnard, F. M.   16, 87
Barnes, H. E.   87
Barnouw, J.   1, 4, 6, 10, 11, 16, 17, 68, 108
Baron, N. S.   16, 87
Bartlett, J.   73
Barzar, J.   87
Bass, T. A.   87
Bassett, B. D.   16
Bate, J.   5
Battafarano, I. M.   65
Battistini, A.   16, 65, 82, 164
Baum, R. F.   87
Bazargan, S.   88
Bear, G.   88
Beardsley, M.   88
Beatty, J.   1
Becker, E.   88
Beckett, S.   16, 34
Bedani, G. L. C.   1, 7, 17, 61, 79, 164
Begnal, M. H.   88
Behrenberg, P.   17
Beiner, R.   88
Beitscher, H.   6, 9

Belaval, Y.  17
Belgioioso, C.  44, 81
Bell, D.  88
Belsey, A.  7, 10
Benaduci, L. B.  65
Bender, J.  88
Benin, S. D.  88
Benstock, B.  17, 88
Bentley, J. H.  88
Benvenuto, B.  88
Berenson, B.  89
Bergel, L.  9, 17, 73
Bergin, T. G.  3, 73, 77, 78, 89, 108
Bergstrom, T.  70, 126, 164
Berlin, I.  1, 10, 15, 17, 18, 59, 89, 90
Bernardo, A.  90
Bernstein, R.  90
Berquist, G. F.  113
Berrigan, J. R.  18
Berrone, L.  90
Berry, T. M.  2, 4
Bertalanffy, L. von  90
Bertland, A.  164
Bertolini, A.  18, 61
Betti, E.  18, 44, 63, 90
Bevilacqua, V. M.  6, 9, 11, 12, 18
Bhattacharya, N.  16, 18, 90
Biasin, G. P.  90
Bickman, M.  85
Bidney, D.  18, 90
Billigheimer, R. C.  90
Bird, L. J.  48
Birns, D. K.  18
Bishop, J. M.  13, 18, 19, 90
Bitz, D.  4
Black, D. W.  19, 32, 90
Black, V.  91
Blackwell, J.  114
Blakey, R.  91
Blanchard, P.  91
Blanchard, W. S.  91
Blasi, A.  12, 19
Bleicher, J.  91
Bloom, H.  91
Bloomer, J.  91

Blumenberg, H.  17, 39, 91
Boas, G.  92
Bobbio, N.  92
Bobick, M. T.  9
Bodin, J.  23, 30, 66
Boers, H.  148
Bolt, S.  92
Bonaparte, F.  19, 92
Bonfante, G.  66
Boorstin, D. J.  92
Bore, P. A.  92
Borges, J. L.  92
Borgman, A.  92
Borradori, G.  92
Bosanquet, B.  92
Bosinelli, R. M.  19, 92
Boucher, D.  92
Bousset, J.-B.  22
Bove, P. A.  149
Bowen, Z.  93
Bowle, J.  19
Boylan, F. X.  93
Bradbury, M.  93
Braham, A.  118
Brandeis, I.  78
Braudel, F.  93
Bray, P.  19, 93
Breisach, E.  19, 93
Bridenthal, R.  93
Bridges, J. H.  93
Brivic, S.  93
Brockway, R. W.  93
Brombert, B. A.  93
Bronowski, J.  93
Brooks, C.  160
Brown, E. A. R.  93
Brown, J. L.  66, 93
Brown, M. E.  93
Brown, N. O.  3, 94
Brown, R.  94
Brown, R. H.  94
Brown, R. L.  94
Brownson, O. A.  94
Broyard, A.  94
Bruner, J.  27

Brunius, T.  9
Bruno, G.  16, 94
Bryan, F. J.  19, 94
Brzozowski, S.  5, 37, 53, 63
Buber, M.  94
Buckle, H. T.  94, 121
Bueno, A. A.  148
Buford, T.  5
Buford, T. O.  19, 95
Bultmann, R.  95
Bunsen, C. J.  95
Burbank, R.  95
Burckhardt, J.  95
Burger, R.  95
Burgess, A.  95
Burke, J. J. Jr.  133
Burke, M. L.  95
Burke, P.  3, 5, 13, 19
Bury, J. B.  95
Byatt, A. S.  95
Bynagle, H. E.  164

Caesar, M.  19
Cahnman, W. J.  20
Cain, S.  12
Cairns, G. E.  20, 95
Calendrillo, L. T.  95
Cambon, G.  10, 20, 95
Cameron, J. M.  95
Cammett, J. M.  96
Campanella, T.  65
Campbell, J.  18, 96
Campbell, J. A.  96
Campbell, R. J.  20, 96
Campion, N.  96
Campo, V.  20
Cantelli, G.  20, 24, 66
Caponigri, A. R.  3, 6, 9, 12, 20, 96, 136
Caramella, S.  21
Carens, J. F.  93
Carlin, J.  96
Carmine, J. D.  96
Carpanetto, D.  21
Carr, D.  96
Carr, T. M.  96

Carravetta, P.  21, 96
Carritt, E. F.  77
Carroll, D.  159
Carruccio, E.  97
Casagrande, J. B.  9
Cascardi, A. J.  97
Caserta, E. G.  21, 23, 97
Casserly, J. V. L.  21
Cassirer, E.  17, 21, 29, 45, 56, 97
Castoriadis, C.  97
Cecchetti, G.  130
Cellerino, M.  21, 97, 154
Ceñal, R.  21
Cesarotti, M.  22
Chambliss, J. J.  3, 21, 97
Chambliss, R.  21
Chase, R.  97
Cheng, V. J.  97
Chiajese, G. A.  30
Child, A.  3, 77
Chill, E.  97
Chisholm, R.  98
Cho, H.  21, 61
Chomsky, N.  24, 36, 98
Church, M.  21, 22, 98
Cicovacki, O.  98
Cixous, H.  98
Clark, G. N.  98
Clark, J. S.  98
Clark, M. A.  22
Clark, P. P.  98
Clark, R. T. Jr.  22, 98
Clemons, W.  89
Cleveland, C.  6
Clive, J.  98
Cobb, E.  98
Cochrane, E. W.  98
Cochrane, L. C.  8
Coers, K. F.  22
Coffin, D. R.  118
Cohen, G. A.  98
Cohen, J. B.  98
Cohen, M. R.  3, 98
Cohen, S.  98
Colbert, J. G.  12

Cole, W. E.  99
Coleman, W. E.  113
Coleridge, H. N.  28, 77
Coleridge, S.  99
Coleridge, S. T.  28, 51, 58, 99
Collingwood, R. G.  3, 22, 35, 38, 54, 99
Collins, J.  9, 10, 99
Comte, A.  13, 21, 59, 99
Connelly, F. S.  61
Cono, J.  3, 27, 54
Conte, A.  22
Cook, A.  99
Cook, P.  13, 57, 73, 99
Cope, J. I.  99
Copleston, F.  22
Cormier, R.  8
Cornecelli, G. M.  61
Corsano, A.  22
Cosford, R. H.  73
Costa, G.  1, 6, 8, 9, 22, 23, 65, 66, 67, 69, 70, 71, 79, 81, 82, 83, 93, 99, 100, 117, 118, 164, 165
Costa-Lima, L.  100
Cotroneo, G.  23
Cousin, V.  23
Covino, W. A.  100
Cowan, B.  100
Cowell, F. R.  100
Cragh, H.  101
Craig, R. P.  23
Cranston, M.  1
Crease, R.  23, 68, 163
Crifò, G.  82
Cristofolini, P.  23
Croce, B.  3, 15, 23, 24, 25, 28, 33, 35, 45, 53, 56, 58, 64, 73, 101, 163, 164
Croff, B. L.  101
Cross, R. K.  101
Crossley, C.  101
Cruz, J. C.  67
Cua, A. S.  101
Culler, J.  101
Curran, C. P.  101
D'Alfonso, A.  24

D'Amico, R.  102
D'Arcy, M. C.  25
D'Entrèves, A. P.  104
Daffina, P.  24
Dalle Vacche, A.  102
Dallmayr, F. R.  2, 24, 34, 102
Dane, E.  102
Dane, J. A.  24
Danesi, M.  3, 7, 8, 13, 24, 25, 36, 66, 102, 103
Daniel, S. H.  1, 25, 103, 105
Dante  7, 16, 19, 20, 25, 46, 48, 63, 79
Danto, A.  103
Dasenbrock R. W.  25
Daus, H. J.  67
David, Z. V.  73
Davidson, A.  103
Davies, S. G.  103
Davis, P. J.  103
Davis, S.  103
Day, P. W.  25
Day, S. J.  103
de Bolla, P.  104
de Condillac, È.  63
De Gennaro, A.  25, 104
de Groot, H.  33
de La Roche, M.  25
de Maistre, J.  4, 62
De Man, P.  57, 104
De Mas, E.  25, 26
de Mauro, T.  26, 104
De Michelis, C.  67
de Ruggiero, G.  104
de Sanctis, F.  104
De Santillana, G.  26
de Vries, J.  104
de Waal Malefijt, A.  9, 11, 104
Deane, S.  103
Della Volpe, G.  104
Denham, R. R.  104
Derrida, J.  29, 40, 41, 55, 104
Descartes, R.  9, 21, 26, 31, 37, 45, 57, 79
Descombes, V.  104
Dewey, J.  3, 39
Di Pietro, R. J.  10, 26, 102, 105

INDEX / 171

Di Salvo, J.  105
Diamond, S.  26, 104
Dickinson, G.  4
Dieckman, L.  26
Dillworth, D. A.  104
Dilthey, W.  34, 49, 55, 105
Dismukes, W. P.  61
Dockhorn, K.  105
Dogana, F.  105
Don Quixote  22
Donadoni, E.  105
Donagan, A.  26, 105
Donagan, B.  26
Donati, B.  67
Donato, E.  105
Donoghue, D.  105
Donzelli, M.  163
Dorfles, G.  26, 106
Doria, P. M.  21, 53
Dostoevsky, F.  67, 142
Downs, R. B.  26
Dray, W. H.  2, 106
Dunn, J.  89
Dupree, R.  12, 31
Durant, A.  26
Durant, W.  26
Duro, A.  67, 106
Dutu, A.  106
Dye, J. W.  10
Dyson-Hudson, N.  106

Eberhard, J. P.  26
Eckley, G.  88
Eco, U.  51, 56, 106
Edel, A.  106
Eder, R.  106
Edie, J. M.  26, 77, 106
Eichhorn, I. E.  27
Einstein, A.  42
Eliade, M.  56
Eliot, G.  19
Ellmann, R.  27, 106, 107
Ellul, J.  39
Ellwood, C. A.  27
Emerson, R. W.  40

Engell, J.  27, 79, 107
Engels, F.  134
Entwistle, H.  107
Essick, R. N.  107
Evangeliou, C.  12
Evans, S. D.  107
Everett, A. H.  107

Failla, D. S.  61
Fáj, A.  27, 67
Falzon, P. L.  163
Farrar, C. C. S.  107
Farrington, B.  107
Fassò, G.  27
Faucci, D.  27
Faur, J.  27, 107
Feder, L.  28
Feibleman, J. K.  28, 107
Feldman, B.  28
Fellmann, F.  68, 81
Fellows, O.  108
Femia, J. V.  108
Ferretti, S.  108
Ferry, L.  108
Fiamingo, G.  108
Ficino, M.  34
Fido, F.  108
Field, M.  122
Fink, K. J.  4
Finkel, C. A.  61
Fisch, M. H.  3, 28, 45, 69, 77, 78, 81, 108, 163
Fischer, K. P.  108
Fisher, P. F.  109
Fitzmorris, T. J.  28
FitzPatrick, P. J.  28
Flanagan, T. E.  12
Fletcher, A.  13, 28, 29, 109
Flew, A.  73
Flint, R.  4, 41, 109
Forbes, D.  7, 10, 109
Formigari, L.  109
Foss, K. A.  109
Foss, S. K.  109
Foucault, M.  53, 109

Fox, J.   9, 10, 29
Franchini, R.   29, 164
Frank, J.   110
Frankel, M.   29, 32, 54, 71, 121, 150
Frascari, M.   4, 110
Fraser, G. S.   110
French, M.   110
Freud, S.   6, 31
Frier, B. W.   124
Fromm, E.   110
Frye, N.   16, 29, 46, 109, 110
Fuentes, C.   59, 111
Fugate, J. K.   111
Fulco, A.   11, 29, 62
Fuller, S.   111
Funkenstein, A.   29, 39, 111
Fyvel, T. R.   2

Gabin, R. J.   32, 111, 149
Gadamer, H.-G.   50, 111
Gadol, E. T.   29
Gaius   36
Galiani   53
Gallie, W. B.   111
Gaonkar, D. P.   111
Gardels, N.   90
Gardiner, P.   2, 7, 8, 9, 30, 74
Gardiner-Janik, L.   29
Gardner, H.   111
Garin, E.   30
Garrison, J. W.   111
Garver, E.   111
Garvin, J.   112
Gash, H.   30
Gates, B. T.   10
Gauguin, P.   61
Gaukroger, S.   30
Geertz, C.   112
Gehlen, A.   112
Gellner, E.   11, 112
Gentile, G.   5, 35, 112
Giannone, P.   63, 67
Gianturco, E.   1, 4, 9, 30, 62, 65, 67, 69, 77, 78, 152, 163
Giarrizzo, G.   66

Gibbon, E.   44, 57
Giddens, A.   11, 112
Gifford, D.   112
Gilbert, K. E.   112
Gilbert, S.   112
Giles, H.   112
Gillespie, M. P.   112
Gilman, S. L.   13
Gilson, É.   30
Ginsberg, R.   112
Giorgi, A. P.   5, 9, 10, 30, 41, 113
Giovene, A.   113
Giuliani, A.   30
Goethe, J. W. von   17, 113
Goetsch, J. R. Jr.   6, 62
Goldberg, S. L.   113
Golden, J. L.   113
Goldfein, A.   3
Goldie, M.   1
Goldstein, L. G.   12
Goldstein, L. J.   113
Goodfield, J.   54, 113
Gordon, J.   113
Goretti, M.   31
Gorman, D.   31, 113
Gorman, H.   113
Gorman, J. L.   7, 31, 113
Gose, E. B.   113
Gottfried, R. K.   113
Gottschalk, L.   113
Goudge, T. A.   9
Gould, W.   113
Gracia, J. J. E.   114
Graff, H. F.   87
Grafton, A.   5, 31, 114
Gramsci, A.   35, 53, 114
Grande, F.   9
Grassi, E.   4, 31, 32, 37, 46, 114, 156
Grasso, A. R.   114
Gratton, C.   114
Gravelle, S. S.   114
Gray, J.   115
Greenberg, P.   32
Greenblatt, S. J.   115
Greenleaf, W. H.   115

Gregory, T.   81
Griffin, R.   32
Grilli, M.   115
Grimaldi, A. A.   4, 62
Grimsley, R.   115
Groden, M.   115
Grose, K.   115
Gross, J.   115
Grosso, M.   115
Grote, G.   115
Grotius, H.   27
Grottanelli, V.   115
Grun, B.   115
Gruner, R.   115
Guardiani, F.   115
Guardini, R.   115
Gueroult, M.   115
Guerry, H.   74
Gullace, V.   115
Gungov, A.   32
Gunn, P.   116
Gunnell, J. G.   116
Günsberg, M.   79
Gustaitis, J.   2
Gutmann, J.   9, 116
Guzmán, J.   32

Haac, O. A.   32, 71, 116
Haber, R. C.   8
Habermas, J.   116
Haddad, L.   32
Haddock, B. A.   1, 2, 4, 6, 8, 32, 62, 79, 94, 116, 122
Haddock. B. A.   12
Haines, J.   5
Hall, R. A. Jr.   33
Hall, V.   116
Halper, N.   116
Hamilton, K. G.   116
Hamilton, P.   116
Hamlyn, D. W.   33, 116
Hammurabi   21
Hampshire, S.   3, 33, 116, 117
Hampson, N.   117
Haney, D. A.   7, 10

Hardy, H.   117, 125
Harris, H. S.   9, 33, 74, 117
Harris, M.   117
Harrison, A.   117
Harrison, B. G.   117
Harrison, R. P.   4
t'Hart. A. C.   33, 68
Hart, C.   117
Hartmann, G.   117
Haskell, F.   117
Haskell, R. E.   33, 117
Hassan, I.   117
Hatton, R.   117
Hausheer, R.   89
Hausman, B.   107
Hawkes, T.   118
Hawkins, R. L.   118
Hayek, von F. A.   39, 118
Hayes, C. H.   74
Hayne, T.   45
Hazard, P.   118
Heade, M. F.   33
Headlam, C.   118
Heath, S.   118
Hebraeus, L.   42
Hegel, G. W. F.   5, 8, 9, 23, 46, 47, 50, 57, 63
Heidegger, M.   4, 21, 31, 32
Hemel, U.   12
Henderson, J. L.   9
Henderson, R. D.   33
Henke, S. A.   118
Henri, C.   82
Henry, A.   82
Henseler, D. L.   62
Heracles   42
Herberg, W.   118
Hercules   39
Herder, J. G.   1, 2, 16, 17, 22, 27, 55, 58, 71
Herkless, J. L.   71, 118
Hermans, H. J. M.   118
Heron, D. C.   33
Herr, C.   13, 118
Herring, P. F.   25
Hersey, G. L.   33, 118
Hersh, R.   103

Hershbell, J. P.  6, 9
Hershenson, D. B.  33
Herzen, A.  119
Herzfeld, M.  119
Hesse, M. B.  34
Hidalgo-Serna, E.  34, 119
Highwater, J.  119
Hill, M. A.  119
Hillensheim, J. W.  23
Hillman, J.  34, 119
Himmelfarb, G.  89
Hintikka, J.  52, 119
Hirsch, E. D. Jr.  119
Hirschman, A. O.  119
Hobbes, T.  3, 16, 20, 29, 62
Hobsbawm, E. J.  119
Hodgart, M.  34, 119
Hodgen, M. T.  119
Hodges, H. A.  34, 120
Holborn, H.  120
Holbrook, P. E. Jr.  120
Hollinger, D. A.  120
Holm, B. J.  153
Holmes, G. F.  120
Holmes, S. T.  34
Holub, R.  7, 62, 120
Homer  25, 32, 37, 38, 43, 52
Hone, J.  120
Hooke, S.  8, 70
Hopper, S. R.  120
Horkheimer, M.  24, 34, 38
Hornstein, A. D.  34
Hösle, V.  82
Houck, J. K.  26
Howard, R. J.  120
Hoyningen-Huene, P.  120
Hughes, H. S.  34, 120
Hughes, P.  6, 29, 34, 120
Hume, D.  8, 39, 58
Humphries, J.  121
Hundert, E. T.  121
Huppert, G.  121
Husserl, E.  35
Hutchins, P.  121
Huth, A. H.  121

Hutton, P. H.  4, 8, 34, 35, 89, 109, 121, 125, 154

ibn-Khaldun  37
ibn-Verga  27
Iggers, G. G.  74, 121
Ijsseling, S.  121
Ilie, P.  50
Illiano, A.  78
Ingram, D.  11
Inman, B. A.  122
Isidore of Seville  15

Jackson, R.  103
Jacobelli, A. M.  35, 68
Jacobik, G.  13
Jacobitti, E. E.  7, 21, 35, 65, 97, 122, 154
Jacoby, R.  122
James, P.  122
Jameson, F.  122, 159
Janusko, R.  13
Jauss, H. R.  122
Jay, M.  35, 122
Jaynes, J.  33
Jennings, J. R.  35, 122
Jermann, C.  82
Jessop, T. E.  1
John-Steiner, V.  122
Johnson, D. A.  11
Johnston, W. H.  122
Johnston, W. M.  35, 159
Joll, J.  123
Jones, V.  79
Jordan, R. W.  35, 55
Joseph, R.  35
Joubert, J.  57
Joyce, J.  3, 13, 16, 17, 18, 19, 20, 21, 22, 25, 27, 32, 33, 34, 35, 36, 38, 39, 40, 41, 43, 45, 46, 48, 50, 51, 52, 53, 56, 58, 62, 64, 123
Jung, H. Y.  36, 56, 123

Kadir, D.  36, 123
Kaempffert, W.  123
Kahler, E.  123
Kahn, B. H.  123

Kain, R. M.   132
Kamenka, E.   12, 36
Kanai, Y.   123
Kann, R. A.   123
Kant, I.   29, 50, 61, 63
Kateb, F.   2
Kaufmann, E. Jr.   123, 152
Kearns, S. M.   123
Keats, J.   3
Kelley, D. R.   1, 2, 5, 7, 10, 31, 36, 66, 106, 123, 124, 125, 137
Kellner, H.   12, 94, 125
Kelly, A.   125
Kennedy, R.   88
Kenner, H.   36
Kenrick, J.   36
Kessler, E.   2, 36, 81, 147
Kiernan, S.   37, 125
Kim, S.-K.   125
King, J. T.   129
Kinsley, J.   125
Kippur. S. A.   125
Kitch, S. L.   125
Klein, A. M.   125
Klein, J.   125
Klemm, D. E.   125
Klibansky, R.   125
Kline, G. L.   37, 68
Knapp. W. F.   125
Knight, M. L.   153
Knight, W.   126
Knox, T. M.   74, 126
Kolakowski, L.   126
Komesu, O.   126
Korte, P.   70
Kosik, K.   126
Kovacs, B. J.   126
Krader, L.   126
Krausz, M.   24
Kreiswirth, M.   126
Krieger, L.   126
Kristeller, P. O.   126
Krois, J. M.   2, 10, 37, 68, 71, 126
Kuhn, H.   112
Kukathas, C.   127

Kunze, D. E. Jr.   5, 11, 37, 62, 127
Kurzweil, E.   91
Kuypers, K.   127
Kuzminski, A.   127

La Capra, D.   127
Labio, C.   37
Labriola, A.   23, 127
Lacan, J.   127
Lacey, A. R.   74
Lachterman, D. R.   11, 37, 127, 140
Ladner, G. B.   127
Lafargue, P.   127
Lafitau   42
Lamparska (Syska), R. A.   5, 37, 53, 63, 65, 68
Lana, R. E.   37, 127
Land, S. K.   38, 127
Lang, B.   128
Langan, T.   30
Langer, S.   19
Lansbury, C.   38
Lasch, C.   128
Laudan, R.   8
Le Peyrère, I.   47
Leach, E.   38, 79, 116, 128, 129
Lecky, E.   128
Lee, V.   128
LeGoff, J.   128
Lehmann-Haupt, C.   95
Leibniz, G. W.   21, 45, 50
Leinfellnerrupertsberger, E.   71
Lentricchia, F.   128
Leonard, J.   132
Leopardi, G.   61
Levi, A. W.   128
Lévi-Strauss, C.   38, 68, 128
Levin, H.   128
Levin, S. R.   38
Levine, J.   38, 92
Levy, Z.   38
Lewes, G. H.   19
Lewis, P.   38
Lichtheim, G.   129
Liebel-Weckowicz, H.   38

Lieberson, J.  129
Lifshitz, M.  38
Lilla, M.  5, 38, 62, 129
Lion, A.  5, 38
Littleford, M.  5, 10, 38, 39, 129
Litz, A. W.  39, 129
Lively, J.  2
Livingston, D. W.  8, 12, 39, 129
Lobner, C. del Greco  129
Locke, J.  57, 63, 79
Logan, O.  3
Long, W.  3
Longfellow, H. W.  57
Lorch, M.  32
Lovejoy, A. O.  129
Lovekin, D.  12, 39, 130
Löwith, K.  39, 68
Lubasz, H.  12
Lucente, G. L.  39, 67, 130, 155, 158
Luft, S. R.  7, 10, 11, 39, 40, 107, 130
Lukàcs, J.  130
Lyons, R.  40
Lyotard, J. F.  37

Mac Cannell, J. F.  130
MacCabe, C.  130
Machiavelli, N.  1, 21, 23, 24, 43, 53, 66
Machievich, W.  131
MacIntyre, A.  2, 22, 40, 51, 131
MacNeice, L.  132
Madden, E. H.  3
Maddox, J. H., Jr.  132
Madera, R.  40
Madison, G. B.  132
Maestro, M.  132
Magalaner, M.  132
Mahootian, F.  132
Maier, J.  40
Mailer, N.  132
Maimonides  27
Mainberger, G. K.  68
Major-Poetzl, P.  132
Makkai, A.  132
Makkreel, R. A.  40, 133
Mali, J.  5, 40

Mandelbaum, M.  133
Manganiello, D.  40, 133
Manglaviti, L. M.  25
Manion, C.  133
Manson, R.  6
Manuel, F. E.  41, 133
Manuel, F. P.  133
Manzoni, A.  133
Marassi, M.  133
Marcel, G.  133
Marchand, J. W.  4
Márcus, G.  133
Marcus, J. T.  134
Marcus, P. L.  134
Marengo Vaglio, C.  41
Margalit, A.  134
Margalit, E. U.  134
Marias Aguilera, J.  41
Marigold, W. G.  65
Marino, J. A.  134
Marrocco, O.  42
Martin, K.  134
Martindale, C.  134
Marvin, F. S.  134
Marwick, A.  134
Marx, K.  11, 12, 15, 16, 18, 23, 29, 31, 34, 35,
  37, 38, 39, 40, 42, 43, 44, 46, 47, 49, 51, 54,
  56, 63, 110, 134
Mascioli, F. P.  78
Mason, E. G.  41, 62, 106
Masur, G.  134
Mathieu, V.  41
Matteo, S.  1, 41
Maurice, F. D.  41
May, R.  41
Mayer, J. P.  41
Mayr, E.  134
Mazlish, B.  6, 93
Mazzarino, S.  41
Mazzeo, J. A.  41, 134
Mazzini, G.  63
Mazzola, R.  66, 165
Mazzotta, G.  41, 134
McAllister, D. W.  5
McCabe, J.  130

McCalla, A.   40
McCarthy, P. A.   130
McCarthy, T.   130
McClintock, R.   10
McCormack, W. J.   130
McCormick, J. O.   40
McCormick, P.   130
McFarlane, J.   93
McGee, P.   131
McHugh, R.   131
McInnes, N.   131
McKeon, R.   131
McLain, E. N.   131
McLuhan, E.   132
McLuhan, M.   46, 58, 62, 131, 132
McMullen, R.   132
McMullin, E.   40, 46
McNeil, L. D.   132
McRae, D. G.   9
McReynolds, J. W.   40
Mead, C. L.   7
Megill, A.   42, 135, 138, 153
Meinecke, F.   42
Meisel, J. H.   135
Melczer, W.   42
Melia, T.   148
Melko, M.   135
Mellor, R.   135
Melotti, U.   135
Mendlewitsch, D.   68
Merquior, J. G.   42, 129, 135
Meskill, M. F.   62
Mestastasio, A. P.   62
Meszaros, I.   135
Meyerhoff, H.   135
Michelet, J.   22, 32, 34, 61, 81, 135
Middleton, R.   135
Milbank, J.   6, 11, 12, 42, 135
Mill, J. S.   13, 59, 135
Miller, C.   6, 62
Miller, D. L.   120
Mills, W. J.   42
Milman, H. H.   135
Mink, L. O.   136
Minogue, K.   12, 42

Mitzman, A.   136
Miuccio, G.   42
Modica, G.   68
Mohan, R. P.   10, 136
Molinaro, J. A.   163
Momigliano, A.   2, 7, 42, 100, 136
Monas, S.   42
Monboddo, J. B.   46
Montagu, M. F. A.   136
Montano, R.   21, 42
Montesquieu   36, 48, 55
Montgomery, J. W.   42
Montuori, A. M.   43
Mooney, M.   4, 6, 11, 43, 62, 136, 163
Mora, G.   10, 37, 43
Moravia, S.   136
Morgenbesser, S.   129
Morison, G. B.   136
Morrall, J. B.   136
Morris, W.   137
Morrison, J. C.   2, 4, 8, 10, 43, 68
Morse, J. M.   137
Moseley, V.   137
Moses   52
Mosley, D. L.   43
Moss, J. D.   6
Moss, M. E.   67, 137
Mueller, L. E.   137
Mueller-Vollmer, K.   137
Muldoon, P.   43
Mumford, L.   137, 156
Munk, A.   12
Munn, E. C.   71
Munz, P.   43, 137, 138
Munzel, G. F.   1
Murillo, L. A.   138
Murray, M.   138
Murrin, M.   43
Musto, D. F.   9

Nakamura, Y.   68
Nash, R. H.   44
Natoli, J.   138
Neff, E.   44, 138
Negro, S. P.   62

Nehamas, A.   157
Nelli, A.   164
Nelson, B.   44
Nelson, J. S.   138
Nelson, R. S.   11, 12
Neruda, P.   32
Neumann, F.   138
Newton, I.   50
Nichols, S. G. Jr.   138
Nicolini, F.   69, 81, 163
Niebuhr, R.   44
Nietzsche, F.   24, 42, 44, 45, 61
Nisbet, R.   9, 22, 44, 138
Noakes, S.   44, 138
Noether, E. P.   9, 44
Noland, A.   138
Nordau, M.   139
Nordenhaug, E.   48
Norris, A. T.   44
Norris, M.   19, 139
Novak, E. E.   139
Novikov, N. V.   74
Nun, J.   139
Nutkiewicz, M. E.   62
Nuzzo, E.   69

O'Banion, J.   139
O'Brien, C. C.   89
O'Hara, D.   149
O'Neill, J.   44, 139
O'Shea, M. J.   140
Oakeshott, M.   139
Olbrechts-Tyteca, L.   141
Oliver, I.   11
Ollman, B.   139
Olney, J.   13
Olsson, G.   139
Ong, W. J.   139
Orelli, J. K.   44
Orpheus   23
Orr, L.   45
Orsini, G. N.   9, 140
Osborne, R.   45
Otto, S.   37, 81
Ovid   33

Pachter, H.   140
Paci, E.   45, 140
Pacifici, S.   140
Padover, S. K.   140
Page, C.   127, 136, 140
Paglia, C.   140
Palmer, H.   113
Palmer, L. M.   3, 9, 45, 59, 68, 79, 132, 140, 149, 154, 163
Palmieri, M.   45
Panofsky, E.   140
Pap, A.   140
Paparella, E.   45
Paparella, E. L.   63
Papini, M.   45, 69
Parker, D.   2
Parker, T.   140
Parry, Adam   140
Parry, D. M.   45
Parsons, T.   45
Pasotti, R.   10
Pasotti, R. N.   63
Patel, C. R. K.   140
Patella, G.   82
Pater, W.   122
Paton, H. J.   125
Peaden, C. L. H.   63
Peake, C. H.   141
Peer, L. A.   141
Peirce, C. S.   28, 37, 109
Pelzel, T.   118
Pennachetti, L.   11, 13, 32, 63
Pennisi, A.   69
Percival, W. K.   45
Perelman, C. H.   32, 141
Perkins, R. L.   8
Perkinson, H. J.   9, 45, 46, 63, 138, 141
Perlove, S.   141
Perniola, M.   141
Perotta, P. C.   46
Pesciarelli, E.   141
Peterfreund, S.   46
Peterson, R. F.   141
Phinney, A. W.   141
Piaget, J.   43

Piccolomini, M.  46, 70, 116, 125, 141, 156
Piccone, P.  141
Pickles, J.  5
Pietropaolo, D.  7, 20, 46, 63, 79, 141, 164
Pinton, G. A.  63, 80
Piovani, P.  7, 23, 46, 70
Pipa, A.  46, 69, 141
Pizzamiglio, G.  67
Plato  3, 21, 61
Plotinus  34
Pocock, J. G. A.  124, 142
Poe, E. A.  67
Polkinghorne, D. E.  142
Pompa, L.  1, 2, 7, 8, 10, 13, 28, 46, 47, 78
Pons, A.  47, 70, 82, 142
Poole, R.  2
Popkin, R. H.  47, 124, 142
Popper, K. R.  142
Porter, R.  8, 70, 142
Potts, W.  142
Pound, E.  25
Poviliunas, A.  47
Prati, G.  28
Preus, J. S.  47, 48
Prezzolini, G.  48, 142
Price, D.  5
Price, M.  142
Procacci, G.  142
Pruitt, R. D.  1, 142
Psathas, G.  142
Pufendorf, S.  62
Pugliatti, P.  92
Puhvel, J.  142
Punter, D.  142
Purdy, S. B.  48
Putnam, H.  143

Quartermain, P.  143
Quigley, H.  143
Quinton, A.  2

Rabate, J. M.  13
Radman, Z.  143
Rafferty, M.  48
Ramos, P.  143

Rand, C.  143
Randall, J. H. Jr.  48
Rappaport, R.  8
Rasula, J.  143
Read, H.  48, 143
Rearick, C.  136, 143
Rée, J.  143
Reese, W. L.  74, 143
Reichert, K.  48
Rella, F.  48
Renaldo, J. J.  48
Reynolds, B.  74
Reynolds, M. T.  48, 129, 143
Rhea, B.  10, 11, 49
Ricci, G. R.  144
Ricciardelli, M.  144
Rice, T. J.  143
Richards J.  144
Richardson, R. C.  144
Richardson, R. D.  28
Richter, P. E.  144
Rickman, H. P.  49, 144
Ricuperati, G.  21
Riddel, J.  144
Riesterer, B.  144
Rigol, M. N.  70
Riley, P.  21
Rimbaud, A.  22
Riquelme, J. P.  144
Riverso, E.  49, 70, 144
Roberts, D. D.  49, 144
Robertson, G. F.  144
Robertson, J.  5
Robertson, J. G.  49
Robertson, J. M.  144
Robinson, D. S.  9
Robinson, H. C.  144
Robinson, H. M.  96
Rockey, P. L.  3, 63
Rockmore, T.  49, 145
Rolfs, D.  66
Romano, C.  49
Romanyshyn, R. D.  145
Rome, H. P.  10
Rorty, R.  51, 145

180 / VICO: A BIBLIOGRAPHY

Rosen, S.  89
Rosnow, R. L.  49, 51, 145
Rosolowski, T. A.  63
Rosselli, J.  2
Rossi, P.  8, 70, 145
Rossides, D. W.  49
Rotenstreich, N.  50, 145
Rousseau, J.-J.  3, 29, 48, 55, 61, 63, 71
Rubanowich, R. T.  145
Rubel, M.  145
Rubinoff, L.  50
Rumble, V.  164
Russell, B.  145
Russo, J. P.  145
Rust Murray, J.  164
Rust, E. C.  145
Rutherford, I.  68
Ryan, A.  2, 145
Rykwert, J.  145

Sabine, G. H.  28
Sahlins, M.  146
Said, E. W.  3, 41, 50, 146
Sailer, S. S.  146
Saintsbury, G. A.  146
Saisselin, R. G.  50, 118
Salamone, R.  70
Salomone, W.  50
Salstrom, P.  50
Samuels, M. S.  50
Sanborn, F. B.  146
Sanchez, F.  27
Sandulescu, C. G.  50, 146
Sanna, M.  66, 83, 165
Sapir, E.  24
Saunders, J. J.  50
Scaglione, A.  7, 146
Schaeffer, J. D.  2, 6, 8, 10, 11, 12, 13, 32, 48, 50, 51, 147
Schaeffer, S.  8
Schefer, J. L.  82
Schellhase, K.  67
Schiffman, Z. S.  147
Schmidt, J.  147
Schmidt, R. W.  70

Schmitt, C. B.  147
Schneck, S.  112
Schneer, C. J.  8
Schneider, H. W.  9, 65
Schopenhauer, A.  13, 59
Schras, F.  147
Schrift, A. D.  24
Schumann, R.  43
Schumpeter, J. A.  147
Schwab, G. B.  110
Schwartz, A.  3
Scott, B. K.  147
Scott, J. A.  67
Scott, N. A. Jr.  147
Scott, W.  147
Scouten, A. H.  2, 17
Scruton, R.  148
Sebba, H.  148
Secord, J. A.  8
Seebohm, T. M.  148
Seidel, M.  148
Seidman, R. J.  112
Senn, F.  148
Sennet, R.  148
Sevilla, J. M.  67, 71
Sewell, E.  51, 78, 148
Shackleton, R.  148
Shanahan, W. O.  3
Shapiro, G.  157
Shelley, P. B.  46
Shenker, I.  51
Shepherd, M.  148
Shibles, W. A.  148
Shimizu, I.  81
Shimizu, J.  81
Shin, S.  51
Shiner, L. E.  9
Shippee, A. W.  80
Shotter, J.  49, 51, 148
Simon, L. H.  1, 51, 63, 116
Simons, H. W.  148
Simonsuuri, K.  52
Simpson, E.  149
Singer, B. J.  145
Singer, J. L.  52

Singleton, C.   149
Sipiora, M. P.   5
Sirignano, A. C.   78
Sitter, J.   149
Skagestad, P.   52, 149
Skinner, B. F.   149
Skinner, Q.   147
Skotnicki, T. P.   63
Slaniceanu, A.   149
Slavens, T. P.   153
Slomich, S. J.   63
Smith, C.   164
Smitten, J.   149
Snukal, R.   149
Snyder, H. R.   149
Snyder, L. L.   149
Sorel, A.   149
Sorel, G.   23, 35, 46
Sorensen, D.   52
Sorokin, P. A.   149
Spanos, W. V.   149
Sparshott, F.   149
Spengler, O.   28
Spenser, E.   25
Spinoza, B.   13, 29, 43, 48, 57, 59, 62, 79
Sprinker, M.   150
Stabb, M. S.   150
Stadelmann, R.   52
Stafford, B. M.   150
Stam, J. H.   52, 150
Stanford, W. B.   150
Stanley, J. L.   150
Stapleton, L.   150
Stark, W.   7, 52, 150
Stead, A.   130
Steadman, J. M.   150
Steegmuller, F.   150
Steinberg, M.   150
Steiner, G.   2, 9, 148, 150, 151
Steinke, H.   52
Steinman, M.   151
Stephens, W.   151
Stephenson, C. L.   8
Stevenson, D. R.   52
Stevenson, W. T.   52

Stewart, C.   119
Stewart, J. I. M.   151
Stillman, E.   151
Stock, B.   151
Stockton, C. N.   151
Stone, H.   52, 53, 63, 124, 151
Strassfeld, R.   73
Stromberg, R. N.   9
Strong, E. F.   12
Struever, N. S.   2, 3, 6, 8, 10, 48, 53, 86, 88, 92, 99, 148, 151, 152, 157
Suarez, F.   30
Sullivan, E. V.   152
Sullivan, K.   152
Sumberg, T. A.   53
Sumner, C.   152
Suttle, B. B.   152
Swearingen, J.   152
Swinny, S. H.   53
Swoboda, W.   2
Synge, J.   25
Szacki, J.   152

Tacitus   21
Tagliacozzo, G.   8, 10, 11, 12, 38, 39, 53, 54, 67, 82, 152, 163, 164
Tagliagambe, S.   70
Tanner, T.   152
Tarnas, R.   152
Tatarkiewicz, W.   152
Tedder, J. D.   78
Teggert, F. J.   153
Tejera, V.   153
Terras, V.   67
Tessitore, F.   66, 70, 71, 83
Thompson, E. P.   153
Thompson, J. H.   153
Thompson, J. W.   153
Thompson, W. I.   153
Thornton, W.   153
Throop, W. M.   153
Tice, T.   153
Timaeus   41
Timpanaro, S.   153

Tindall, W. Y.  153
Titone, R.  54
Todd, J.  54
Todd, J. M.  3, 27
Todorov, T.  153
Toennies, F.  20
Tokarczyk, R.  54
Tolomeo, D.  154
Tonelli, G.  154
Topolsky, J.  154
Toulmin, S.  35, 45, 52, 54, 154
Toynbee, A. J.  135, 154
Trabant, J.  55
Trapp, R.  109
Treves, P.  78
Trilling, L.  154
Tristram, R. J.  55
Trompf, G. W.  154
Trotsky, L. D.  154
Trousdale, M.  154
Tsanoff, R. A.  3
Tuan, Y. F.  5
Tubino, F.  63
Tucker, L. A. S.  154
Tully, J.  154
Tursman, R.  155
Tusiani, J.  79
Tuttle, H. N.  55, 155
Tyrrell, R. E. Jr.  155
Tysdahl, B. J.  155

Uemura, T.  51, 55
Ullmann, S.  155
Ulysses  25
Unamuno, M. de.  155
Ungaretti, G.  32
Updike, J.  2, 155

Valdès, M. J.  55
Valery, P.  68
Valesio, P.  155
Valla, L.  53
Valone, J. J.  2, 10, 55
Van Atta, J. R.  155
van der Dussen, J.  155

Van Nostrand, C. A.  64
Vasoli, C.  6, 11
Vattimo, G.  58, 155
Vaughan, C. E.  55
Vaughan, F.  4, 12, 55
Veit, W.  155
Veneziani, M.  81
Venturi, F.  156
Venturi, L.  156
Verdicchio, M.  55, 56, 64
Verdicchio, P.  79
Verene, D. P.  4, 8, 9, 10, 11, 12, 13, 17, 31, 36, 40, 56, 57, 68, 74, 75, 78, 79, 80, 82, 105, 156, 164
Verene, M. B.  163
Verri, A.  18, 71, 156
Vickers, B.  57, 157
Viechtbauer, H.  37, 57, 71, 81
Vignoli, T.  157
Visconti, G. G.  80, 82
Vittorini, D.  57
Voegelin, E.  77, 157
von Bertalanffy, L.  157
von Glaserfeld, E.  30, 144, 157
von Leyden, W.  8
Vossius, G. J.  23
Vucinich, A.  157

Wainwright, E. H.  57
Walker, J. M.  81
Walsh, J. V.  3
Walsh, W. H.  2, 12, 57, 157
Walton, C.  57
Ward, P. A.  57
Ward, R. S.  57
Warneke, G.  157
Warnock, M.  2
Warren, A.  158
Wartofsky, M. W.  158
Watson, J.  13
Weatley, O. K.  64
Weber, E.  158
Weber, M.  15
Weinberg, K.  158
Weintraub, K. J.  57

Weir, L.   58, 132, 158
Weiss, P.   158
Wellberg, D. E.   88
Wellek, R.   58, 158
Wells, G. A.   58
Wescott, R. W.   58
Wesseley, A.   58
West, C.   158
Westfall, R.   8
Whalley, G.   58, 158
White, D. A.   158
White, H. V.   2, 7, 8, 11, 58, 75, 119, 155, 159
White, M.   159
White, P. T.   58, 64
White, S. H.   58
Whitfield, J. H.   3, 6
Whitney, C.   159
Whitt, J. R.   5
Whittaker, T.   13, 59, 69
Whitton, B. J.   159
Whyte, L. L.   159
Widgery, A. G.   159
Wiener, P. P.   159
Wieseltier, L.   91
Wiggins, D.   159, 160
Wilcox, D. J.   59, 160
Wilder, T.   160
Wilkerson, K. E.   160
Wilkins, E. H.   160
Williams, R.   160
Wilson, E.   160
Wilson, F. A. C.   160
Wilson, J.   164
Wilson, R. A.   160
Wilson, W. A.   160
Wimsatt, W. K.   160
Winch, P.   24, 160
Windelband, W.   160
Wittgenstein, L.   49
Wittram   27
Wohlfhart, G.   71
Wolf, F. A.   43
Wolff, K. H.   6
Wolfgazo, E.   68
Wright, O. W.   161

Wundt, W. M.   20, 161
Wyatt, T.   25

Yeats, W. B.   27, 161
Yoneyama, Y.   81
Young, L. M.   161

Zacchi, R.   92
Zagorin, P.   59, 161
Zamora, L. P.   59
Zhang, L.   59, 161
Zhu Guangqian   59, 82, 161
Zimmer, L. B.   2
Zobermann, P.   6